WITHDRAWN

THE LOEB CLASSICAL LIBRARY

FOUNDED BY JAMES LOEB 1911

EDITED BY

JEFFREY HENDERSON

EDITOR EMERITUS

G. P. GOOLD

AUSONIUS
I

LCL 96

AUSONIUS

VOLUME I

WITH AN ENGLISH TRANSLATION BY

HUGH G. EVELYN WHITE

HARVARD UNIVERSITY PRESS
CAMBRIDGE, MASSACHUSETTS
LONDON, ENGLAND

First published 1919
Reprinted 1951, 1961, 1968, 1988, 2002

LOEB CLASSICAL LIBRARY® is a registered trademark
of the President and Fellows of Harvard College

ISBN 0-674-99107-9

*Printed in Great Britain by St Edmundsbury Press Ltd,
Bury St Edmunds, Suffolk, on acid-free paper.
Bound by Hunter & Foulis Ltd, Edinburgh, Scotland.*

CONTENTS

INTRODUCTION

THE works of Ausonius were held in high esteem by the poet's contemporaries: Symmachus protests that he classes the *Mosella* as equal with the poems of Virgil, and Paulinus of Nola has grave doubts as to whether "Tully and Maro" could have borne one yoke with his old master. Extravagant as such judgments may be,[1] they have their value as indicating wherein (from the modern point of view) the importance of Ausonius really lies. As poetry, in any high or imaginative sense of the word, the great mass of his verse is negligible; but the fact that in the later fourth century men of letters and of affairs thought otherwise, establishes it as an example and criterion of the literary culture of that age. The poems of Ausonius are in fact a series of documents from which we may gather in what poetry was then assumed to consist, what were the conditions which determined its character, and the models which influenced it.

In a definite sense, therefore, the chief value of the works of Ausonius is historical; but not for the history of intellectual culture alone. The poet does not, indeed, throw light on the economic fabric of

---

[1] *cp.* Gibbon's epigram "The poetical fame of Ausonius condemns the taste of his age" (*Decline and Fall*, ed. Bury, III. p. 134 note 1).

society and conditions of life in his day ; but he re-
veals to us certain sides of social life which are at
least curious—as in the picture which he draws of the
typical agent who "managed" the estates of the
Roman landowner of his day (*Epist.* xxvi.), or when
he shows what manner of folk were the middle-class
people, officials, doctors, professors and their woman-
kind, amongst whom so large a part of his life was
spent.

Both these aspects of Ausonius' work, the literary
and the social, are explained by the facts of his life.

LIFE OF AUSONIUS

Decimus Magnus Ausonius was born about 310 A.D.
His father, Julius Ausonius, a native of Bazas and
the scion apparently of a race of yeomen (*Do-
mestica* i. 2, *Grat. Act.* viii.), is introduced to us as a
physician of remarkable skill and discreet character
who had settled at Bordeaux, where he practised and
where his son was born. Aemilia Aeonia, the mother
of the future consul, was of mixed Aeduan and
Aquitanian descent, the daughter of one Caecilius
Argicius Arborius, who had fled to Dax in the an-
archic days of Victorinus and the Tetrici and had
married a native of that place. Whatever the reason,
her son speaks of her in the coolest and most unim-
passioned terms as if possessing no other virtues than
conjugal fidelity and industry in wool-working (*Parent.*
ii.). Though she seems to have lived until about

353 A.D., the upbringing of her son devolved upon
various female connections of the family, notably upon
Aemilia Corinthia Maura, of whose strict discipline
the poet seems to have retained painful recollections
(*Parent.* v. 7–8).

The boy's education was begun at Bordeaux; and
amongst his early instructors in "grammar" (Greek
and Latin language and literature) he mentions
Macrinus, Sucuro, and Concordius, who taught him
Latin (*Proff.* x. 11), and Romulus and Corinthius who
were hard put to it to overcome his dislike for Greek
(*Proff.* viii. 10 ff.). About 320 A.D. he was transferred
to the care of his maternal uncle, Aemilius Magnus
Arborius, then professor at Toulouse, where the lad
resided until his relative was summoned (*c.* 328 A.D.)
to Constantinople, to become tutor to one of the sons
of Constantine. Ausonius then returned to Bordeaux
and continued his studies in rhetoric under Miner-
vius Alcimus and perhaps Delphidius, the ill-starred
son of the ex-priest of Bellenus and a descendant of
the old Druids (*Proff.* i., ii., v.).

Ausonius started on his own professional career
about 334 A.D. as *grammaticus* at the University of
Bordeaux (*Praef.* i. 20), and about the same time
wedded Attusia Lucana Sabina, daughter of a leading
citizen. By this marriage he had three children,
Ausonius who died in infancy, Hesperius, and a
daughter whose name is not mentioned. In due time
he was promoted to a professorship in rhetoric, and
though he practised for a while in the courts, his real

bent was towards teaching (*Praef.* i. 17). One event only, so far as we know, disturbed the monotonous but not wholly restful (*cp. Epist.* xxii. 77 ff.) course of his professional life—the death (*c.* 343 A.D.) of his wife, who had inspired the best of his shorter poems (*Epigram* xl.). How sorely he felt this loss is shown by the real though somewhat egotistical feeling with which he wrote of her more than thirty years later (*Parent.* ix.); and his words gain weight from the fact that he never married again.

It was in 364 A.D., or thereabouts, after thirty years of class teaching, that Ausonius was summoned to the " golden palace " to become tutor to the youthful Gratian (*Praef.* i. 24 ff.); and the next ten years were spent in guiding the prince through the orthodox courses of " grammar " and " rhetoric." On one occasion at least the monotony of such a life was relieved for both tutor and pupil by a change to more stirring scenes. For Ausonius and Gratian both accompanied Valentinian I. on the expedition of 368–9 A.D. against the Germans, when the former was commissioned to celebrate the more spectacular results of the campaign (*Epigr.* xxviii., xxxi.). The preface to the *Griphus* gives us a glimpse of the professor on active service, and the *Bissula* adds a singular detail to the same episode.

In 370 A.D. the title of *comes* was conferred upon him, and five years later he took the first step in his official career, becoming *quaestor sacri palatii*. When at the end of 375 A.D. his pupil Gratian ascended the throne,

INTRODUCTION

his advancement became rapid and his influence very marked. His hand, for instance, has been traced in the legislation of this period (see Cod. Theod. xiii. 3. 11, xv. 1. 19 and *cp.* Seeck, *Symmachus,* p. lxxix.). In his rise the soaring professor drew a train of relatives after him. His father, then nearly 90 years of age, was granted the honorary rank of prefect of Illyricum in 375 A.D. (*Dom.* iv. 52); his son Hesperius was proconsul of Africa in 376 A.D. and *praefectus praetorio* of Italy, Illyricum and Africa in 377–380; his son-in-law, Thalassius, succeeded Hesperius in the proconsulship of Africa; while a nephew, Aemilius Magnus Arborius, was appointed *comes rerum privatarum* in 379 A.D. and promoted *praefectus urbi* in the year following. Ausonius himself was raised to the splendid post of *praefectus Galliarum* in 378, the office being united by special arrangement with the prefecture of Hesperius to enable father and son to share between them the toils and rewards of both posts. But the crowning honour was reserved for 379 A.D., when the ex-professor attained the consulship—an absorbing theme discussed from all its bearings in the *Gratiarum Actio.* At the close of 379 A.D. Ausonius retired to Bordeaux (*Domestica* i. : title), no doubt to take possession of the ancestral estate which had come to him on the death of his father in 378 A.D.

But in 383 the mainspring of the family fortunes was rudely broken. The army in Britain revolted with Maximus at its head: Trèves was occupied, Gratian slain at Lyons, Valentinian II. driven out of

INTRODUCTION

Italy, and the usurper was master of the Western Empire. The prospects of the favourites of the old régime were definitely at an end. What Ausonius did during the domination of Maximus is unknown. From the explanatory note prefixed to *Epist.* xx. we learn that when the storm burst he was at Trèves (he had no doubt returned to the court there) and it is possible that his continued stay in the city was in fact a detention at the order of Maximus. But if this is so, it is likely that he was soon permitted to return to his native Bordeaux.

When at length Theodosius overthrew Maximus (388 A.D.) Ausonius may indeed have visited the court (*cp. Praef.* iii.), but was too old for public life. Henceforth his days were spent in his native province, where he lived chiefly on his own estates, paying occasional visits, which he disliked or affected to dislike, to Bordeaux (*Domest.* i. 29 ff., *Epist.* vi. 17 ff.). Here he passed his time in enjoyment of the sights and sounds of the country (*Epist.* xxvii. 90 ff.), in dallying with literary pursuits, and in the company of friends similarly disposed.

The date of his death is not definitely known, but may be presumed to have occurred at the close of 393 or in 394, since nothing from his hand can be assigned to a later year. He was then over eighty years of age.

In connection, however, with his life something must be said on his attitude towards Christianity.

INTRODUCTION

When and how he adopted the new religion there is nothing to show ; but certain of his poems make it clear that he professed and called himself a Christian, and such poems as the *Oratio* (*Ephemeris* iii.) and *Domestica* ii., which show a fairly extensive knowledge of the Scriptures, sometimes mislead the unwary to assume that Ausonius was a devout and pious soul. But in these poems he is deliberately airing his Christianity : he has, so to speak, dressed himself for church. His everyday attitude was clearly very different. When Paulinus began to conform his life to what he believed to be the demands of Christianity, Ausonius is totally unable to understand his friend's attitude and can only believe that he is crazed. A devout and pious Christian might have combated the course chosen by Paulinus, but he would certainly have sympathised with the principle which dictated it. Nor does Christianity enter directly or indirectly into the general body of his literary work (as distinguished from the few " set pieces "). In the *Parentalia* there is no trace of Christian sentiment—and this though he is writing of his nearest and dearest : the rite which gives a title to the book is pagan, the dead " rejoice to hear their names pronounced " (*Parent.* Pref. 11), they are in Elysium (*id.* iii. 23) or in Erebus (*id.* xxvii. 4) or amongst the Manes (*id.* xviii. 12) according to pagan orthodoxy; but in his own mind Ausonius certainly regards a future existence as problematical (*Parent.* xxii. 15 and especially *Proff.* i. 39 ff.).

Further, the conception of the Deity held by Ausonius was distinctly peculiar—as his less guarded references show. In the *Easter Verses* (*Domest.* ii. 24 ff.) the Trinity is a power transcending but not unlike the three Emperors; and in the *Griphus* (l. 88) the "tris deus unus" is advanced to enforce the maxim "ter bibe" in exactly the same tone as that in which the children of Rhea, or the three Gorgons are cited : for our author the Christian Deity was not essentially different from the old pagan gods.

There is a marked contrast, therefore, between Ausonius' formal professions and his actual beliefs. This is not to accuse him of hypocrisy. Conventional by nature, he accepted Christianity as the established religion, becoming a half-believer in his casual creed : it is not in the least likely that he ever set himself to realize either Christianity or Paganism.

The Literary Work of Ausonius

The adult life of Ausonius may be divided into three periods : the first, extending from *c.* 334 to 364 A.D., covers the thirty years of professorial work at Bordeaux ; the second (*c.* 364–383) includes the years spent first as Gratian's tutor and then as his minister ; while the last ten years of his life constitute the third. His circumstances during each of these periods necessarily affected his literary work, which may therefore be correspondingly divided.

The First Period.—The first period in the career

of Ausonius is a long one, yet the output, so far as it can be identified, is small in the extreme; and since Ausonius was by no means the man to suppress anything which he had once written, we may believe that his professional duties left him little or no leisure for writing. Some of his extant work, however, can be identified as belonging to this period. Possibly his earliest work (since he seems to have married *c.* 334 A.D.) is the letter written to his father *On the Acknowledgment of his Son* (*Epist.* xix.)—a copy of forty elegiacs, very correct but very obvious and conventional in sentiment. To the first eight years of this period we must also assign the epigrams relating to his wife (*Epigr.* xxxix., xl., liii.–lv.), and those on certain "lascivae nomina famae" (*Epigr.* xxxviii. and lxv.), which seem to have caused Sabina some misgiving. It is also probable that a considerable number of the remaining epigrams—especially those dealing with academic persons or topics (*e.g. Epigr.* vi.–xiii., lx., lxi.)—were composed during this period; and it is at least a possible conjecture that some of the mnemonic verses on the Roman Calendar, the Greek Games, etc. (*Ecl.* ix.–xxvii.), were written by Ausonius when *grammaticus* to assist his pupils at Bordeaux,[1] though worked up for formal publication at a much later date.

The Second Period.—The years spent at the imperial court were more prolific. The *Easter Verses,* an

---

[1] Compare the mnemonics of some modern Latin Grammars.

imperial commission, were written in or after 368 A.D. (*Domestica* ii. 25), and were followed by three of Ausonius' most characteristic works, the *Griphus*, the *Cento Nuptialis*, and the *Bissula*.

The first of these, composed in 368 A.D.[1] while the poet was with the expedition against the Alamanni, celebrates the universality of the mystic number Three. Though so trivial a theme is no subject for poetry at all, it must be admitted that Ausonius here shows at his best as an ingenious versifier : partly by the immense range and skilful selection of his examples, partly by variety of rhythm, and partly by judicious use of assonance, the author succeeds in evading monotony—and this though ninety hexameters are devoted to so unpromising a topic.

The *Cento Nuptialis* was likewise compiled when Ausonius was on active service ;[2] but neither that " military licence " of which he speaks elsewhere as permissible at such a period, nor the plea that he wrote at the direction of the Emperor, can excuse the publication of this work at a much later date. As its title implies, it is a description of a wedding festival made up of tags, whose length is determined by certain fixed rules, from the works of Virgil. In the nature of the case, the result is shambling and

---

[1] It was dedicated to Symmachus and published some years later, but before 383 A.D.

[2] If the words " sub imperatore meo tum merui " at the close of the preface are to be taken—as no doubt they are— in their strict military sense.

awkward as to sense, and disgraced by the crude and brutal coarseness of its closing episode. Neither the thorough knowledge of Virgil's text, nor the perverse ingenuity displayed in the compilation can redeem this literary outrage.

In the third work of this group, the *Bissula*, Ausonius sung the praises of a young German girl of that name, who had been assigned to him as his share in the spoils of the Alamannic War. Of the series of short poems or epigrams, which once constituted the work, only a brief preface addressed to Paulus, another to the reader, and the three opening poems have (perhaps fortunately: cp. *Biss.* II. 3 ff.) survived. Since the heroine is represented as already thoroughly Romanized, the composition cannot well be earlier than *c.* 371–2 A.D.

The poet's most ambitious and certainly his best work, the *Mosella*, is also loosely connected with the German War (see *Mosella* 423 ff.), which probably occasioned the journey described at the beginning of the poem (ll. 1–11). It was not finished before 371 A.D., the date of the consulship of Probus and Gratian and of the birth of Valentinian II., both of which events are alluded to (*Mosella* 409 ff., 450). After sketching his route from Bingen to Neumagen, Ausonius breaks into a eulogistic address to the Moselle, and settles to serious work with an exhaustive catalogue of the fish to be found in its waters. Next he sings of the vine-clad hills bordering the river valley and the general amenities of the stream, which make it a favourite haunt of superhuman and human beings alike. The aquatic sports and pastimes to be seen upon the river having been described, the poet dilates upon the stately mansions which stud the banks and celebrates the numerous tributaries which swell its waters. After a promise to devote his future leisure to praise of the country through which the river flows, Ausonius commits the Moselle to the Rhine, closing his poem with an exaltation of the former above the streams of Gaul such as the Loire, the Aisne, and the Marne.

The years following 375 A.D. must have involved Ausonius in much public business, and this doubtless accounts for an interval of comparative barrenness. Except *Epist.* xiii., written in 377 when Ausonius was quaestor, and the *Epicedion* [1] (*Domest.* iv.) of 378, nothing noteworthy seems to have been produced during the busiest period of his official life. But the consulship of 379 A.D. brought leisure and revived the inspiration of the poet, who celebrates the beginning of his term of office with a prayer in trochaic septenarians and another in hexameters (*Domest.* v., vi.): both these are wholly pagan in sentiment; but the elect were doubtless propitiated by a third and portentous prayer in rhopalic hexameters, written (it seems) during the consulship itself, which is purely Christian in tone. At the close of his year of office Ausonius rendered thanks to the Emperor in an elaborate oration, the *Gratiarum Actio.* This, the only

---

[1] A second and enlarged edition was prepared later.

extant specimen of Ausonius' oratory, is of the class
which must be read to be appreciated.

The Third Period.—After the consulship, Ausonius
found himself free from the ties of public duties,
and was able to devote himself wholly to his literary
pursuits. In 379 or 380 he retired to Aquitaine to
take possession of the estate left him by his father.
The occasion is celebrated in a short poem *On his
Patrimony* (*Domest.* i.). At the close of 379 A.D. he
published the first edition of his *Fasti,* dedicated to
his son Hesperius. Originally the main part of this
work was a list of the kings and consuls of Rome
from the foundation of the city down to the author's
own consulate. The list however, is not extant,[1] and
all that remains of this production are the short
addresses in verse which accompanied it. A second
edition brought up to date (and probably corrected)
was issued in 383 A.D. with a new dedication to
Gregorius.

Kinship of subject makes it probable that the
Caesares was written at about the same time as
the *Fasti.* In its first edition this book comprised
only the Monosticha i.–iv. and the Tetrasticha on the
Emperors from Nerva to Commodus; the second
edition was enlarged by (*a*) a series of Tetrasticha
on the twelve Caesars, and (*b*) new Tetrasticha
bringing the list down to the times of Heliogabalus.
Another work of about the same date is the

---

[1] It was apparently never included in the *Opuscula.*

Protrepticus (*Epist.* xxii.), an exhortation addressed to the poet's grandson and namesake.

We have seen that Ausonius returned from Aquitaine to Trèves somewhere between 380 and 383 A.D. It was perhaps during these years that he wrote the *Cupid Crucified*, the subject of which was suggested by a wall-painting at Trèves.

In 383 A.D. Maximus seized the Empire of the West, and Ausonius' pupil, Gratian, was done to death. The poet, as we have seen, was possibly detained for a while at Trèves; and the revolution seems to have profoundly affected him. A fragment (*Epist.* xx.) written at this period clearly shows the gloom and foreboding which had settled upon his spirits, and possibly checked for a time the flow of his poetic vein. Nevertheless, in or after 385 A.D. a noteworthy group of works was completed and published. The first of these, indeed, the *Parentalia*, was written at intervals (*e.g.* iv. 31 *c.* 379, and xxiv. 5, 16 in 382 A.D.) and may have been actually finished in 382; but the preface to the *Professores* indicates that the two works were issued together.[1] The *Parentalia* is a collection of thirty poems, mostly in elegiacs, celebrating the memory of the author's deceased relatives. Whether superstition or mere love of verse-making be the cause, even remote connections whom the poet had hardly or never met are duly commemorated (*Parent.* xxi.

[1] Unless this preface belongs to the Collected Edition alone.

1–2): the semi-historical interest of these poems has already been alluded to (pp. vii. f.). The *Professores* is a similar collection of memorial verses, though distinguished by greater metrical variety, and commemorates the public teachers of the University of Bordeaux. A reference to the execution of Euchrotia with the Priscillianist martyrs (v. 37) shows that the work was not finished earlier than 385 A.D. Here again, if we except the verses on Nepotianus (*Prof.* xv.), Ausonius' verse is more interesting as a document for social history than as poetry. The *Epitaphs,* a series of epigrams on the chief heroes of the Trojan War, was finished after the *Professores* and appended to it, as the author himself states, owing to the similarity of the two works in tone. The presence of the miscellaneous epitaphs which follow will be explained below (p. xxxvi.).

The *Genethliacos* (*Epist.* xxi.), a letter of congratulation to his grandson Ausonius on the occasion of his fifteenth birthday, may be dated *c.* 387 A.D.

At this point mention must be made of the *Ephemeris,* the date of which is by no means clear, though it has been variously fixed at *c.* 368 and *c.* 379–380. It is not easy to decide whether the poet was writing in the city (*i.e.* at Trèves) or in the country (Aquitaine): the former is suggested by iv. 4 ff., v. 3, the latter by viii. 42 f. Consequently the period to which the composition is to be assigned is doubtful: probably, however, it was late; for the *Oratio* which forms part of it is but a revised and expanded edition of an earlier and independent poem. The *Ephemeris*, when complete, described the daily routine of the poet's life. He wakes and calls his servant (unsuccessfully) in sapphics, only rousing the laggard by the substitution of iambics: he demands his clothes and water for washing and gives orders for the chapel to be opened. After reciting the prayer already mentioned, which in its revised form runs to eighty-five hexameters, Ausonius decides that he has "prayed enough" (*satis precum datum deo*) and prepares to go out, but somehow failing to do so, first dispatches a servant to remind certain friends that they are invited to lunch, and then visits his kitchen to animate the cook Here unfortunately a considerable portion of the text has been lost, and only[1] the concluding poem (imperfect) which deals with troublesome dreams is now extant.

The usurper Maximus was overthrown by Theodosius in 388 A.D., and the exultation with which Ausonius hails the event in the *Order of Famous Cities* (ix. 1, 5 ff.) suggests that this book was finished in 388 or 389. But from the opening words of the poem on Aquileia, "non erat iste locus" it may be inferred that most of the series was written before the end of Maximus and that the alteration was

[1] Peiper inserts in the lacuna an address to a secretary (*Ephem.* vii.): this is at best purely conjectural, and the piece seems rather to have been intended to stand at the head of a collection of poems.

made in order to admit a reference to the avenging of Gratian. As the title partly indicates, Ausonius here celebrates the twenty most remarkable cities of the Empire in a series of descriptive notices, the longest and warmest of which is naturally that dealing with Bordeaux.

A very characteristic but by no means attractive work is the *Technopaegnion*, a classified list of (probably) all the monosyllabic nouns in the Latin language so contrived as to form the last syllables of 164 hexameters. This, like the *Fasti*, the *Caesares*, the *Oratio*, the *Epicedion* and certain of the *Epitaphs*, is extant in two editions. The former of these, dedicated to Paulinus, must have been issued before 389, when the estrangement between Ausonius and his former pupil began : the second was addressed to Pacatus in 390, and contains a new dedication, one entirely new section, xiii. (*On Monosyllabic Letters*), besides a considerable number of alterations in the original matter.[1]

Far more attractive than the dreary work just named is the *Masque of the Seven Sages*, again dedicated to Pacatus in 390 A.D. The famous Seven are here forced to appear upon the stage in turn to deliver each his wise precept and to expound its

---

[1] Miss Byrne (*Prolegomena*, p. 60) considers that the first edition contained only the dedication to Paulinus and the initial section (*Techn.* ii. and iii.) ; but surely the frequent alterations evidenced by the *V* and *Z* groups of MSS., above all the variants *Pauline* and *Pacate* in xiii. 21, show that the two editions were *nearly* co-extensive.

practical application. Action of any sort there is none (for the characters appear singly), and the "dramatic" form is therefore a mere screen to allow Ausonius to turn the wisdom of the Sages into verse. But the artificiality is agreeably relieved by touches of parody (as in ll. 131-2), or of humour (ll. 201, 213, &c.).

Only the more salient landmarks in the literary history of Ausonius are here noticed, and this imperfect sketch must close with some reference to the noteworthy correspondence between the poet and his former pupil Paulinus. Pontius Meropius Paulinus, born in 357 A.D., belonged to a noble and distinguished family in Aquitaine. He was educated at Bordeaux under Ausonius, by whose influence he was subsequently elected *consul suffectus* in 378. In the following year he married Therasia (the "Tanaquil" of *Epist.* xxviii. 31, xxxi. 192). At first there is no trace of a shadow upon the friendship between Paulinus and his old tutor (see *Epist.* xxiii.–xxvi.); but in 389 Paulinus retired to Barcelona where he began to strip himself of his wealth and to lead a life of asceticism. Ausonius tried to combat this strange madness on the part of his friend, which he compares with Bellerophon's aberration : he deplores the growing estrangement of his friend, and rashly but not obscurely blames the influence of "Tanaquil" (Therasia). These appeals were conveyed in four letters, one of which never reached Paulinus : the remaining three reached their destination together in 393 A.D. and were answered by Paulinus. Of this part of the correspondence two letters by Ausonius with the reply of Paulinus are extant (*Epist.* xxviii., xxix. and xxxi.). In 393 Ausonius wrote once again and received a reply conciliatory indeed but unyielding from his friend (*Epist.* xxvii., xxx.). It was the death, probably, of the older man which prevented the subject from being further pursued.

LITERARY CHARACTER OF AUSONIUS

The influences which determined Ausonius' literary quality were perhaps three in number, his age in general and social surroundings in particular, his education and profession, and his racial stock.

Whatever the salient characteristics of the fourth century may be, intellectual freshness, imagination and a broad human outlook are not amongst them. The old literary forms and methods were outworn, and there was no spiritual force to reanimate or to reshape them. The accessible realms of the intellect had been delimited, mapped out, and explored as definitely as the Roman Empire itself; and outside (it was now tacitly assumed) was nothing but chaos, just as beyond the political and military frontiers of the state lay nothing but barbarism. In such an age was Ausonius born. His family surroundings were not such as to exert a compensating influence, as the family portraits sketched in the *Parentalia* unmistakably show : the men and women whom he depicts are indeed excellent social units, examples of domestic and civic virtue, but no less surely conventional and unimaginative. With such surroundings, it may be said, Ausonius was not more heavily handicapped than Shakespeare probably was; but the age of Ausonius was emphatically not Elizabethan, and in himself he was far from being a prodigy: he could not but conform to the mould of his early circumstances.

The conventional type which he inherited and which his upbringing reimpressed, was stamped yet deeper by the educational system of his day. In this the masterpieces of ancient literature were made subordinate to the demands of rhetoric and studied not so much for the sake of the thoughts or ideas which they embodied as of the mode of expression; while rhetoric itself from a vehicle for the statement of facts had degenerated into a mere display of verbal dexterity.

The effect of these two influences, his general surroundings and his education, on the work of Ausonius is clear. From first to last his verse is barren of ideas: not a gleam of insight or of broad human sympathy, no passion, no revolt: his attitude towards life is a mechanical and complacent acceptance of things as they are. To appreciate this it is only necessary to read Ausonius' *Lament for his Father* (*Epicedion*), beginning with a mechanical catalogue of everyday virtues and leading up to a glorification of the writer's own success—and then to turn to

Rugby Chapel. The same defects, narrowness in out-
look and egoism, make sterile even those poems which
commemorate keener sorrows than a man of seventy
might be expected to feel at the death of his father
at the ripe age of ninety: a favourite grandson is
accidentally killed, and the cry is not "O the pity of
it," but "Alas, all *my* hopes are upset" (*Parent.* xi.
13). This is common, very common, human nature,
but it is not great poetry. And again, grief for the
loss of his wife (*Parent.* ix.), deeply felt as it was and
much as its expression may command our pity, is too
self-centred to engage entire respect. It is in the
verses *To his Wife* (*Epigr.* xl.) alone that an entirely
natural and universal expression of human feeling is
to be found; and even here the pedant must needs
drag in the stiff lay-figures of Nestor with his "triple
span" and Deiphobe of Cumae to chill the atmosphere
of brave optimism and tenderness.

Insensible, broadly speaking, to sentiment and
unappreciative of the human sympathy which should
pervade true poetry, Ausonius regarded the art (in
practice at any rate) as the rhetorical treatment of
any subject in verse—with the inevitable rider that
the harder the subject, the better the poetry. His
Muse, therefore, was not of Helicon but essentially
of the schools, and from the schools he derived both
his subjects and his mode of treatment. The names
of the days of the week, the Roman calendar, tabloid
histories of the Roman Emperors, a catalogue of mono-
syllables in Latin, or of the Trojan War heroes—such

were the themes in which Ausonius delighted: the *Parentalia* and the *Mosella*, indeed, are notable exceptions; but even in these the mania for versified lists manifests itself, here in a complete catalogue of the poet's relatives, there in an exact enumeration of the fishes to be found in the stream.

But if we could admit for a moment that these and similar matters were legitimate objects for poetic treatment, we should also have to admit that Ausonius was a master of his craft. The skill displayed in working out the unpromising theme of the *Griphus* has already been noticed, and it is exerted to the full in the impossible task of making palatable the *Technopaegnion*. Ausonius, indeed, brought to his task many qualities and accomplishments which a brighter genius might have envied: his acquaintance with the letter, if not with the spirit, of classic authors was intimate; his memory was clearly of unusual strength, as the quotations or reminiscences occurring on almost every page will show; and his rhetorical skill stands him in good stead in his more ambitious works, the *Moselle* and *Cupid Crucified*. The peroration of the former (ll. 438–468) may indeed be singled out as a really impressive example of this art. To these he adds the half-poetical, half-rhetorical gift for epigram —as when he writes of Tiberius (*Caesares*, Tetr. iii. 4),

> quae prodit vitiis credit operta locis,

or of Otho (*id.* viii. 4),

> hoc solum fecit nobile quod periit;

and the more dubious turn for various forms of assonance such as "ignoscenda... cognoscenda," "legenda ... tegenda" (*Ludus* i. 1, 3 f.), "faciendo ... patiendo" (*Caesares*, Tetr. v. 4); or in "Leonine" verses (often emphasising an antithesis) as

> fleta prius lacrim*is* nunc memorabo mod*is*
>
> (*Parent.* Pref. 2),

or again (*id.* 7-8),[1]

> quae Numa cognat*is* sollemnia dedicat umbr*is*
> ut gradus aut mort*is* postulat aut gener*is*.

Sometimes this degenerates into actual punning, as in *Caesares*, Tetr. iv. 4, "qui super*avit avum*" (unless this is accidental), or "non est quod mireris ... est quod misereris" (*Techn.* ii.).

Education and long scholastic experience influenced Ausonius in yet other directions.

As *grammaticus* he was familiar with ancient authors, and, bound as he was by convention, to these he turned for models. Catullus and Horace are his masters in lyric, Plautus and Terence in the pseudo-dramatic *Ludus*, Virgil and Horace again in hexameter verse, and Martial and the Greek Anthology in epigram. In shorter passages and phraseology his debt to these and to others of his predecessors is immense. Unhappily this dependence is not confined to matters of technique or form. The literary bent of Ausonius was, in one of its aspects, towards

---

[1] In this preface the assonance is frequently used and its significance is clearly funereal.

the epigram; and he conscientiously imitates the
masters of this form of composition in that obscenity
of subject and grossness of expression which, as the
younger Pliny (*Epist.* IV. xiv. 4 ff., v. iii. 1 ff.) informs
us, was regarded as essential even by the greatest
and most staid worthies.

Rhetoric had a profound effect upon the literary
work of Ausonius. For him a simple statement was
an opportunity (for verbal display) missed; and no
feature is so characteristic of his poems as duplica-
tions like

> set neque tu viduo longum cruciata sub aevo
>   protinus optato fine secuta virum.
>
> (*Parent.* xxx. 9 f.)

More than this, for a necessary word or two Ausonius
loves to substitute an elaborate *tour de force.* Thus
in *Epist.* xvi. 3–14 the simple complaint "you have
not visited me for three months" is expanded into six
elegiac couplets; in *Epist.* xv. 5–35 the word "thirty"
is transmuted into as many lines of mixed verse; in
Epist. xiii. 7–24 it needs eighteen verses adequately
to say "six." In another place Ausonius complacently
admits this tendency, and instead of telling his book
that it is destined for Probus, observes (*Epist.* xii. 7 ff.)

> possem absolute dicere,
> sed dulcius circumloquar
> diuque fando perfruar,

—and devotes the next twenty-four lines to a defini-
tion of Probus through his attributes.

INTRODUCTION

Hitherto we have been dealing with the effect of his age and training upon Ausonius: the third factor, if not so potent, is far more interesting. Ausonius was of Celtic blood; and, extravagantly as Celtic claims are often overrated, it is possible that an element in his work, which is not due to his classical culture, should be ascribed to the genius of his race. This is a distinct appreciation for the beauties of Nature without reference to the comfort and gratification which they may afford to mankind. In the nature of the case such an element rarely finds its way through the crust which unimaginative surroundings and a thoroughly artificial education and career had imposed upon the nature of Ausonius; but the subject of the *Mosella* afforded it some outlet. The *locus classicus* is, of course, *Mosella* 63 ff., where the poet describes the dark weeds rooted in the rippled sands of the river bed, how they bend and sway in the under-current of the waters, revealing and again concealing the bright pebbles which lie amid them. Elsewhere, in a passage less distinctive, perhaps, but of a richer tone (ll. 192 ff.), he dwells upon the beauty of the Moselle at evening when "Hesperus drives on the lingering shadows" and the steep sides of the valley are mirrored in the still waters, when the boat gliding with the stream seems to be moving over the vines which clothe the hills. In the remainder of his work Ausonius by his choice of subjects, forbade himself the use of this his most genuine poetic quality: yet here and there, like the pebbles in the Moselle, it gleams out for a moment and is hidden again, as in *Ephem.* iii. 38 f.

> puri qua lactea caeli
> semita ventosae superat vaga nubila lunae,

or in the passage rapidly sketching his rural life near Bordeaux (*Epist.* xxvii. 93), where "nemus umbris mobilibus" betrays a touch of the same spirit.

Perhaps this naturalistic gift accounts for the vividness with which some of the personages sketched by Ausonius stand out. The pictures of his grandfather, the shy astrologer, of his grandmother, who would stand no nonsense, and of his aunt Cataphronia, the needy but generous old maid (*Parent* iv., v., xxvi.) are excellent examples ; but perhaps the best, because the most varied, are to be found amongst the *Professores.* There we have the brilliant but restless Delphidius, ruined by his own ambitions (*Proff.* v.); Phoebicius (*id.* x. 23 ff.), offspring of Druids, who, finding the service of the god Belenus unremunerative, became a professor; Citarius, grammarian and poet, who was equal with Aristarchus and Zenodotus on the one hand and with Simonides of Ceos on the other (*id.* xiii.); Victorius (*id.* xxii.), the zealous student of antiquities, who died, unhappily, before he had worked his way down to such modern authors as Cicero and Virgil ; and Dynamius, who left Bordeaux under a cloud but fell on his feet in Spain (*id.* xxiii.). Unhappily Ausonius has not condescended to depict the peasantry (*coloni*) of his day ; but in compensation he introduces us to two rustic figures whom we could ill spare. The first of these is a squireen, Theon, who lives in Médoc in a thatched farm-house near the sea coast: he has a weakness for making verses—not of the best—out of tags filched from another bard, Clementinus. What does he do all day? asks Ausonius. Is he buying up for a song tallow, wax, pitch and waste paper to resell at a thumping profit? Or is he more heroically chasing robbers until they admit him to a share in their spoils? Or does he spend his time in hunting or fishing? This curious person sends Ausonius rustic presents from time to time, such as oysters and apples, and still more rustic verses; occasionally he seems to have borrowed the poet's money and then (as Ausonius complains) to have kept well out of his way. The letters to Theon (*Epist.* xiv.–xvii.) give us, in fact, a very good idea of the life and pursuits of the small "local gentry" in the remoter parts of Gaul. The second character is the bailiff (or, as he prefers to be called, the factor) on the estate of Ausonius. In personal appearance he is grey-haired, bristly, truculent, with plenty of assurance—just such a one as Phormio in Terence (*Epist.* xxvi.). He is a Greek whom Juvenal would have had no difficulty in recognizing. Through his ignorance of agriculture the crops have turned out a failure, and he has the effrontery to cast the blame upon the gods and the poverty of the soil. But the disaster has restored him to his natural element. Commissioned

to purchase grain to relieve the famine threatening
the poet's household, he "comes out strong as a new
corn-dealer," traverses the whole countryside buying
up corn and attending all the markets. So adroitly
does he manage this congenial business, complains
Ausonius, that "he enriches himself and beggars
me."

The place to be assigned to Ausonius as a poet is not
a high one. He lacked the one essential, the power
of penetrating below the surface of human nature;
indeed his verse deals rather with the products of
man than with mankind itself. His best quality—
appreciation for natural and scenic beauty—is rarely
indulged; and this, after all, is an accessory, not an
essential, of poetry. In his studies of persons (such
as the *Parentalia* and *Professores*) he gives us clever
and sometimes striking sketches, but never portraits
which present the inner as well as the outer man.

Textual History

Ausonius did not necessarily publish a poem imme-
diately after composition. Though it is evident that
the first edition of the *Fasti* must have been formally
issued as soon as completed in 379, the prefatory
letters introducing the *Cento* and the *Griphus* show
that each of these works was held back for some time
before its definitive publication. At the same time
the second of these documents speaks of the *Griphus*
as " secreta quidem sed vulgi lectione laceratus,"

i.e. as being surreptitiously circulated; and from
the letter of Symmachus appended to the *Mosella*
it appears that the poet sometimes sent copies of
his most recent work to friends before he made it
public property.   These "advance copies" were
issued in confidence, as the words of Symmachus,
"libelli tui (me) arguis proditorem" (*Epist.* i.), imply,
and were not published in the full sense of the term.
It was only after he had revised a poem to his
satisfaction that Ausonius "published" it. This was
usually done by sending it to a friend with an epistle
prefixed, in which the author went through the
polite farce[1] of inviting the recipient to correct its
faults and so let it live, or to suppress it altogether
(*Ludus* i. 1–4, 13–18).

Ausonius sometimes revised, supplemented, and
reissued poems already published, usually (but not
always) adding a new dedication. Thus the *Techno-
paegnion*, originally dedicated to Paulinus, underwent
some alterations and additions before being re-
published with its new dedication to Pacatus; but
in the second edition of the *Fasti* the prefatory
poem, originally addressed to Hesperius, was merely
adapted by slight verbal alterations to suit Gregorius.

In the prefatory note to his second edition of the
Epicedion (*Domest.* iv.) Ausonius writes: "imagini
ipsius (*sc.* patris) hi versus subscripti sunt neque

---

[1] Ausonius, of course, would have been surprised and
annoyed had any of his correspondents taken him at his
word.

minus in opusculorum meorum seriem relati. Alia omnia mea displicent mihi ; hoc relegisse amo "— clearly showing that he kept by him a collection of *all* his published or finished work. The fruits thus garnered were reissued in three " collected editions." The first of these, prefaced by a dedication to Gratian (*Epigr.* xxvi.), appeared in or just before 383 A.D. ; the second was drawn up *c.* 390 A.D. at the request of the Emperor Theodosius (*Praefat.* iii., iv.) ; and finally a collection, including second editions of old poems and works hitherto unpublished or which had appeared only in separate form, was issued after Ausonius' death by his son Hesperius or some intimate friend, probably in 393.[1] This conclusion may be drawn from the lemma of *Epist.* xx. which is in the third person (contrary to Ausonius' practice) and, after mentioning the circumstances in which the letter was written, states that it is " unfinished and copied as it stands from the rough draft " : similarly the lemma to the *de Herediolo* (*Domest.* i.) is in the third person. In both cases it is clear that Ausonius is not the writer, but someone (such as Hesperius) very intimately acquainted with the details of his life. To this editor the intrusion of the miscellaneous epitaphs (*Epitaphs* xxvii.–xxxv.) at the end of the series on the Trojan War heroes may be due ; though it is possible that they were placed there by the author himself who intended to expand them into a distinct work standing next to the original series.

[1] According to Seeck.

INTRODUCTION

In the fourth century, therefore, there were current
(*a*) early or "advance" copies of individual works,
(*b*) formally published copies of the same, possibly
containing small improvements, (*c*) three "collected"
editions of the works. What is the relation between
these possible sources and the extant MSS.? We
may say at once that there is no means of determin-
ing whether our MSS. are to any extent dependent
upon either the "advance" copies or the published
editions of single works; and it is tolerably certain
that the collected edition prepared for Theodosius is
no longer extant and probably was never available
to the public. It is apparently from the collected
editions of 383 and 393 A.D. that the surviving
MSS. are derived. These MSS. are classified in four
groups: (1) The *Z* or Tilianus group, represented
by the Codex Tilianus (Leidensis Vossianus lat.
Q. 107). The numerous MSS. of this class all present
the same works in the same order and contain no poem
assignable to a date later than 383 A.D. (2) The *V*
group, a single MS. of the ninth century (Leidensis
Vossianus lat. 111) containing for the most part the
poet's later works and "remains" together with
second editions of some earlier poems, and some
material (*e.g.* the *Griphus* and the *Versus Paschales*) in
the same shape which it wears in the *Z* group. (3)
The *P* group, represented by Parisinus 8500, contain-
ing selections. (4) The *Excerpts* (so called from the
title of the MSS.), a further series of extracts.

The exact history of the third and fourth groups

cannot be traced; but since they contain nothing in common they are probably to be regarded as complementary to one another. Further, most of their contents are common to *V*, but include nothing peculiar to the *Z* group as contrasted with *V*. Consequently it is probable that *P* and *Exc.* are related to *V*; and the presence in them of some matter not to be found in *V*, *e.g.* the letter of Theodosius (*Praef.* iii.) and the *Moselle*, suggests that they were derived from a more complete representative of this collection than the extant Leyden MS.

If this is so, the groups may be reduced to two—on the one side the *Z* MSS., and on the other *V* and the selections. Of these two main groups, *Z*, which opens with a dedication to Gratian and contains nothing later than 383 A.D., represents the first collected edition, and *V*, with related MSS., reproduces the "posthumous" edition of 393 A.D.

Such in its broad outlines appears to be the history of the text. Peiper, however, has put forward a very different theory. All the MSS. were derived (he holds) from a single copy of the final collected edition, and this archetype was split into two parts, the former being the ancestor of the *Z* group, the latter of *V*, which was supplemented by the remains of another copy (perhaps the ancestor of *Z*) in a very decayed condition. As for *P* and *Exc.*, they are to be traced to a defective MS. akin to, but earlier than the ancestor of *V*, since it contained the *Mosella* and other matter not preserved in that MS.

INTRODUCTION

This theory cannot be upheld. The poems common to *Z* and *V* frequently differ so markedly that the variants cannot possibly be attributed to the fortunes of the MSS. The *Epicedion* may be cited first in illustration. Here *Z* omits the lemma, ll. 13–16, 19–26 (all found in *V*), and in l. 38 reads "gnatos tris numero genui" (for "gnatos quattuor edidimus" of *V*), omitting further ll. 39–40.

In the *Epitaphia* the same phenomena occur: in xxxi. 1 *Z* reads "et odoro perlue nardo" for the "bene olentis et unguine nardi" of *V*; and in l. 6 *Z* has "felix seu memini sive nihil memini" as against the "seu meminisse putes omnia, sive nihil" of *V*. And in xxxii. 1 *Z* gives "Lucius: una quidem geminis sed dissita punctis" for *V*'s "una quidem, geminis fulget set dissita punctis." In xxxv. 5 we find "Quis mortem accuset? Complevit munia vitae" (*Z*) and "Quis mortem accuset? Quis non accuset in ista" (*V*).

An example of another kind is afforded by the *Oratio* (*Ephemeris* iii.). In *Z* this is an independent poem, in *V* it is embodied as an episode in the *Daily Round*; and further the text shows more than accidental changes. In l. 1 *Z* has "Omnipotens, quem mente colo, pater unice rerum": *V*, "Omnipotens, solo mentis mihi cognite cultu"; ll. 8–16 are found in *V* but not in *Z*; and in l. 84 *Z* reads "Consona quem celebrat modulato carmine plebes," but *V*, "C. q. celebrant modulati carmina David."

So, too, in the *Fasti*. The initial poem is addressed

to Gregorius in *Z* and begins l. 9 " exemplo confide
meo"; whereas in *V* it is addressed to Hesperius
and substitutes " exemplum iam patris habes." And
of the remaining three pieces ii. is found in *V* only,
iii. and iv. in *Z* only.

The *Technopaegnion* affords yet more striking in-
stances of variation between *Z* and *V*. The original
dedication to Paulinus (*Techn.* ii.) is found in *Z*
alone, the later dedication to Pacatus (*Techn.* i.) in
V only : of the sections in this work that on *Mono-
syllabic Letters* (*Techn.* xiii.) occurs in *V*, but not in *Z*,
while the texts of the two groups show well-marked
differences. Thus in x. 26 *Z* has " nota et parvorum
cunis " which is changed in *V* into " nota Caledoniis
nuribus"; for xiv. 3 (according to *V*) *Z* reads
" et quod nonnunquam praesumit laetificum gau,"
placing this after xiv. 19 ; and for xiv. 5 f. (of *V*) *Z*
has the single line " scire velim Catalepta legens
quid significet tau." Lastly and most significantly
(if we remember the alternative prefaces) *V* has
" indulge *Pacate* bonus " in xiv. 21 in place of the
" indulge *Pauline* bonus " of *Z*. These variants can
only be due to deliberate revision on the part of
the author; in other words the matter common to
Z and *V* follows one edition in the former group,
and another in the latter. Peiper's theory of a single
archetype consequently collapses.

It has been necessary to dwell on this matter at
some length for the following reason. Owing
primarily to an error of judgment on the part of the

translator, and subsequently to the difficulty of
introducing a radically new system in a series of this
nature, the text of the present edition is Peiper's
(Teubner, Leipzig, 1886), in which (1) the two
distinct collections were thrown into one and the
resultant mass rearranged according to the Editor's
notion of what was plausible ; (2) the two recensions
of individual works were fused together confound-
ing the two series. As a result Ausonius' literary
methods are somewhat obscured ; but the fact that
the order of the "opuscula" is without significance,
makes this disadvantage less serious.

The Manuscripts

The MSS. cited at the foot of the text are as
follows (the symbols being substituted for the
confusing system adopted by Peiper):

Z = Tilianus and its fellows.

T = Tilianus (Leidensis Voss. lat. Q. 107).

V = Leidensis Voss. lat. 111.

B = Bruxellensis 5369/73.

C = Cantabrigiensis Kk. v. 34.

G = St. Gall 899.

L = Laurentianus 51, 13.

M = Maglibecchianus i. 6, 29.

P^1 = Parisinus 8500.

P^2 = Parisinus 7558.

P^3 = Parisinus 4887.

R = Rhenaugiensis (Turicensis) 62.

INTRODUCTION

SELECT BIBLIOGRAPHY

(1) *Early Printed Editions.*

 Bartholomaeus Girardinus, Venice, 1472 (*editio princeps*).

 Julius Aemilius Ferrarius, Milan 1490 (reprinted at Venice 1494 and reissued by Avantius at Venice in 1496).

 Thaddaeus Ugoletus, Parma, 1499; Venice, 1501.

 Hieronymus Avantius, Venice, 1507.

 Iodocus Ascensius, Paris, 1511, 1513, 1517.

 Richard Croke, Leipzig, 1515.

 Richard Croke, Florence, 1517 (Juntine Edition).

 H. Avantius, Venice, 1517 (Aldine Edition).

 Nicolaus Borbonius, Lyons, 1549.

 Stephanus Charpinus⎫
 R. Constantinus ⎬, Lyons, 1558.

 Joseph Scaliger, Lyons, 1574–5.

 E. Vinetus, Bordeaux, 1580.

(2) *Later Editions.*

 J. Toll, Amsterdam, 1669.

 Fleury ⎫
 Souchay⎬, Paris, 1730.

 Karl Schenkl, Berlin, 1883 (*Mon Germ. Hist.*, Auctores Antiquissimi, V. ii.).

 Rudolf Peiper, Leipzig, 1886 (Teubner Series).

(3) *Translations.*

There appears to be no English translation of
Ausonius. A French version is by—
Etienne François Corpet, Paris, 1842, and 1887.

(4) *General.*

F. Marx, *s.v.* Ausonius in Pauly-Wissowa, *Real-
Encyclopädie*, ii. cols. 2562–2580.

Teuffel and Schwabe, *Hist. of Rom. Lit.* (trans.
Warr) ii. § 421.

Samuel Dill, *Roman Society in the Last Century of
the Western Empire*, ch. v. and *passim.*

T. R. Glover, *Life and Letters in the Fourth
Century*, pp. 102 ff.

J. E. Sandys, *Hist. of Class. Scholarship*, i. 221 ff.

Marie José Byrne, *Prolegomena to an Edition
of the Works of Ausonius*, New York, 1916.

BIBLIOGRAPHICAL ADDENDUM

Editions:

Ausonius, ed. S. Prete (Bibliotheca Teub-
neriana), Leipzig 1978

Ausonii Opera, ed. by R. P. H. Green (Oxford
Classical Texts), Oxford 1999

*Die Moselgedichte des Decimus Magnus Aus-
onius und des Venantius Fortunatus*, ed. with
commentary by C. Hosius, Marburg 1926[3]
(repr. 1967)

INTRODUCTION

Ausonius, Mosella, ed. with commentary by C. M. Ternes (Erasme series), Paris 1973

Ausonii Mosella, ed. by B. K. Weis, Wissenschaftliche Buchgesellschaft: Darmstadt 1989

Ausonii Mosella, ed. with commentary by M. E. Consoli, Congedo 1998

Ausonii Parentalia, ed. with commentary by M. Lolli (Collection Latomus 232), Brussels 1997

Decimus Magnus Ausonius. *Technopaegnion*, introduction, text, and commentary by Carlo Di Giovine, Bologna 1996

Reference:

R. Browning in *The Cambridge History of Classical Literature*, vol. II, Cambridge 1982, pages 698–704

H. Sivan, *Ausonius of Bordeaux: Genesis of a Gallic Aristocracy*, Routledge: London/New York 1993

AUSONIUS

OPUSCULA

D. MAGNI AUSONII

OPUSCULA

LIBER I

[PRAEFATIUNCULAE][1]

I.—Ausonius Lectori Salutem

Ausonius genitor nobis, ego nomine eodem :
   qui sim, qua secta, stirpe, lare et patria,
adscripsi, ut nosses, bone vir, quicumque fuisses,
   et notum memori me coleres animo.
Vasates patria est patri, gens Haedua matri   5
   de patre, Tarbellis set genetrix ab Aquis,
ipse ego Burdigalae genitus : divisa per urbes
   quattuor antiquas stirpis origo meae.
hinc late fusa est cognatio ; nomina multis
   ex nostra, ut placitum, ducta domo veniant :   10
derivata aliis, nobis ab stemmate primo
   et non cognati, sed genetiva, placent.
set redeo ad seriem.   genitor studuit medicinae,
   disciplinarum quae dedit una deum.

[1] Omitted in the MSS.

AUSONIUS

BOOK I

PREFATORY PIECES

I.—Ausonius to his Reader, Greeting

My father was Ausonius, and I bear the same name. Who I am, and what is my rank, my family, my home, and my native land, I have written here, that you might know me, good Sir, whoever you may have been, and when you know me, might honour me with a place in your memory. Bazas[1] was my father's native place; my mother was of Aeduan[2] race on her father's side, though her mother came from Aquae Tarbellae;[3] while I myself was born at Bordeaux : four ancient cities contribute to the origin of my family. Thus my connexions are widely spread : many, if so they please, may adopt names which are derived from my house. Others like names brought in from outside; I like such as are taken from the main line and are not names of connexions, but proper to the family. But I return to my main theme. My father practised medicine—the only one of all the arts which produced a god;[4] I gave myself up

---

[1] In Aquitania.   [2] The capital of the Aedui was at Autun.
[3] Dax, in the Dép. des Landes.   [4] sc. Aesculapius.

nos ad grammaticen studium convertimus et mox 15
  rhetorices etiam, quod satis, attigimus.
nec fora non celebrata mihi, set cura docendi
  cultior, et nomen grammatici merui
non tam grande quidem, quo gloria nostra subiret
  Aemilium aut Scaurum Berytiumve Probum,   20
sed quo nostrates, Aquitanica nomina, multos
  conlatus, set non subditus, adspicerem.
Exactisque dehinc per trina decennia fastis
  deserui doctor municipalem operam,
aurea et Augusti palatia iussus adire   25
  Augustam subolem grammaticus docui,
mox etiam rhetor.   nec enim fiducia nobis
  vana aut non solidi gloria iudicii.
cedo tamen fuerint fama potiore magistri,
  dum nulli fuerit discipulus melior.   30
Alcides Atlantis et Aeacides Chironis,
  paene Iove iste satus, filius ille Iovis,
Thessaliam Thebasque suos habuere penates :
  at meus hic toto regnat in orbe suo.
cuius ego comes et quaestor et, culmen honorum, 35
  praefectus Gallis et Libyae et Latio

---

[1] Probably Aemilius Asper, commentator on Terence and
Virgil : cp. *Epist.* xiii. 27.
[2] Q. Ter. Scaurus flourished under Hadrian, and wrote an
Ars Grammatica and commentaries on Virgil, Plautus, and
others.
[3] M. Valerius Probus, of Beyrût, failing to win promotion,
left the army and became a grammarian.   Jerome dates his

to Grammar, and then to Rhetoric, wherein I gained
sufficient skill. I frequented the Courts as well,
but preferred to follow the business of teaching, and
won some repute as a grammarian; and though my
renown was not of so high a degree as to approach
that of Aemilius,[1] or Scaurus,[2] or Probus of Beyrût;[3]
yet it was high enough to let me look upon the
teachers of my day, men famous in Aquitaine, as
their equal rather than their inferior.

[23] Afterwards, when three decades with all their
festivals were passed, I left my toils as a provincial
teacher, receiving the command to enter the Em-
peror's golden palace. There I taught the young
prince Grammar, and in due time Rhetoric; for, in-
deed, I have good reason for satisfaction and my
boasting rests upon firm ground. Yet I confess that
there have been tutors of greater fame, so but 'tis
granted that there has been to none a nobler pupil.
Alcaeus' offspring was taught by Atlas, and the son
of Aeacus by Chiron[4]—the first Jove's own son, and
the other well-nigh sprung from Jove—and these
had Thebes and Thessaly for their homes. But this
my pupil reigns over the whole world, which is his
own. He created me Companion and Quaestor,[5] and
crowned my honours with the prefectship of the pro-
vinces of Gaul, Libya, and Italy.[6] I became consul,[7]

prime 56–57 A.D., and calls him *eruditissimus grammaticorum*.
He is perhaps confused here with the later (second century)
Probus, the editor of Virgil.   [4] Hercules and Achilles.
    [5] In 370 and 375. On the title *comes* see Seeck in Pauly-
Wissowa, *Real-Encyclopädie*, iv.: in this instance it seems to
have been a purely honorary title.   [6] In 378.   [7] In 379.

et, prior indeptus fasces Latiamque curulem,
   consul, collega posteriore, fui.
Hic ergo Ausonius : sed tu ne temne, quod ultro
   patronum nostris te paro carminibus.   40

II.—Ausonius Syagrio

Pectoris ut nostri sedem colis, alme Syagri,
   communemque habitas alter ego Ausonium :
sic etiam nostro praefatus habebere libro,
   differat ut nihilo, sit tuus anne meus.

III.—Epistula Theodosi Augusti

[Theodosius Augustus Ausonio parenti salutem.][1]

Amor meus qui in te est et admiratio ingenii
atque eruditionis tuae, quae multo maxima sunt,
fecit, parens iucundissime, ut morem principibus
aliis solitum sequestrarem familiaremque sermonem
autographum ad te transmitterem, postulans pro
iure non equidem regio, sed illius privatae inter
nos caritatis, ne fraudari me scriptorum tuorum
lectione patiaris. quae olim mihi cognita et iam
per tempus oblita rursum desidero, non solum ut,
quae sunt nota, recolantur, sed etiam ut ea, quae
fama celebri adiecta memorantur, accipiam. quae

---

[1] Suppl. *Avantius.*

too, and was given the precedence on assuming the
insignia and the curule chair, so that my colleague's
name stood after mine.

[39] Such, then, is Ausonius: and you, on your part,
do not despise me because I ask your favour for
these songs of mine, without your seeking.

II.—Ausonius to Syagrius

Gentle Syagrius,[1] even as you have a home within
my heart and, like another self, inhabit the Ausonius
we both share, so also shall your name stand on the
front page of my book, that there may be no differ-
ence whether it be mine or yours.

III.—A Letter of the Emperor Theodosius

The Emperor Theodosius to his father Ausonius,
greeting.

My affection for you, and my admiration for your
ability and learning, which could not possibly be
higher, have caused me, my dearest father, to adopt
as my own a custom followed by other princes and
to send you under my own hand a friendly word
asking you—not in right of my kingship, but of our
mutual affection for each other—not to let me be
cheated of a perusal of your works. Once I knew
them well, but with time they have been forgotten;
and now I long for them again, not only to refresh
my memory as to those which are commonly known,
but also to receive those which general report de-
clares that you have added to the former. As you

---

[1] Apanius Syagrius was praetorian praefect in 380 and 382,
consul in 382. He was a close friend of Symmachus.

tu de promptuario scriniorum tuorum, qui me amas, libens imperties, secutus exempla auctorum optimorum, quibus par esse meruisti : qui Octaviano Augusto rerum potienti certatim opera sua tradebant, nullo fine in eius honorem multa condentes. qui illos haut sciam an aequaliter atque ego te admiratus sit, certe non amplius diligebat. vale parens.

IV.—Domino Meo et Omnium Theodosio Augusto Ausonius Tuus

Agricolam si flava Ceres dare semina terrae,
   Gradivus iubeat si capere arma ducem,
solvere de portu classem Neptunus inermem :
   fidere tam fas est, quam dubitare nefas.
insanum quamvis hiemet mare crudaque tellus   5
   seminibus, bello nec satis apta manus,
nil dubites auctore bono.   mortalia quaerunt
   consilium.   certus iussa capesse dei.
scribere me Augustus iubet et mea carmina poscit
   paene rogans : blando vis latet imperio.   10
non habeo ingenium, Caesar sed iussit : habebo.
   cur me posse negem, posse quod ille putat ?
invalidas vires ipse excitat et iuvat idem,
   qui iubet : obsequium sufficit esse meum.

8

love me, then, consent to favour me with those treasures stored away in your desk, and so follow the example of the choicest writers, with whom you have earned an equal place. For when the Emperor Octavianus was reigning, they vied with one another in presenting him with their works, and set no limit to the number of the poems which they composed to his praise. You may be sure that though he may perhaps have admired these authors as much as I do you, he certainly did not have a greater personal affection for them. Farewell, my father.

IV.—To my Lord and the Lord of All, Theodosius the Emperor, from Ausonius, your Servant

If yellow Ceres should bid the husbandman commit seed to the ground, or Mars order some general to take up arms, or Neptune command a fleet to put out to sea unrigged, then to obey confidently is as much a duty as to hesitate is the reverse. However much the wintry sea may rage with storms, or the land be yet unready for the seed, or the host still untrained for war, do not hesitate with such good councillors. Behests of mortals call for deliberation : what a god commands perform without wavering. The Emperor bids me write, and asks for my verse—nay, almost begs for it; power is masked under a courteous command. I have no skill to write, but Caesar has bidden me ; well, I will have it. Why should I deny that I can do what he thinks that I can do ? He by his own influence stirs up my feeble power, and he who bids me aids me as well ; it is enough for me to obey. It is not

non tutum renuisse deo. laudata pudoris   15
   saepe mora est, quotiens contra parem dubites.
Quin etiam non iussa parant erumpere dudum
   carmina. quis nolit Caesaris esse liber,
ne ferat indignum vatem centumque lituras,
   mutandas semper deteriore nota?   20
tu modo te iussisse, pater Romane, memento
   inque meis culpis da tibi tu veniam.

safe to disoblige a god; though delay due to modesty often deserves praise, when we hold back despite the entreaties of our peers.

17 Nay more, these songs of mine have long been ready to break out unbidden: and what book would not be Caesar's own in the hope to escape thereby the countless erasures of a wretched bard, always emending and emending for the worse? Remember only, father of the Romans, that you gave me the command, and where I fail you must bestow forgiveness on yourself.

LIBER II

EPHEMERIS

ID EST

TOTIUS DIEI NEGOTIUM

I

MANE iam clarum reserat fenestras,
iam strepit nidis vigilax hirundo:
tu velut primam mediamque noctem,
    Parmeno, dormis.

dormiunt glires hiemem perennem,   5
sed cibo parcunt: tibi causa somni,
multa quod potas nimiaque tendis [1]
    mole saginam.

inde nec flexas sonus intrat aures
et locum mentis sopor altus urget   10
nec coruscantis oculos lacessunt
    fulgura lucis.

annuam quondam iuveni quietem,
noctis et lucis vicibus manentem,
fabulae fingunt, cui Luna somnos   15
    continuarit.

      [1] *V*: caedis, *Peiper*.

BOOK II

THE DAILY ROUND

OR

THE DOINGS OF A WHOLE DAY

I

Already bright Morn is opening her windows, already the watchful swallow twitters from her nest; but you, Parmeno, sleep on as if it were the first or the middle watch of the night. Dormice sleep the winter round, but they leave food alone; while you slumber on because you drink deep, and swell out your paunch with too great a mass of food. And so no sound enters the winding channels of your ears, a deep stupor presses on your consciousness, and all the dazzling beams of light do not vex your eyes. Old tales pretend that once upon a time a youth [1] slept on year in, year out, untroubled by the interchange of night and day, because Luna made his slumbers unending.

[1] *sc.* Endymion.

surge, nugator, lacerande virgis :
surge, ne longus tibi somnus, unde
non times, detur : rape membra molli,
      Parmeno, lecto.   20

fors et haec somnum tibi cantilena
Sapphico suadet modulata versu?
Lesbiae depelle modum quietis,
      acer iambe.

II.—Parecbasis

Puer, eia, surge et calceos
et linteam da sindonem.
da, quidquid est, amictui
quod iam parasti, ut prodeam.
da rore fontano abluam   5
manus et os et lumina.
pateatque, fac, sacrarium
nullo paratu extrinsecus :
pia verba, vota innoxia,
rei divinae copia est.   10
nec tus cremandum postulo
nec liba crusti mellei,
foculumque vivi caespitis
vanis relinquo altaribus.
Deus precandus est mihi   15
ac filius summi Dei,
maiestas unius modi,
sociata sacro spiritu.
et ecce iam vota ordior :
et cogitatio numinis   20
praesentiam sentit pavens.
pavetne quidquam spes, fides ? [1]

---

[1] Added in margin of *V* by the first hand. Some editors
reject the verse as an interpolator's correction.

[17] Up with you, you waster! What a thrashing you deserve! "Up, or a long, long sleep will come on you from where you dread it least."[1] Out with you, Parmeno, from your downy bed!

[21] Perchance this ditty, tuned to the Sapphic mode, encourages your sleep? Come you then, brisk Iambus, and banish hence the restful Lesbian strain.

II.—THE INTERLUDE

HI, boy! Get up! Bring me my slippers and my tunic of lawn: bring all the clothes that you have ready now for my going out. Fetch me spring water to wash my hands and mouth and eyes. Get me the chapel opened, but with no outward display: holy words and guiltless prayers are furniture enough for worship. I do not call for incense to be burnt nor for any slice of honey-cake: hearths of green turf I leave for the altars of vain gods. I must pray to God and to the Son of God most high, that co-equal[2] Majesty united in one fellowship with the Holy Spirit. And lo, now I begin my prayers: my heart feels Heaven is near and trembles. Have faith and hope, then, anything to fear?

---

[1] Quoted from Horace, *Odes*, III. xi. 38.
[2] *lit.* " of one extent."

III.—Oratio

Omnipotens, solo mentis mihi cognite cultu,
ignorate malis et nulli ignote piorum :
principio extremoque carens, antiquior aevo,
quod fuit aut veniet : cuius formamque modumque
nec mens conplecti poterit nec lingua profari :   5
cernere quem solus coramque audire iubentem
fas habet et patriam propter considere dextram
ipse opifex rerum, rebus causa ipse creandis,
ipse dei verbum, verbum deus, anticipator
mundi, quem facturus erat : generatus in illo   10
tempore, quo tempus nondum fuit : editus ante
quam iubar et rutilus caelum inlustraret Eous :
quo sine nil actum, per quem facta omnia :[1] cuius
in caelo solium, cui subdita terra sedenti
et mare et obscurae chaos insuperabile noctis :   15
inrequies, cuncta ipse movens, vegetator inertum :
non genito genitore deus, qui fraude superbi
offensus populi gentes in regna vocavit,
stirpis adoptivae meliore propage colendus :
cernere quem licuit proavis, quo numine viso   20
et patrem vidisse datum :[2] contagia nostra
qui tulit[3] et diri passus ludibria leti
esse iter aeternae docuit remeabile vitae :
nec solam remeare animam, sed corpore toto
caelestes intrare plagas et inane sepulcri   25
arcanum vacuis adopertum linquere terris.

---

[1] cp. *John* i. 3.   [2] cp. *John* xiv. 9.
[3] cp. 1 *Cor.* xv. 3.

THE DAILY ROUND

III.—The Prayer

ALMIGHTY One, whom through the worship of my heart alone I know, to the wicked unknown, yet known to every devout soul, thou art without beginning and without end, more ancient than time past and time to come: thy fashion and extent no mind can ever grasp, nor tongue express. He only may behold thee and, face to face, hear thy bidding and sit at thy fatherly right-hand who is himself the Maker of all things, himself the Cause of all created things, himself the Word of God, the Word which is God, who was before the world which he was to make, begotten at that time when Time was not yet, who came into being before the Sun's beams and the bright Morning-Star enlightened the sky. Without him was nothing made, and through him were all things made: his throne is in Heaven; and beneath his seat lie Earth and the Sea and the invincible Chaos of darkling Night: unresting, he is the very mover of all things, the quickener of the lifeless. He is God, the begotten of the unbegotten, who being provoked by the guile of his scornful people, called the nations into his kingdom—the worthier offshoots of an ingrafted stock to worship him. To our forefathers it was granted to behold him; and whoso discerned his Godhead, to him it was given to have seen the Father also. He bare our sinful stains and suffered a death with mockery, thus teaching us that there is a road to lead back to eternal life, and that the soul returns not alone, but with the body complete enters the realms of Heaven and leaves the secret chamber of the grave empty, covered with earth which cannot hold it.

17

Nate patris summi nostroque salutifer aevo,
virtutes patrias genitor cui tradidit omnes,
nil ex invidia retinens plenusque datorum,
pande viam precibus patriasque haec perfer ad
    aures.   30

Da, pater, invictam contra omnia crimina mentem
vipereumque nefas nocituri averte veneni.
sit satis, antiquam serpens quod prodidit Aevvam
deceptumque adiunxit Adam : nos sera nepotum
semina, veridicis olim praedicta prophetis,   35
vitemus laqueos, quos letifer inplicat anguis.

Pande viam, quae me post vincula corporis aegri
in sublime ferat, puri qua lactea caeli
semita ventosae superat vaga nubila lunae,
qua proceres abiere pii quaque integer olim   40
raptus quadriiugo penetrat super aera curru
Elias et solido cum corpore praevius Enoch.

Da, pater, aeterni speratam luminis auram,
si lapides non iuro deos unumque verendi
suspiciens altare sacri libamina vitae   45
intemerata fero : si te dominique deique
unigenae cognosco patrem mixtumque duobus,
qui super aequoreas volitabat spiritus undas.[1]

Da, genitor, veniam cruciataque pectora purga :
si te non pecudum fibris, non sanguine fuso   50

---

[1] *Genesis* i. 2.

[27] Son of the all-highest Father, Bringer of salvation to our race, thou unto whom thy Begetter has committed all the powers of his Fatherhood, keeping none back in envy but giving freely, open a way for these my prayers and safely waft them to thy Father's ears.

[31] Grant me a heart, O Father, to hold out against all deeds of wrong, and deliver me from the Serpent's deadly venom, sin. Let it suffice that the Serpent did beguile our old mother Eve and involved Adam also in his deceit[1]: let us, their late-born progeny once foretold by sooth-speaking Prophets, escape the snares which the death-dealing Serpent weaves.

[37] Prepare a road that I, being freed from the fetters of this frail body, may be led up on high, where in the clear heaven the Milky Way stretches above the wandering clouds of the wind-vexed moon —that road by which the holy men of old departed from the earth; by which Elias,[2] caught up in the chariot, once made his way alive above our lower air; and Enoch,[3] too, who went before his end without change of body.

[43] Grant me, O Father, the effluence of everlasting light for which I yearn, if I swear not by gods of stone, and, looking up to one altar of awful sacrifice alone, bring there the offering of a stainless life; if Thee I recognize as Father of the Only-Begotten, our Lord and God, and, joined with both, the Spirit who brooded over the waters' face.

[49] Grant me thy pardon, Father, and relieve my anguished breast, if I seek thee not with the bodies of slain beasts nor with blood poured forth, nor

[1] 1 *Tim.* ii. 14.   [2] 2 *Kings* ii. 11.   [3] *cp. Hebrews* xi. 5.

19

quaero nec arcanis numen coniecto sub extis:
si scelere abstineo errori obnoxius et si
opto magis, quam fido, bonus purusque probari.
confessam dignare animam, si membra caduca
execror et tacitum si paenitet altaque sensus   55
formido excruciat tormentaque sera gehennae
anticipat patiturque suos mens saucia manes.[1]

    Da, pater, haec nostro fieri rata vota precatu.
nil metuam cupiamque nihil:[2] satis hoc rear esse,
quod satis est; nil turpe velim nec causa pudoris 60
sim mihi; non faciam cuiquam, quae tempore eodem
nolim facta mihi.[3] nec vero crimine laedar
nec maculer dubio: paulum distare videtur
suspectus vereque reus. male posse facultas
nulla sit et bene posse adsit tranquilla potestas.   65
sim tenui victu atque habitu, sim carus amicis
et semper genitor sine vulnere nominis huius.
non animo doleam, non corpore: cuncta suetis
fungantur membra officiis: nec saucius ullis
partibus amissum quidquam desideret usus.   70
pace fruar, securus agam, miracula terrae
nulla putem. suprema dii cum venerit hora,
nec timeat mortem bene conscia vita nec optet.
purus ab occultis cum te indulgente videbor,
omnia despiciam, fuerit cum sola voluptas   75
iudicium sperare tuum; quod dum sua differt

---

[1] *cp.* Virgil, *Aen.* vi. 743.
[2] *cp.* Horace, *Ep.* i. 16, 35.
[3] *cp. Matth.* vii. 12.

divine heaven's will from the secrets of their entrails: if I, though prone to stray, hold off from wrong, and if I long, rather than trust, to be approved upright and pure. Accept a soul which makes its confession, if I abhor these my frail limbs, if I repent me inwardly, and if deep-seated dread racks all my nerves and foretastes the final torments of Gehenna, and the stricken mind suffers its own ghostly doom.

[58] Grant, then, O Father, that these petitions may be fulfilled as I pray. Naught let me fear, and naught desire: let me feel that to be enough which is enough; let me seek nothing vile, nor be the cause of my own shame; let me not do to any that which at the same time I would not have done to me. May no real crime bring me to ruin, nor suspicion tarnish my name: small difference there seems between the real and supposed guilt. Keep thou from me the means to do ill deeds, and let me ever have the calm power to do well. Let me be moderate in food and dress, dear to my friends, and ever careful to do naught to shame the name of father. In mind and body let me be free from pain: let all my limbs perform their wonted functions, and let not crippled habit mourn the loss of any part. Let me enjoy peace and live quietly, counting as nothing all that astounds on earth. And when the hour of my last day shall come, grant that the conscience of a life well spent suffer me not to fear death, nor yet long for it. When, through thy mercy, I shall appear cleansed from my secret faults, let me despise all else, and let my one delight be to await in hope thy judgment. And if that season

tempora cunctaturque dies, procul exige saevum
insidiatorem blandis erroribus anguem.
    Haec pia, sed maesto trepidantia vota reatu,
nate, aput aeternum placabilis adsere patrem,   80
salvator, deus ac dominus, mens, gloria, verbum,
filius, ex vero verus, de lumine lumen,
aeterno cum patre manens, in saecula regnans,
consona quem celebrant modulati carmina David :[1]
et responsuris ferit aera vocibus amen.   85

IV.—Egressio

Satis precum datum deo,
quamvis satis numquam reis
fiat precatu numinis.
habitum forensem da, puer.
dicendum amicis est have   5
valeque, quod fit mutuum.
quod cum per horas quattuor
[cursum citatis sol equis][2]
inclinet ad meridiem,
monendus est iam Sosias.

V.—Locus Invitationis

Tempus vocandis namque amicis adpetit ;
ne nos vel illis demoremur prandium,
propere per aedes curre vicinas, puer.
scis ipse, qui sint : iamque dum loquor, redi.
quinque advocavi ; sex enim convivium   5
cum rege iustum : si super, convicium est.
abiit ; relicti nos sumus cum Sosia.

---

[1] *VP*[2] : *C* has also the variant line " consona quem cele-
brat modulato carmine plebes."
[2] Suppl. *Translator.*

tarries and the day delays, keep far from me that fierce tempter, the Serpent, with his false allurements.

[79] These prayers of a soul devout, albeit trembling with dark sense of guilt, claim for thine own before the eternal Father, thou Son of God who mayest be entreated, Saviour, God and Lord, Mind, Glory, Word and Son, Very God of Very God, Light of Light, who remainest with the eternal Father, reigning throughout all ages, whose praise the harmonious songs of tuneful David echo forth, until respondent voices rend the air with " Amen."

IV.—Going Out

Now I have prayed enough to God, albeit we sinful men can never entreat Heaven enough. Boy ! Bring me my morning coat. I must exchange my " Hail " and " Farewell " with my friends. But since the sun for four full hours has urged on his steeds and now verges towards noon, I needs must speak a word with Sosias.[1]

V.—The Time for giving Invitations

And now the time for inviting my friends draws on. So, that no fault of mine may make them late for lunch, hurry at your best pace, boy, to the neighbours' houses—you know without my telling who they are—and back with you before these words are done. I have invited five to lunch; for six persons, counting the host, make the right number for a meal: if there be more, it is no meal but a *mêlée*. Ah, he is off! And I am left to deal with Sosias.

[1] It being now ten o'clock and two hours to lunch-time, Ausonius remembers that he must give directions (which follow in § vi.) to his cook Sosias.

AUSONIUS

VI.—Locus Ordinandi Coqui.

Sosia, prandendum est.   quartam iam totus in horam
    sol calet: ad quintam flectitur umbra notam.
an vegeto madeant condita opsonia gustu
    (fallere namque solent), experiundo proba.
concute ferventes palmis volventibus ollas,   5
    tingue celer digitos iure calente tuos,
vibranti lambat quos umida lingua recursu [1]

     *   *   *   *   *   *

VII.—[In Notarium in Scribendo Velocissimum]

    Puer, notarum praepetum
    sollers minister, advola.
    bipatens pugillar expedi,
    cui multa fandi copia,
    punctis peracta singulis,   5
    ut una vox absolvitur.
    ego volvo libros uberes
    instarque densae grandinis
    torrente lingua perstrepo:
    tibi nec aures ambigunt,   10
    nec occupatur pagina
    et mota parce dextera
    volat per aequor cereum.
    cum maxime nunc proloquor
    circumloquentis ambitu,   15
    tu sensa nostri pectoris
    vix dicta iam ceris tenes.
    sentire tam velox mihi
    vellem dedisset mens mea,

[1] The remainder of this poem together with much else has
been lost.

VI.—The Time for Directing the Cook

Sosias, I must have lunch. The warm sun is already passed well on into his fourth hour, and on the dial the shadow is moving on towards the fifth stroke. Taste and make sure—for they often play you false—that the seasoned dishes are well soused and taste appetisingly. Turn your bubbling pots in your hands and shake them up : quick, dip your fingers in the hot gravy and let your moist tongue lick them as it darts in and out . . .

VII.—To his Stenographer, a Ready Writer

Hi, boy ! My secretary, skilled in dashing short-hand, make haste and come ! Open your folding tablets wherein a world of words is compassed in a few signs and finished off as it were a single phrase. I ponder works of generous scope ; and thick and fast like hail the words tumble off my tongue. And yet your ears are not at fault nor your page crowded, and your right hand, moving easily, speeds over the waxen surface of your tablet. When I declaim, as now, at greatest speed, talking in circles round my theme, you have the thoughts of my heart already set fast in wax almost before they are uttered. I would my mind had given me power to think as

quam praepetis dextrae fuga   20
tu me loquentem praevenis.
   Quis, quaeso, quis me prodidit?
quis ista iam dixit tibi,
quae cogitabam dicere?
quae furta corde in intimo   25
exercet ales dextera?
quis ordo rerum tam novus,
veniat in aures ut tuas,
quod lingua nondum absolverit?
doctrina non hoc praestitit   30
nec ulla tam velox manus
celeripedis compendii:
natura munus hoc tibi
deusque donum tradidit,
quae loquerer, ut scires prius   35
idemque velles, quod volo.

VIII

[Discutiunt nobis placidos portenta sopores,
qualia miramur, cum saepius aethere in alto
conciliant varias coetu vaga nubila formas][1]
quadrupedum et volucrum, vel cum terrena marinis
monstra admiscentur; donec purgantibus euris
difflatae liquidum tenuentur in aera nubes.
nunc fora, nunc lites, lati modo pompa theatri
visitur: et turmas equitum caedesque latronum   5
perpetior: lacerat nostros fera belua vultus
aut in sanguinea gladio grassamur harena.

---

[1] Schenkl observes that a leaf containing the end of the
Ephemeris and the beginning of this poem has fallen out of
the archetype.   The Translator's supplement (in brackets) is
intended to suggest the general sense immediately preceding.

swiftly as you outstrip me when I speak, and as your dashing hand leaves my words behind.

[22] Who, prithee, who is he who has betrayed me? Who has already told you what I was but now thinking to say? What thefts are these that your speeding hand perpetrates in the recesses of my mind? How come things in so strange an order that what my tongue has not yet vented comes to your ears? No teaching ever gave you this gift, nor was ever any hand so quick at swift stenography: Nature endowed you so, and God gave you this gift to know beforehand what I would speak, and to intend the same that I intend.

VIII

[Strange monsters disturb our calm slumbers, like those we marvel at when, sometimes, in the high upper air the wandering clouds unite and blend together the various shapes] of four-footed beasts and winged creatures; when monstrous shapes of earth and sea are mingled in one, until the cleansing eastern winds blow the clouds to shreds and thin them out into the clear air. Now the courts pass before my eyes with suits at law, and now the spacious theatre with its shows. Here I endure the sight of troops of cavalry cutting down brigands: or in the bloody arena some wild beast tears my face, or I am butchered with the sword. I go afoot across the

27

per mare navifragum gradior pedes et freta cursu
transilio et subitis volito super aera pinnis.
infandas etiam veneres incestaque noctis   10
dedecora et tragicos patimur per somnia coetus.
perfugium tamen est, quotiens portenta soporum
solvit rupta pudore quies et imagine foeda
libera mens vigilat : totum bene conscia lectum
pertractat secura manus : probrosa recedit   15
culpa tori et profugi manascunt crimina somni.
cerno triumphantes inter me plaudere : rursum
inter captivos trahor exarmatus Alanos.
templa deum sanctasque fores palatiaque aurea
specto et Sarrano videor discumbere in ostro   20
et mox fumosis conviva adcumbo popinis.

 Divinum perhibent vatem sub frondibus ulmi
vana ignavorum simulacra locasse soporum
et geminas numero portas : quae fornice eburno
semper fallaces glomerat super aera formas :   25
altera, quae veros emittit cornea visus.
quod si de dubiis conceditur optio nobis,
desse fidem laetis melius quam vana timeri.
ecce ego iam malim falli ; nam, dum modo semper
tristia vanescant, potius caruisse fruendis,   30
quam trepidare malis. satis est bene, si metus absit.
sunt et qui fletus et gaudia controversum
coniectent varioque trahant eventa relatu.

wrecking sea, bound at a stride across the straits, and flit above the air on new-found wings. Then, too, in dreams we undergo amours unspeakable, and night's foul shames, and unions which are the themes of tragedy. Yet there is escape from these whenever shame bursts through the bonds of sleep, scattering the horrors of our dreams, and the mind freed from filthy fancying keeps watch. Then the hands untainted feel about the bed nor find cause for remorse : the sinful guilt of luxury departs, and as the dream fades from us, so its stain. Now, I see myself applauding, one of a triumphant throng : again I am dragged through the streets a disarmed Alan prisoner of war. And now I gaze upon the temples of the gods, their sacred portals and golden palaces; or seem to recline at a feast upon a couch of Sarran (Tyrian) purple, and presently sit feasting at the table of some steamy eating-house.

²² They say the heavenly bard[1] set for the empty phantoms of sluggish sleep a place beneath an elm-tree's leaves, and appointed them two gates: that which is arched with ivory ever pours forth upon the air a host of deceptive shapes : the second is of horn and sends forth visions of the truth. But if dreams of doubtful import leave us the choice, better that cheerful sights deceive us than we should fear with a cause. Look you, I would even rather be deceived ; for, if only gloomy dreams always prove void, it is better to have missed what might have been enjoyed than to tremble at ill-fortune. 'Tis well enough if only fear be far from us. Some there are also who argue their woe and weal by contraries, and who forecast results by opposite interpretation.

---

[1] sc. Virgil (*Aen.* vi. 282 ff.).

Ite per oblicos caeli, mala somnia, mundos,
inrequieta vagi qua difflant nubila nimbi ;   35
lunares habitate polos : quid nostra subitis
limina et angusti tenebrosa cubilia tecti ?
me sinite ignavas placidum traducere noctes,
dum redeat roseo mihi Lucifer aureus ortu.
quod si me nullis vexatum nocte figuris   40
mollis tranquillo permulserit aere somnus,
hunc lucum, nostro viridis qui frondet in agro
ulmeus, excubiis habitandum dedico vestris.

[34] Away, you evil dreams, through the sloping firmaments of heaven, where wandering storms scatter the still-vexed clouds; dwell in the moon-lit skies. Why steal you in at my doors and haunt the darkling couch in my confined dwelling? Leave me to pass night unexcited in calm repose till golden Lucifer comes back for me in the rosy east. But if soft sleep shall soothe me with his gentle breath, nor any shapes trouble my rest by night, this grove —the elm which spreads its green leaves on my estate—I dedicate for you to dwell in on your night watches.

LIBER III

[DOMESTICA]

I.—De Herediolo

Cum de palatio post multos annos honoratissimus,
quippe iam consul, redisset ad patriam, villulam,
quam pater reliquerat, introgressus his versibus lusit
Luciliano stilo:

Salve, herediolum, maiorum regna meorum,
  quod proavus, quod avus, quod pater excoluit,
quod mihi iam senior properata morte reliquit:
  eheu nolueram tam cito posse frui!
iusta quidem series patri succedere, verum   5
  esse simul dominos gratior ordo piis.
nunc labor et curae mea sunt; sola ante voluptas
  partibus in nostris, cetera patris erant.
parvum herediolum, fateor, set nulla fuit res
  parva umquam aequanimis, adde etiam unanimis. 10
ex animo rem stare aequum puto, non animum ex re.
  cuncta cupit Croesus, Diogenes nihilum:

---

[1] Of Cyrene, a disciple of Socrates. For the anecdote here
related *cp.* Horace, *Sat.* ii. iii. 100.

BOOK III

PERSONAL POEMS

I.—On his Little Patrimony

When the author had left the court after many
years' enjoyment of the highest distinctions, having
even become consul, he returned to his native place
and settled down in the little property which his
father had left him. Thereupon he wrote the following
playful verses in the manner of Lucilius:

Hail, little patrimony, the realm of my forebears,
which my great-grandfather, which my grandfather,
which my father tended so carefully, which the last-
named left to me when he died all too soon, albeit
in a ripe old age. Ah me! I had not wished to be
able to possess you so early. 'Tis indeed the natural
order when the son succeeds the father; but where
there is affection, it is a more pleasing course for
both to reign together. Now all the toil and trouble
falls on me: of old the pleasure only was my share,
the rest was all my father's. It is a tiny patri-
mony, I allow; but never yet did property seem
small to those whose souls are balanced, nay more,
whose souls are one. Upon the soul—it is my
balanced judgment—wealth depends, and not a
man's soul upon his wealth. A Croesus desires every-
thing, a Diogenes, nothing; an Aristippus[1] strews

spargit Aristippus mediis in Syrtibus aurum,
  aurea non satis est Lydia tota Midae.
cui nullus finis cupiendi, est nullus habendi :   15
  ille opibus modus est, quem statuas animo.
Verum ager iste meus quantus sit, nosce, etiam ut me
  noveris et noris te quoque, si potis es.
quamquam difficile est se noscere ; γνῶθι σεαυτόν
  quam propere legimus, tam cito neclegimus.   20
agri bis centum colo iugera, vinea centum
  iugeribus colitur prataque dimidio,
silva supra duplum, quam prata et vinea et arvum ;
  cultor agri nobis nec superest nec abest.
fons propter puteusque brevis, tum purus et amnis ;   25
  naviger hic refluus me vehit ac revehit.
conduntur fructus geminum mihi semper in annum.
  cui non longa penus, huic quoque prompta fames.
Haec mihi nec procul urbe sita est, nec prorsus ad
    urbem,
  ne patiar turbas utque bonis potiar.   30
et quotiens mutare locum fastidia cogunt,
  transeo et alternis rure vel urbe fruor.

II.—Versus Paschales pro Augusto Dicti

Sancta salutiferi redeunt sollemnia Christi
et devota pii celebrant ieiunia mystae.
at nos aeternum cohibentes pectore cultum
intemeratorum vim continuamus honorum.
annua cura sacris, iugis reverentia nobis.   5

his gold abroad in the midst of the Syrtes, all Lydia turned to gold cannot content a Midas. The man who sets no bounds to his greed, sets none to his possessions: that is the limit to wealth, which you decree in your own soul.

[17] But now you must know of what size is this estate of mine, that you may also know me and know yourself too, if you are capable. And yet how difficult this is, to know oneself! KNOW THYSELF: as hastily as we read that motto, so quickly we forget it. I keep in tillage two hundred acres: a hundred more are grown with vines, and half as much is pasture. My woodland is more than twice as much as my pasture, vineyard and tilth together: of husbandmen I have neither too many nor too few. A spring is near my house and a small well, besides the unsullied river, which on its tides bears me by boat from home and back again. I have always fruits in store to last me two whole years: who has short victual by him, he too has famine at hand.[1]

[29] This my estate lies not far from the town, nor yet hard by the town, to rid me of its crowds while reaping its advantages. And so, whenever satiety moves me to change my seat, I pass from one to the other, and enjoy country and town by turns.

II.—EASTER VERSES COMPOSED FOR THE EMPEROR

Now return the holy rites of Christ, who brought us our salvation, and godly zealots keep their solemn fasts. But we, guarding within our hearts an unending worship, maintain without a break the strength of an inviolate homage: rites are observed once a year; but our devotion is continual.

[1] cp. Hesiod, W. and D. 31, 363.

Magne pater rerum, cui terra et pontus et aer
Tartaraque et picti servit plaga lactea caeli,
noxia quem scelerum plebis tremit almaque russum
concelebrat votis animarum turba piarum :
tu brevis hunc aevi cursum celeremque caducae   10
finem animae donas aeternae munere vitae.[1]
tu mites legum monitus sacrosque prophetas
humano impertis generi servasque nepotes,
deceptum miseratus Adam, quem capta venenis
implicuit socium blandis erroribus Aevva.[2]   15
tu verbum, pater alme, tuum, natumque deumque,
concedis terris totum similemque paremque,
ex vero verum vivaque ab origine vivum.
ille tuis doctus monitis hoc addidit unum,
ut, super aequoreas nabat qui spiritus undas,[3]   20
pigra inmortali vegetaret membra lavacro.
trina fides auctore uno, spes certa salutis
[da veniam et praesta speratae munera vitae [4]]
hunc numerum iunctis virtutibus amplectenti.

Tale et terrenis specimen spectatur in oris
Augustus genitor, geminum sator Augustorum,   25
qui fratrem natumque pio conplexus utrumque
numine partitur regnum neque dividit unum,
omnia solus habens atque omnia dilargitus.
hos igitur nobis trina pietate vigentes,

---

[1] *cp. Romans* viii. 18.   [2] *cp.* 1 *Timothy* ii. 14.
[3] *cp. Genesis* i. 2.
[4] A line such as is here supplied appears to have dropped
out of the text.

⁶ O mighty Father of all things; to whom are subject earth, sea, and air, and hell, and all the expanse of heaven emblazoned with the Milky Way; before thee tremble the folk guilty of offences, and contrariwise the blameless company of righteous souls extols thee with prayer and praise. Thou dost reward our course through these few years and the swift close of our frail being with the prize of ever-lasting life. Thou dost bestow upon mankind the gentle warnings of the Law together with the holy Prophets; and, as thou didst pity Adam when be-guiled by Eve, on whom the poison seized so that she drew him by her smooth enticements to be the fellow of her transgression, so thou dost keep us, their progeny. Thou, gracious Father, grantest to the world thy Word, who is thy Son, and God, in all things like thee and equal with thee, very God of very God, and living God of the source of life. He, guided by thy behests, added this one gift alone, causing that Spirit which once moved over the face of the deep to quicken our dull members with the cleansing waters of eternal life. Object of our faith, Three, yet One in source, sure hope of our salvation! Grant pardon and bestow on me the gift of life for which I yearn, if I embrace this diversity of Persons united in their powers.

²⁴ Even on this earth below we behold an image of this mystery, where is the Emperor, the father, begetter of twin Emperors, who in his sacred majesty embraces his brother and his son, sharing one realm with them, yet not dividing it, alone holding all though he has all distributed. These, then, we pray, who, though three, flourish as one in natural

rectores terrae placidos caelique ministros,   30
Christe, aput aeternum placabilis adsere patrem.

III.—Oratio Consulis Ausonii Versibus Rhopalicis [1]

Spes, deus, aeternae stationis conciliator :
si castis precibus veniales invigilamus,
his, pater, oratis placabilis adstipulare.

   Da, Christe, specimen cognoscier inreprehensum,
rex bone, cultorum famulantum vivificator.   5
cum patre maiestas altissima, non generato.[2]

   Da trinum columen paraclito consociante,
ut longum celebris devotio continuetur :
ad temet properant vigilatum convenienter.

   Nox lucem revehet funalibus anteferendam,   10
nox lumen pariens credentibus indubitatum,
nox flammis operum meditatrix sidereorum.

   Tu mensis dirimis ieiunia relligiosa,
tu bona promittens surgentia concelebraris :
da, rector, modicos effarier omnipotentem.   15

   Fons tuus emundat recreatu iustificatos,
dans mentem oblitam positorum flagitiorum,
dans agnos niveos splendescere purificatos.

   Lux verbo inducta,[3] peccantibus auxiliatrix,   21
ut nova Iordanis ablutio, sanctificavit,   19

---

[1] *Scaliger* and most edd. reject this as a work of Ausonius.
[2] *Heinsius, Schenkl* : ingenerato, *V, Peiper.*
[3] *St. John* i. 4 ff.

ties, these mild rulers of the earth and instruments of Heaven, claim them for thine own in presence of thine eternal Father, O Christ most merciful.

III.—A Prayer of Ausonius the Consul In Rhopalic[1] Verse

O God, our hope, who dost provide for us an endless home; if we by holy prayer and vigil win thy pardon, then, Father, in thy mercy grant us our petitions. Grant us, O Christ, to know thy faultless pattern, O gracious King, thou quickener of thy servants who adore thee—thou, who with the Father, the Unbegotten, art one Majesty most high. Grant through the fellowship of the Comforter a triple stay to aid us, that throngs of worshippers may ceaselessly prolong thy praise: to thee it is they haste fitly to keep vigil. Night shall bring back a light far beyond any taper's ray; night which sends forth a beam in which believers put their trust; night which broods o'er the tasks of the fiery stars. Thou at thy table endest our solemn fasts; thou, who dost promise still increasing blessings, art praised by all with one accord: O thou, our Ruler, give us poor worthless mortals power to express the greatness of the Almighty.

[16] Thy fount cleanseth the sinner made justified by new creation: it bringeth the heart forgetfulness of sins now laid aside: it causeth thy cleansed lambs to shine white as the snow. The light, brought in by the Word, the sinner's stay, even as a new washing clean in Jordan, hath sanctified them,

[1] Rhopalic ("clublike") verse is that in which the first word is a monosyllable, the second a disyllable, the third a trisyllable, and so on.

cum sua dignati tinguentia promeruerunt.   20

Et Christus regimen elementis inrequietis
fert undam medici baptismatis intemerati,
ut noxam auferret mortalibus extenuatam.

Crux poenae extremum properata inmaculato,   25
ut vitam amissam renovaret mortificatus,
tot rerum titulis obnoxius immodicarum.   28

Quis digne domino praeconia continuabit?   27
an terra humano locupletat commemoratu,   29
quem vocum resonant modulatus angelicarum?   30

Dans aulam Stephano pretiosam dilapidato,
dans claves superas cathedrali incohatori,
quin Paulum infestum copulasti adglomeratu.

Fit doctor populi lapidantum constimulator,
ut latro confessor paradisum participavit,   35
sic, credo, adnectens dirissima clarificandis.

Nos seros famulos adcrescere perpetieris
sub tali edoctos antistite relligionis;
da sensum solida stabilitum credulitate.

Fac iungar numero redivivo glorificatus,   40
ad caelum invitans consortia terrigenarum,
SPES, DEUS, AETERNAE STATIONIS CONCILIATOR!

IV.—Epicedion in Patrem

Post deum semper patrem colui secundamque re-
verentiam genitori meo debui. sequitur ergo hanc
summi dei venerationem epicedion patris mei. titulus

when by their merits they are grown worthy of its blessed unction. And Christ, who ruled the restless elements, bringeth the healing waters of stainless baptism to minish and take away the guilt of men. The Sinless One was hurried to the cross of direst penalty, that by his death he might renew the life we forfeited, himself the theme of praise for all his matchless deeds. Who can worthily express the praises of the Lord? Can earth with its human tongues enrich his renown which tuneful choirs of angels echo forth above? Thou didst open thy splendid palace for Stephen stoned, thou didst give the keys of heaven to that first founder of the Apostolic Throne: much more, thou didst add Paul the persecutor to thy flock. He who urged on the men who stoned Stephen, became a teacher of the people, as the thief who confessed thee received a place in Paradise, so, methinks, following up his heinous deeds with acts worthy of renown. Thou wilt suffer us thy servants of these latter days to grow in grace, led by the teaching of that great prelate of our creed: give us an heart established with firm faith. Grant that I, being glorified, may join the company of them that live again, when thou shalt call the fellowship of earth-born men to Heaven, O God, our hope, who dost provide for us an endless home!

IV.—An Elegy upon his Father

I always revered my father next to God, and felt that I owed my parent the second place after Him in my veneration. And so this hymn of worship to God most high is followed by an *epicedion* upon my

a Graecis auctoribus defunctorum honori dicatus,
non ambitiosus, sed religiosus: quem commendo lec-
tori meo, sive is filius est seu pater sive utrumque.
neque, ut laudet, exigo; set, ut amet, postulo. ne-
que vero nunc patrem meum laudo, quod ille non
eget et ego functum oblectatione viventium onerare
non debeo. neque dico nisi quod agnoscunt, qui
parti aetatis eius interfuerunt. falsum me autem
morte [eius] obita dicere et verum tacere eiusdem
piaculi existimo. imagini ipsius hi versus subscripti
sunt neque minus in opusculorum meorum seriem
relati. alia omnia mea displicent mihi; hoc relegisse
amo.

Nomen ego Ausonius, non ultimus arte medendi
 et, mea si nosses tempora, primus eram.
vicinas urbes colui patriaque domoque,
 Vasates patria, sed lare Burdigalam.
curia me duplex et uterque senatus habebat   5
 muneris exsortem, nomine participem.
non opulens nec egens, parcus sine sordibus egi:
 victum, habitum, mores semper eadem habui.
sermone inpromptus Latio, verum Attica lingua
 suffecit culti vocibus eloquii.   10
optuli opem cunctis poscentibus artis inemptae
 officiumque meum cum pietate fuit.

father. It is a title consecrated by Greek writers to the honour of the departed, and is expressive not of vanity but of devotion. And this poem I commend to my reader, be he son, or father, or both. I do not demand that he should praise it, but I do ask him to love it. And indeed I do not here sing the praises of my father; for he needs no praise, and I have no right to burden the dead with the entertainment of the living. Furthermore, I say nothing more of him than what those who were to some degree his contemporaries recognize as fact. For me to say what is untrue about him because he is dead, and to disguise what is true, I consider to be equally heinous. These verses were written under his portrait, and likewise entered in the collection of my works. I am dissatisfied with all else of mine; but this poem I love to read over and over again.

My name was Ausonius, of no mean repute in the art of healing; nay, if you but knew my age, I was the foremost. I was born and had my dwelling in two neighbouring towns; Bazas was my birthplace, but Bordeaux was my home. I was a senator in the council[1] of both towns, although I filled no office and my rank was honorary. Not wealthy nor yet needy, I lived thriftily yet not meanly: as to my table, dress, and habits, I have always followed the same way. For Latin I never had a ready tongue; but the speech of Athens supplied my need with words of choice eloquence. To all who asked I brought the aid of my art without fee, and pity bare a large share in my work.

---

[1] Every *municipium* had a senate of one hundred members (*decuriones*) who met in a council-chamber called *curia*.

43

iudicium de me studui praestare bonorum:
    ipse mihi numquam, iudice me, placui.
officia in multos diverso debita cultu   15
    personis, meritis, tempore distribui.
litibus abstinui: non auxi, non minui rem;
    indice me nullus, set neque teste, perit.
invidi numquam; cupere atque ambire refugi;
    iurare aut falsum dicere par habui.   20
factio me sibi non, non coniuratio iunxit:
    sincero colui foedere amicitias.
felicem scivi non qui, quod vellet, haberet,
    set qui per fatum non data non cuperet.
non occursator, non garrulus, obvia cernens,   25
    valvis et velo condita non adii.
famam, quae posset vitam lacerare bonorum,
    non finxi et, veram si scierim, tacui.
ira procul, spes vana procul, procul anxia cura
    inque bonis hominum gaudia falsa procul.   30
vitati coetus eiuratique tumultus
    et semper fictae principum amicitiae.
deliquisse nihil numquam laudem esse putavi
    atque bonos mores legibus antetuli.
irasci promptus properavi condere motum   35
    atque mihi poenas pro levitate dedi.
coniugium per lustra novem sine crimine concors
    unum habui: gnatos quattuor edidimus.
prima obiit lactans; at qui fuit ultimus aevi,
    pubertate rudi non rudis interiit.   40

I strove to fulfil the judgment good men formed of me; I myself was a judge who never satisfied myself. Upon many I bestowed such acts of kindness as their various walks in life, persons, deserts, or the occasion demanded. I kept clear of lawsuits, and neither increased nor lessened my estate: none ever died accused by me, or even on my testimony. I envied none; greed and self-seeking I shunned: false-speaking I abhorred as deeply as perjury. Parties and cabals never found an ally in me, and I honoured loyally the bond of friendship. I saw full well that he is not the happy man who has all that he would, but he who does not long for what fate has not given. No busybody, no tattler, seeing only what was before my eyes, I did not intrude upon what door or curtains screened. I dished up no scandal to wound the life of worthy men; or if I knew such to be true, I held my tongue. Anger, and idle hopes, and carking cares—all these were far from me, as were all hollow joys in what men count as goods. Meetings I shunned, and riots I forswore along with the ever-false friendships of the great. I never held it to my credit that I transgressed in naught, ever regarding good habits above mere laws. Being quick of temper, I made haste to crush this impulse, and did violence to myself to maintain an unruffled soul. For nine full lustres (forty-five years) I lived without reproach as without quarrel with one wife; and of our union four children were born. The eldest girl died in infancy; but our youngest boy died e'er he ripened into boyhood, though not unripe in parts. Our elder

maximus ad summum columen pervenit honorum,
   praefectus Gallis et Libyae et Latio,
tranquillus, clemens, oculis, voce, ore serenus,
   in genitore suo mente animoque puer.
huius ego et natum et generum pro consule vidi; 45
   consul ut ipse foret, spes mihi certa fuit.
matronale decus possedit filia, cuius
   egregia et nuptae laus erat et viduae,
quae nati generique et progeneri simul omnium
   multiplici inlustres vidit honore domos.   50
ipse nec adfectans nec detrectator honorum
   praefectus magni nuncupor Illyrici.
haec me fortunae larga indulgentia suasit
   numine adorato vitae obitum petere,
ne fortunatae spatium inviolabile vitae   55
   fatali morsu stringeret ulla dies.
optinui auditaeque preces: spem, vota, timorem
   sopitus placido fine relinquo aliis.
inter maerentes, sed non ego maestus, amicos
   dispositis iacui funeris arbitriis.   60
nonaginta annos baculo sine, corpore toto
   exegi, cunctis integer officiis.
haec quicumque leges, non aspernabere fari:
   talis vita tibi, qualia vota mihi.

---

[1] Ausonius himself was properly prefect of the Gauls (in 378); but his prefecture was combined with that held by Hesperius (of Italy, Illyricum, and Africa).

son rose to the highest pinnacle of dignity, as prefect of all Gaul, Libya, and Latium,[1] calm and kindly, gentle of glance and speech and mien, in bearing towards his father he was still a boy in mind and heart. I lived to see his son and son-in-law proconsuls,[2] and my hope was always sure that he himself would be consul. My daughter enjoyed the pride of the wedded state, and won the highest praise both as wife and widow. She lived to see her son, her son-in-law, and her granddaughter's husband all bring glory to their house in titles manifold. And I, although I neither angled for distinctions nor affected to disdain them, bore the title of prefect of the great Illyricum. Such lavish kindness on fortune's part moved me to praise my God, and pray that my life might end before any day with fell tooth should fret the unmarred span of so fortunate a life. My prayers were heard and my request was granted: now I am fallen asleep after a peaceful end, and leave to others hopes, and prayers, and fears. And so, after the allowances [3] for my funeral had been allotted, I lay amid grieving friends, myself not grieving. Ninety years I lived, without a staff, my body whole and unfailing in all its functions. Whoe'er you are who shall read these lines, you will not scorn to say : " Your life was such as I pray mine may be."

[2] *sc.* Hesperius and Thalassius, proconsuls of Africa.

[3] *Arbitria* (*cp.* Cic. *de Domo sua*, 37) were so called because their amount was adjudged (*arbitrabantur*) in accordance with the means and rank of the deceased : see Justinian, *Dig.* xi. vii. 12, §§ 5, 6.

AUSONIUS

Iane, veni : novus anne, veni : renovate veni, sol.

* * * * * *

* * * * * *

consulis Ausonii Latiam visure curulem.
ecquid ab Augusta nunc maiestate secundum   5
quod mireris, habes?   Roma illa domusque Quirini
et toga purpurei rutilans praetexta senati
hoc apice aeternis signat sua tempora fastis.
[Iane, veni : novus anne, veni : renovate veni, sol.]¹
Anne, bonis coepte auspiciis, da vere salubri   10
apricas ventorum animas, da roscida Cancro
solstitia et gelidum Boream Septembribus horis.
mordeat autumnis frigus subtile pruinis
et tenuata moris cesset mediocribus aestas.
sementem Notus umificet, sit bruma nivalis,   15
dum pater antiqui renovatur Martius anni.
[Iane, veni : novus anne, veni : renovate veni, sol.]
Spiret odorato florum nova gratia Maio,
Iulius et segetes coquat et mare temperet Euris,
Sirius ardentem non augeat igne Leonem,   20
discolor arboreos variet Pomona sapores,

¹ Suppl. *Peiper.*

---

¹ See Pliny, *N.H.* xv. 3, 4.   In the earliest times, the
Roman year began in March, and there were only ten
months (December being the last): the addition of two new

PERSONAL POEMS

V.—A Solemn Prayer of Ausonius as Consul-desig-
NATE, WHEN HE ASSUMED THE INSIGNIA OF OFFICE
ON THE EVE OF THE KALENDS OF JANUARY

*Come, Janus; come, New Year; come, Sun, with
strength renewed!*

* * * * * *
* * * * * *

soon to behold Ausonius enthroned in state, consul
of Rome. What hast thou now beneath the Imperial
dignity itself to marvel at? That famous Rome, that
dwelling of Quirinus, and that Senate whose bordered
robes glow with rich purple, from this point date
their seasons in their deathless records.

*Come, Janus; come, New Year; come, Sun, with
strength renewed!*

[10] Year, that beginnest with good augury, give us
in healthful Spring winds of sunny breath; when the
Crab shows at the solstice, give us dews, and allay the
hours of September with a cool north wind. Let
shrewdly-biting frosts lead in Autumn and let Sum-
mer wane and yield her place by slow degrees. Let
the south winds moisten the seed corn, and Winter
reign with all her snows until March, father of the
old-style year,[1] come back anew.

*Come, Janus; come, New Year; come, Sun, with
strength renewed!*

[18] Let May come back with new grace and fragrant
breath of flowers, let July ripen crops and give the
sea respite from eastern winds, let Sirius' flames
not swell the heat of Leo's rage, let party-hued
Pomona bring on array of luscious fruits, let Autumn

months (January and February) was traditionally ascribed to
Numa.

mitiget autumnus, quod maturaverit aestas,
et genialis hiems parta sibi dote fruatur.
pacem mundus agat nec turbida sidera regnent.

[IANE, VENI: NOVUS ANNE, VENI: RENOVATE VENI, SOL..]

Nulla tuos, Gradive, offendat stella penates,⠀⠀⠀⠀26
quae non aequa tibi; non Cynthia, non celer Arcas
finitimus terris; non tu, Saturne, supremo
ultime circuitu: procul a Pyroente remotus
tranquillum properabis iter.⠀⠀vos comminus ite,⠀⠀30
stella salutigeri Iovis et Cythereie Vesper:
non umquam hospitibus facilis Cyllenius absit.

IANE, VENI: NOVUS ANNE, VENI: RENOVATE VENI, SOL.

Hostibus edomitis, qua Francia mixta Suebis
certat ad obsequium, Latiis ut militet armis,⠀⠀⠀35
qua vaga Sauromates sibi iunxerat agmina Chuni,
quaque Getes sociis Histrum adsultabat Alanis
(hoc mihi praepetibus victoria nuntiat alis):
iam venit Augustus, nostros ut comat honores,
officio exornans, quos participare cupisset.⠀⠀⠀40

IANE, VENI: NOVUS ANNE, VENI: RENOVATE VENI, SOL.

Aurea venturo, Sol, porrige gaudia Iano:
fascibus Ausonii succedet Caesar in annum,

---

[1] Of the stars mentioned in ll. 26-32 Cynthia is the Moon,
Arcas or Arctophylax (son of Jove and Callisto) is the Bear
Warden, the "Fiery Planet" is Mars, and "Cytherean
Vesper" is Venus as the Evening Star. The "Cyllenian" is
Mercury, reputed to take on the influence of whatever star
happens to be in his "house."

[2] Ausonius is the only authority for Gratian's exploits in
378 after the defeat of the Alemanni at Argentaria (Colmar

mellow what Summer has matured, and let jolly Winter enjoy his portion due. Let the world live at peace, and no stars of trouble hold sway.

Come, Janus; come, New Year; come, Sun, with strength renewed!

[26] Gradivus, let no star but such as favours thee invade thy house—not Cynthia, nor swift Arcas nearest to the earth, nor thou, O Saturn, moving remote in thy distant orbit: far from the Fiery Planet thou shalt move on thy peaceful course. Ye in conjunction move, star of health-bringing Jove, and Cytherean Vesper, nor ever let the Cyllenian,[1] so complaisant to his guests, tarry far off.

Come, Janus; come, New Year; come, Sun, with strength renewed!

[34] All foes now vanquished [2] (where the mixed Frankish and Swabian hordes vie in submission, seeking to serve in our Roman armies; and where the wandering bands of Huns had made alliance with the Sarmatian; and where the Getae with their Alan friends used to attack the Danube—for Victory borne on swift wings gives me the news of this), lo now the Emperor comes to grace my dignity, and with his favour crowns the distinction which he would fain have shared.

Come, Janus; come, New Year; come, Sun, with strength renewed!

[42] Offer thy golden joys, O Sun, to Janus, soon to come. A year, and Caesar shall succeed to the insignia of Ausonius, and wear for the fifth time the

in Alsace). In the *Gratiarum Actio* (ch. ii.) Gratian is credited with having restored peace along the frontiers of the Rhine and the Danube in a single year. The reference to a message here supposed to be brought by Victory is probably anticipatory.

quintam Romulei praetextam habiturus honoris.
ecce ubi se cumulat mea purpura (mitibus audi   45
auribus hoc, Nemesis) post me dignatur oriri
Augustus consul.   plus quam conferre videtur
me sibi, qui iussit nostros praecedere fasces.
  IANE, VENI: NOVUS ANNE, VENI: RENOVATE VENI, SOL.
Tu tropicum soli da[1] cedere, rursus et illum   50
terga dare, ut duplex tropico varietur ab astro
et quater a ternis properet mutatio signis.
aestivos inpelle dies brumamque morantem
noctibus adceleret promissus Caesaris annus.
illum ego si cernam, tum terque quaterque beatus, 55
tunc ero bis consul, tunc tangam vertice caelum.

VI.—ITEM PRECATIO KAL. IANUARIIS

ANNE, bonis coepte auspiciis, felicia cernis
consulis Ausonii primordia: prome coruscum,
Sol aeterne, caput solitoque inlustrior almo
lumine purpureum iubar exere lucis eoae.
anne, pater rerum, quas Iani mense bifrontis   5
volvis in hibernum glaciali fine Decembrem,
alme, veni et festum veteri novus adice Ianum.   7
coge secuturos bis sena per ostia menses;[2]   7a

---

   [1] *Scaliger*: solido da, *V, Peiper*.
   [2] Transferred to this place by Peiper: in the MS. (*V*) this
verse follows l. 49 in the preceding poem.

robe that distinguishes the Roman consul. Lo, how my honours are increased (hear this, O Nemesis, with an indulgent ear): Augustus deigns to appear as consul after me. It is as though he did more than rank me with himself now he has bidden me to bear the insignia before himself.

Come, Janus; come, New Year; come, Sun, with strength renewed!
[50] Cause the one Tropic to give place to the Sun and again, make that other flee; that twice he (the Sun) may move through his changes from the Tropic Star and four times hasten to pass on from the three grouped Signs.[1] Urge on the summer days, and let Caesar's promised year speed the winter with its laggard nights. If I behold that year, then shall I be thrice, nay four times blessed; then shall I be doubly consul, then my head shall touch heaven itself.

VI.—ANOTHER PRAYER FOR THE FIRST OF JANUARY

YEAR, that beginnest with good augury, thou dost behold the opening of Ausonius' consulship. Show forth thy fiery head, eternal Sun, and shine more brilliantly than is thy wont, spreading a glowing beam of light from out the East. O Year, who art the father of all those things which thou dost roll onward from the month of twy-faced Janus to wintry December's icy close, come, gracious New Year, and on the heels of the Old Year bring in merry January. Drive through thy gates the twelve months

---

[1] A close rendering seems impossible. The two Tropics (of Cancer and Capricorn) are to be quickly passed (*cedere . . . terga dare*), that the Sun may run his due course between the *two* Tropic Stars and the *four* groups (of three Signs each) which mark the seasons, and so bring the year to a close.

sollemnes pervade vias bissenaque mundo   8
curricula aequatis varians per tempora signis
praecipitem aeterna perfer vertigine cursum,   10
sic prono raptate polo, contraria Phoebus
ut momenta ferat servata parte dierum
et novus hiberno reparet sua lumina pulsu.
menstrua ter decies redeunt dum cornua lunae,
exortus obitusque manu volvente rotabis,   15
legitimum Phoebi cohibens per signa meatum.

that are to follow. Move on along the accustomed ways, and as thou changest season by season the courses of the twelve even-moving Signs in heaven, bear them along in headlong career with unceasing revolutions, thyself so carried onwards by the steep-sloping heaven, that Phoebus may begin to reverse his motions ere all your days are spent,[1] and through winter's impulse may restore his fires anew. While thrice ten times the hornèd moon returns new born, thy hand shall bring round in succession dawn and eve, still keeping Phoebus to his ordained course amid the signs of heaven.

[1] *i.e.* the days which intervene between the winter solstice (when the Sun begins to "reverse his motions") and the actual end of the year.

LIBER IV

PARENTALIA

Praefatio in Prosa

Scio versiculis meis evenire, ut fastidiose legantur:
quippe sic meritum est eorum. sed quosdam solet
commendare materia et aliquotiens fortasse lectorem
solum lemma sollicitat tituli, ut festivitate persuasus
et ineptiam ferre contentus sit. hoc opusculum nec
materia amoenum est nec appellatione iucundum.
habet maestam religionem, qua carorum meorum
obitus tristi adfectione commemoro. titulus libelli
est Parentalia. antiquae appellationis hic dies et
iam inde ab Numa cognatorum inferiis institutus:
nec quidquam sanctius habet reverentia superstitum,
quam ut amissos venerabiliter recordetur.

Item Praefatio Versibus Adnotata

Nomina carorum iam condita funere iusto,
  fleta prius lacrimis, nunc memorabo modis,

BOOK IV

PARENTALIA [1]

Preface in Prose

I know that it is the fate of my poor poems to be read with a feeling of weariness : that is indeed what they deserve. But some are recommended by their subject-matter ; and at times, perhaps, the explanatory heading alone so attracts the reader that, allured by its gaiety, he cheerfully puts up with its insipidness. This little volume is neither cheerful as regards its subject, nor attractive in title. It is endued with that mournful affection with which I commemorate in sorrowing love the loss of my dear ones. The book is headed *Parentalia*, after the solemn day [2] so called in ancient times, being indeed appointed so long ago as the times of Numa for offerings to departed relatives. The loving respect of the living has, indeed, no more sacred office it can perform than to call to mind with due reverence those who are lost to us.

A Second Preface Cast in Verse

Names of my dear ones long honourably buried—names that were once mourned with tears—shall now be recalled in verse. [3] What though it leave

---

[1] This title is explained in the Preface.
[2] See Ovid, *Fasti*, ii. 533 ff.　　[3] See table at end of volume.

nuda, sine ornatu fandique carentia cultu:
    sufficit inferiis exequialis honos.
nenia, funereis satis officiosa querellis,   5
    annua ne tacitis munera praetereas,
quae Numa cognatis sollemnia dedicat umbris,
    ut gradus aut mortis postulat aut generis.
hoc satis est tumulis, satis est telluris egenis:
    voce ciere animas funeris instar habet.   10
gaudent conpositi cineres sua nomina dici:
    frontibus hoc scriptis et monumenta iubent.
ille etiam, maesti cui defuit urna sepulcri,
    nomine ter dicto paene sepultus erit.
at tu, quicumque es, lector, qui fata meorum   15
    dignaris maestis conmemorare elegis,
inconcussa tuae percurras tempora vitae
    et praeter iustum funera nulla fleas.

I.—Iulius Ausonius Pater

Primus in his pater Ausonius, quem ponere primum,
    etsi cunctetur filius, ordo iubet.
cura dei, placidae functus quod honore senectae
    undecies binas vixit Olympiadas.
omnia, quae voluit, qui prospera vidit: eidem,   5
    optavit quidquid, contigit, ut voluit.
non quia fatorum nimia indulgentia, sed quod
    tam moderata illi vota fuere viro.

---

¹ *i.e.* the tribute paid by calling upon the name of the
dead: *cp.* Vergil, *Aen.* iii. 68, vi. 507.

them bare, undecked, and unadorned with well polished phrase? The funereal tribute[1] is offering enough to the departed. O Dirge, so ready to do service with plaints for the dead, forget not thy yearly tribute to these silent ones—that tribute which Numa ordained should be offered year by year to the shades of our relatives, according as the nearness of their death or kinship demands.[2] For the buried, as for those who lack earth to cover them, one rite suffices: to call on the soul by name counts for the full ceremony. Our dead ones laid to rest rejoice to hear their names: and thus even the lettered stones above their graves would have us do. Even he who lacks the sad urn of burial will be well-nigh as though interred, if his name be uttered thrice. But you, my reader, whosoe'er you be, who deign to recall in these sad plaints the deaths of those I loved, may you pass your span of life without a shock, and never have to mourn a death save in the course of nature.

I.—Julius Ausonius, my Father

First among these I name Ausonius my father; and even if his son should hesitate to place him first, yet natural order will have it so. He was God's special care, seeing that he enjoyed the glory of a calm old age, and lived through twice eleven Olympiads. All that he wished for, he saw fulfilled: likewise whate'er he desired befell him as he wished. It was not that Fate was more kind to him than is her wont, but that this worthy man was so reasonable in all his hopes. His own age matched

---

[2] *i.e.* a remote relative lately dead must be commemorated.

quem sua contendit septem sapientibus aetas,
    quorum doctrinam moribus excoluit,   10
viveret ut potius quam diceret, arte sophorum,
    quamquam et facundo non rudis ingenio.
praeditus et vitas hominum ratione medendi
    porrigere et fatis amplificare moras.
inde et perfunctae manet haec reverentia vitae,   15
    aetas nostra illi quod dedit hunc titulum :
ut nullum Ausonius, quem sectaretur, habebat,
    sic nullum, qui se nunc imitetur, habet.

II.—Aemilia Aeonia Mater

Proxima tu, genetrix Aeonia, sanguine mixto
    Tarbellae matris patris et Haeduici.
morigerae uxoris virtus cui contigit omnis,
    fama pudicitiae lanificaeque manus
coniugiique fides et natos cura regendi   5
    et gravitas comis laetaque serietas.
aeternum placidos manes conplexa mariti,
    viva torum quondam, functa fove tumulum.

III.—Aemilius Magnus Arborius Avunculus

Culta mihi est pietas patre primum et matre vocatis,
    dici set refugit tertius Arborius,
quem primum memorare nefas mihi patre secundo,
    rursum non primum ponere paene nefas.
temperies adhibenda, [et proximus ille vocandus[1]]   5
    ante alios, quamquam patre secundus erit.

---

[1] Suppl. *Translator*.

him with the Seven Sages, whose teaching he so closely practised in his life as to live by the rule of wisdom rather than profess it, albeit he was not unskilled nor lacking in the gift of eloquence. To him was given the power to prolong men's lives by means of medicine, and make the Fates wait their full time. Wherefore, though his life's task is ended, so great a reverence for him lingers yet that our own age has given him this epitaph: "Even as Ausonius had none for him to follow, so he has none who now can match his skill."

II.—Aemilia Aeonia, my Mother

Next will I sing of you, Aeonia, who gave me birth, in whom was mingled the blood of a mother from Tarbellae and of an Aeduan father. In you was found every virtue of a duteous wife, chastity renowned, hands busy spinning wool, truth to your bridal vows, pains to bring up your children : sedate were you yet friendly, sober yet bright. Now that for ever you embrace your husband's peaceful shade, still cheer in death his tomb, as once in life you cheered his bed.

III.—Aemilius Magnus Arborius, my Mother's Brother

Natural affection bade me utter first my father's and my mother's names, and yet Arborius refuses to take third place. Though it were an outrage to mention him first and my father after him, yet again it is scarcely less to deny him the first place. So let us compromise; let him be named next, before all others, although he will be second to my father.

tu frater genetricis et unanimis genitori,
　et mihi qui fueris, quod pater et genetrix,
qui me lactantem, puerum iuvenemque virumque
　artibus ornasti, quas didicisse iuvat—　　　　10
te sibi Palladiae antetulit toga docta Tolosae,
　te Narbonensis Gallia praeposuit,
ornasti cuius Latio sermone tribunal
　et fora Hiberorum quaeque Novem populis.
hinc tenus Europam fama crescente petito　　　15
　Constantinopolis rhetore te viguit.
tu per mille modos, per mille oracula fandi
　doctus, facundus, tu celer, atque memor.
tu, postquam primis placui tibi traditus annis,
　dixisti nato me satis esse tibi.　　　　　　20
me tibi, me patribus clarum decus esse professus
　dictasti fatis verba notanda meis.
Ergo vale Elysiam sortitus, avuncule, sedem:
　haec tibi de Musis carmina libo tuis.

IV.—Caecilius Argicius Arborius Avus

Officiosa pium ne desere, pagina, munus:
　maternum post hos commemoremus avum
Arborium, Haeduico ductum de stemmate nomen,
　conplexum multas nobilitate domus,
qua Lugdunensis provincia quaque potentes　　5
　Haedues, Alpino quaque Vienna iugo.

You, my mother's brother, and one in soul with my father, and to me who were as my father and my mother, who in my infancy, boyhood, youth, and manhood, instructed me in arts which it is a delight to have learned—you the learned gownsmen of Toulouse, that home of Pallas, made their chief, you Gaul of Narbonne—a province whose tribunal you enriched with Roman eloquence, as also the courts of Spain and Novempopulonia.[1] Hence your fame was spread all over Europe, until Constantinople claimed you as its professor and flourished under your instruction. It was you, skilled and eloquent of speech through all its countless devices, through all its countless utterances of majesty; you, quick of wit and sure of memory; you who, when in my earliest years I was committed to your charge and pleased you well, said you needed nothing more since I was in the world. And when you avowed that I was a glory, I an honour to you and to my parents, you dictated words to be entered in the book of my destiny.

[23] And so farewell, my uncle, in the Elysian abode appointed you: I make this offering of verse to you from the cup of your own Muses.

IV.—CAECILIUS ARGICIUS ARBORIUS, MY GRANDFATHER

FORSAKE not your sacred task, my duteous page: next after these let me celebrate the memory of my mother's father, Arborius who derived his name from a line of Aeduan ancestors, uniting the blood of many a noble house, both of the province of Lyons, and of that land where the Aedui held sway, and in the country of Vienne bordered by

[1] A province in the "diocese" of Vienne.

63

invida set nimium generique opibusque superbis
  aerumna incubuit; namque avus et genitor
proscripti, regnum cum Victorinus haberet
  ductor et in Tetricos recidit imperium.   10
tum profugum in terris, per quas erumpit Aturrus
  Tarbellique furor perstrepit oceani,
grassantis dudum fortunae tela paventem
  pauperis Aemiliae condicio inplicuit.
mox tenuis multo quaesita pecunia nisu   15
  solamen fesso, non et opes tribuit.
tu caeli numeros et conscia sidera fati
  callebas studium dissimulanter agens.
non ignota tibi nostrae quoque formula vitae,
  signatis quam tu condideras tabulis,   20
prodita non umquam; sed matris cura retexit,
  sedula quam timidi cura tegebat avi.
tu novies denos vitam cum duxeris annos,
  expertus Fortis tela cavenda deae,
amissum flesti per trina decennia natum   25
  saucius: hoc leto lumine cassus eras.
dicebas sed te solacia longa fovere,
  quod mea praecipuus fata maneret honos.
et modo conciliis animarum mixte priorum
  fata tui certe nota nepotis habes.   30
sentis, quod quaestor, quod te praefectus et idem
  consul honorifico munere conmemoro.

---

[1] One of the "Thirty Tyrants" who bore rule in Gaul
during the days of Gallienus. His "reign" lasted from
267–268 A.D.

Alpine heights. But trouble, all too jealous of lineage and proud wealth, weighed heavy upon him; for my grandfather and his father were proscribed when Victorinus[1] was holding sway as prince, and when the supreme power passed into the hands of the two Tetrici.[2] Then, while in exile in the lands through which the Adour breaks forth to the sea, and where wild Ocean rages on the shore of Tarbellae (Dax), though still he feared the arrows of Fortune who so long had sought his life, he was united in marriage with penniless Aemilia. In time a scanty sum gathered with great pains furnished his wearied age with some relief, though not with wealth. You—though you cloaked your pursuits—had skill in the measures of the heavens and in the stars which keep the secret of man's destiny. Not unknown to you was the outline of my life, which you had hidden in a sealed tablet, and never betrayed; but my mother's forward care revealed that which the care of my shy grandfather sought to conceal. When you had lived a life of ninety years, you found how to be dreaded are the arrows of the goddess Chance, and wounded by her shaft, mourned for a son, lost in his thirtieth year—a death which blotted the light out of your life. Yet you would say that some consolation, though far remote, cheered you, because high distinction awaited my destiny. And now that you join in the assemblies of souls that are gone before, surely you have knowledge of your grandson's fortunes: you feel that a quaestor, that a prefect, and likewise a consul am I who now commemorate you with a tribute in your honour.

[2] The Tetrici (father and son) succeeded Victorinus.

AUSONIUS

V.—Aemilia Corinthia Maura Avia

Aemiliam nunc fare aviam, pia cura nepotis,
    coniunx praedicto quae fuit Arborio.
nomen huic ioculare datum, cute fusca quod olim
    aequales inter Maura vocata fuit.
sed non atra animo, qui clarior esset olore   5
    et non calcata qui nive candidior.
et non deliciis ignoscere prompta pudendis
    ad perpendiculum seque suosque habuit.
haec me praereptum cunis et ab ubere matris
    blanda sub austeris inbuit inperiis.   10
tranquillos aviae cineres praestate, quieti
    aeternum manes, si pia verba loquor.

VI.—Aemilia Hilaria Matertera Virgo Devota

Tuque gradu generis matertera, sed vice matris
    adfectu nati commemoranda pio,
Aemilia, in cunis Hilari cognomen adepta,
    quod laeta et pueri comis ad effigiem,
reddebas verum non dissimulanter ephebum,   5
    *   *   *   *
more virum medicis artibus experiens.
feminei sexus odium tibi semper et inde
    crevit devotae virginitatis amor.
quae tibi septenos novies est culta per annos
    quique aevi finis, ipse pudicitiae.   10

---

[1] *Perpendiculum* is a mason's or carpenter's plumb-line.
The same phrase is used figuratively of severe morality in
Ammianus Marcellinus, xxix. ii. 16.

V.—Aemilia Corinthia Maura, my Grandmother

Now must a grandson's duteous affection tell of
Aemilia, my grandmother, who was the spouse of
that Arborius named above.   Her name was given
her in play, because for her dark complexion she
was called Maura in old days by her girl-friends.
But she was not dark in her soul, which was whiter
than a swan and brighter than untrodden snow.
She was not ready to overlook shameful indulgences,
but kept herself rigidly upright[1] and her household
as well.   When I was torn too soon from my cradle
and my mother's breast, kindly was her early train-
ing though hid beneath stern rule.   Ye ever restful
shades, grant peace to my grandmother's ashes, if I
utter righteous prayer.

VI.—Aemilia Hilaria, my Mother's Sister, an Avowed Virgin

You too who, though in kinship's degree an aunt,
were to me a mother, must now be recalled with
a son's affection, Aemilia, who in the cradle gained
the second name of Hilarus[2] (Blithesome), because,
bright and cheerful after the fashion of a boy, you
made without pretence the very picture of a lad
. . .[3] busied in the art of healing, like a man.   You
ever hated your female sex, and so there grew up
in you the love of consecrated maidenhood.   Through
three and sixty years you maintained it, and your
life's end was also a maiden's end.   You cherished

[2] The masculine is explained by l. 4.
[3] Two verses appear to have fallen out of the text.

67

haec, quia uti mater monitis et amore fovebas,
  supremis reddo filius exequiis.

VII.—Cl. Contemtus et Iulius Callippio Patrui

Et patruos, elegea, meos reminiscere cantu,
  Contemtum, tellus quem Rutupina tegit ;
magna cui et variae quaesita pecunia sortis
  heredis nullo nomine tuta perit ;
raptus enim laetis et adhuc florentibus annis   5
  trans mare et ignaris fratribus oppetiit.
Iulius in longam produxit fata senectam,
  adfectus damnis innumerabilibus.
qui comis blandusque et mensa commodus uncta
  heredes solo nomine nos habuit.   10
Ambo pii, vultu similes, ioca seria mixti,
  aevi fortunam non habuere parem.
discreti quamquam tumulis et honore iacetis,
  commune hoc vobis munus habete, " vale."

VIII.—Attusius Lucanus Talisius Socer

Qui proceres veteremque volet celebrare senatum
  claraque ab exortu stemmata Burdigalae,
teque tuumque genus memoret, Lucane Talisi,
  moribus ornasti qui veteres proavos.
pulcher honore oris, tranquillo pectore comis,   5
  facundo quamvis maior ab ingenio :

me with your precepts and your love as might a
mother; and therefore as a son I make you this
return at your last rites.

VII.—Clemens Contemtus and Julius Callippio, my Uncles

And now, my lay, call back in song the memory
of my uncles, of Contemtus who lies buried in the
soil of Rutupiae[1]; whose great wealth, gained through
various hazards, perished unguarded by the name of
any heir; for dying untimely, when he was still in
the prime and vigour of his years, he met his end
beyond the sea and without his brothers' knowledge.

[7] Julius lived on into extreme old age, o'erwhelmed
with losses beyond reckoning. Cheerful, courteous,
an agreeable host at his well-appointed board, he left
me his heir, though only in name.

[11] Both loving, both alike in countenance, both
mingling grave and gay, they were ill-matched in
their allotted spans of life. Though ye lie far apart
and lack the privilege of a common tomb, yet take
this single offering to you both, my "fare thee well!"

VIII.—Attusius Lucanus Talisius, my Father-in-Law

Whoso would praise the nobles, the ancient
Senate, and the houses of Bordeaux, illustrious from
their first arising, let him tell of you and of your
race, Lucanus Talisius—of you, whose life has added
lustre to your ancient line. Handsome and noble in
features, gentle and kindly in heart, your gift of
eloquence made you yet greater still. You spent all

[1] Richborough, in Kent, an important British port and a
fortress on the "Saxon Shore," here equivalent to Britain.

venatu et ruris cultu victusque nitore
  omne aevum peragens, publica despiciens :
nosci inter primos cupiens, prior esse recusans,
  ipse tuo vivens segregus arbitrio.   10
optabas tu me generum florente iuventa :
  optare hoc tantum, non et habere datum.
vota probant superi meritisque faventia sanctis
  inplent fata, viri quod voluere boni.
et nunc perpetui sentis sub honore sepulcri,   15
  quam reverens natae quamque tui maneam.
caelebs namque gener haec nunc pia munera solvo :
  nam et caelebs numquam desinam et esse gener.

IX.—ATTUSIA LUCANA SABINA UXOR

HACTENUS ut caros, ita iusto funere fletos
  functa piis cecinit nenia nostra modis.
nunc dolor atque cruces nec contrectabile vulnus,
  coniugis ereptae mors memoranda mihi.
nobilis a proavis et origine clara senatus,   5
  moribus atque bonis clara Sabina magis.
te iuvenis primis luxi deceptus in annis
  perque novem caelebs te fleo Olympiadas.
nec licet obductum senio sopire dolorem ;
  semper crudescit nam mihi paene recens.   10
admittunt alii solacia temporis aegri :
  haec graviora facit vulnera longa dies.

your life in hunting, and husbandry, and all the
pleasures of a refined life, despising public affairs.
Eager to be recognized among the foremost, yet you
refused to be the foremost, by living in seclusion
from the throng at your own pleasure. When
youth's heyday was mine, you desired me for your
daughter's husband; but you were suffered only to
desire this, not also to attain it. The Gods above
give effect to prayers, and the Fates looking kindly
on unsullied worth, fulfil what good men desire;
and now, deep in the eternal tomb where rest your
honoured bones, you still feel how constant I abide
to your daughter's memory and to your own. For
unwedded, I, your son-in-law, now pay this tribute
of devotion : nor will I ever cease to be both unwed
and your son-in-law.

IX.—Attusia Lucana Sabina, my Wife

Thus far my dirge, fulfilling its sacred task, has
sung in loving strains of those who, though dear,
were mourned but in the course of nature. Now
my grief and anguish and a wound that cannot bear
a touch—the death of my wife snatched away un-
timely, must be told by me. High was her ancestry
and noble in her birth from a line of senators, but
yet Sabina was ennobled more by her good life. In
youth I wept for you, robbed of my hopes in early
years, and through these six and thirty years, un-
wedded, I have mourned, and mourn you still. Age
has crept over me, but yet I cannot lull my pain;
for ever it keeps raw and well-nigh new to me.
Others receive of time a balm to soothe their grief:
these wounds become but heavier with length of

torqueo deceptos ego vita caelibe canos,
   quoque magis solus, hoc mage maestus ago.
vulnus alit, quod muta domus silet et torus alget, 15
   quod mala non cuiquam, non bona participo.
maereo, si coniunx alii bona ; maereo contra,
   si mala : ad exemplum tu mihi semper ades.
tu mihi crux ab utraque venis : sive est mala, quod tu
   dissimilis fueris ; seu bona, quod similis. 20
non ego opes cassas et inania gaudia plango,
   sed iuvenis iuveni quod mihi rapta viro.
laeta, pudica, gravis, genus inclita et inclita forma,
   et dolor atque decus coniugis Ausonii.
quae modo septenos quater inpletura Decembres 25
   liquisti natos, pignera nostra, duos.
illa favore dei, sicut tua vota fuerunt,
   florent, optatis adcumulata bonis.
et precor, ut vigeant tandemque superstite utroque
   nuntiet hoc cineri nostra favilla tuo. 30

X.—Ausonius Parvulus Filius

Non ego te infletum memori fraudabo querella,
   primus, nate, meo nomine dicte puer :
murmura quem primis meditantem absolvere verbis
   indolis et plenae, planximus exequiis.[1]
tu gremio in proavi funus commune locatus, 5
   invidiam tumuli ne paterere tui.

---

[1] *V*: obsequiis, *Peiper.*

days. I tear my grey hairs mocked by my widowed life, and the more I live in loneliness, the more I live in heaviness. That my house is still and silent, and that my bed is cold, that I share not my ills with any, my good with any—these things feed my wound. I grieve, if one man has a worthy wife; and yet again I grieve if another has a bad: for pattern, you are ever present with me. Howe'er it be, you come to torture me: if one be bad, because you were not like her; or if one be good, because you were like her. I mourn not for useless wealth or unsubstantial joys, but because in your youth you were torn from me, your youthful lord. Cheerful, modest, staid, famed for high birth as famed for beauty, you were the grief and glory of Ausonius your spouse. For ere you could complete your eight and twentieth December, you deserted our two children, the pledges of our love. They by God's mercy, and as you ever prayed, flourish amid an abundance of such goods as you desired for them. And still I pray that they may prosper, and that at last my dust may bring the news to your ashes that they are living yet.

X.—Ausonius, my Son, a Little Child

I will not leave you unwept, my son, nor rob you of the complaint due to your memory—you, my first-born child, and called by my name. Just as you were practising to transform your babbling into the first words of childhood and were of ripe natural gifts we had to mourn for your decease. You on your great-grandfather's bosom lie sharing one common grave, lest you should suffer the reproach of your one lone tomb.

AUSONIUS

XI.—Pastor Nepos ex Filio

Tu quoque maturos, puer inmature, dolores
  interrupisti luctus acerbus avi,
Pastor care nepos, spes cuius certa fuisses,[1]
  Hesperii patris tertia progenies.
nomen, quod casus dederat (quia fistula primum   5
  pastorale melos concinuit genito),
sero intellectum vitae brevis argumentum :
  spiritus adflatis quod fugit e calamis.
occidis emissae percussus pondere testae,
  abiecit tecto quam manus artificis.   10
non fuit artificis manus haec : manus illa cruenti
  certa fuit fati suppositura reum.
heu, quae vota mihi, quae rumpis gaudia, Pastor !
  illa meum petiit tegula missa caput.
dignior o, nostrae gemeres qui fata senectae   15
  et quererere meas maestus ad exequias !

XII.—Iulia Dryadia Soror

Si qua fuit virtus, cuperet quam femina prudens
  esse suam, soror hac Dryadia haud caruit.
quin etiam multas habuit, quas sexus habere
  fortior optaret nobilitasque virum.
docta satis vitamque colu famamque tueri,   5
  docta bonos mores ipsa suosque docens.
et verum vita cui carius unaque cura
  nosse deum et fratrem diligere ante alios.

---

[1] *Translator* : fuit res, *V* (and *Peiper*).

PARENTALIA

XI.—Pastor, my Son's Child

You also, lad of unripe years, have broken this
sequence of laments for riper age, Pastor, my loved
grandson, filling with bitter grief your grandfather,
whose sure hope you would have been, third child
of Hesperius your father. Your name, which chance
had given you (because just when you were born a
pipe sounded some pastoral air), too late was under-
stood to be a symbol of your short life : because
the breath soon passes from the pipes on which a
shepherd blows. You perished stricken down by
the weight of a cast tile, thrown from the roof by
a workman's hand. No workman's hand was that :
that hand of bloody Fate should surely have borne
the blame. Ah me, how many of my hopes, how
many of my joys you broke short, my Pastor '
That tile, carelessly flung, reached my head. O,
how much fitter were you to mourn the end of
my old age, and raise a sad lament at my burial!

XII.—Julia Dryadia, my Sister

If there is any virtue which a discreet woman
could desire to possess, Dryadia, my sister, lacked
it not. Nay more, she had many which the stronger
sex and the nobler heart of men would gladly
have. Well trained with her distaff's aid to main-
tain her life and her good name, and trained in
all good habits, she trained her household too.
To her truth was dearer than life, and her one
thought was to know God and to love her brother

75

coniuge adhuc iuvenis caruit, sed seria vitans
    moribus austeras aequiperavit anus   10
produxitque hilarem per sena decennia vitam,
    inque domo ac tecto, quo pater, oppetiit.

XIII.—Avitianus Frater

Avitianum, Musa, germanum meum
    dona querella funebri.
minor iste natu me, sed ingenio prior
    artes paternas inbibit.
verum iuventae flore laeto perfrui   5
    aevique supra puberis
exire metas vetuit infesta Atropos.
    heu quem dolorem sociis!
heu quanta vitae decora, quem cultum spei,[1]
    germane, pubes deseris,   10
germane carnis lege et ortu sanguinis,
    amore paene filius!

XIV.—Val. Latinus Euromius Gener

O generis clari decus, o mihi funus acerbum,
    Euromi, e iuvenum lecte cohorte gener,
occidis in primae raptus mihi flore iuventae,
    lactantis nati vix bene note pater.
tu procerum de stirpe satus, praegressus et ipsos,   5
    unde genus clarae nobilitatis erat,
ore decens, bonus ingenio, facundus et omni
    dexteritate vigens praecipuusque fide.

---

[1] *Gronovius* : Heu quanta vitae decora | quem cultum spei
quem dolorem sociis, *V.*

above all besides. Albeit she lost her husband while still young, she was a match for any dame in the strictness of life, though shunning sourness, and lived out six decades of cheerful life, dying in the same home and under the same roof as did her father.

XIII.—AVITIANUS, MY BROTHER

MUSE, do thou enrich Avitianus, my brother, with a mournful lay. In years below me, but in gifts of mind above, he learned our father's art. But Atropos, his foe, forbade him fully to enjoy the gladsome bloom of youth or to pass beyond the bounds which mark the end of boyhood. Ah, what grief for his playmates! Ah, from how glorious a life, and what rich hopes you turned away while yet a lad, my brother—my brother by the law of flesh and parentage of blood, in love almost my son!

XIV.—VALERIUS LATINUS EUROMIUS, MY SON-IN-LAW

O GLORY of an illustrious race, O untimely death to me, Euromius, my son-in-law chosen from the company of youths, you perished snatched from me in the very bloom of early youth, a father scarce fully recognized by your son at his mother's breast. You, the scion of noble ancestors, surpassed even them from whom you traced your glorious descent, in features comely, gifted in mind, eloquent, active in all vigorous pursuits, and eminent

hoc praefecturae sedes, hoc Illyris ora
    praeside te experta est, fiscus et ipse cliens.   10
nil aevi brevitate tamen tibi laudis ademptum :
    indole maturus, funere acerbus obis.

XV.—Pomponius Maximus Adfinis

Et te germanum non sanguine, sed vice fratris,
    Maxime, defunctum nenia nostra canet.
coniunx namque meae tu consociate sorori
    aevi fruge tui destituis viduam.
non domus hoc tantum sensit tua : sensit acerbum 5
    saucia, pro, casum curia Burdigalae,
te primore vigens, te deficiente relabens
    inque Valentinum te moriente cadens.
heu quare nato, qui fruge et flore nepotum,
    ereptus nobis, Maxime, non frueris?   10
set frueris, divina habitat si portio manes
    quaeque futura olim gaudia, nosse datur.
longior hic etiam laetorum fructus habetur—
    anticipasse diu, quae modo participas.

XVI.—Veria Liceria Uxor Arborii Sororis Filii

Tu quoque sive nurus mihi nomine, vel vice natae,
    Veria, supremi carmen honoris habe.

in honour. This the prefect's seat, this the Illyrian shore learned when you were governor, and the Treasury itself whose advocate you were. Yet life's short span has robbed you of naught of your praise : ripe were your powers, untimely your end.

XV.—Pomponius Maximus, my Brother-in-Law

You also, not akin to me in blood yet like a brother—you, Maximus, now dead, shall be sung by my dirge. For you were wedded to my sister, only to leave her widowed in the harvest-season of your life. Not your home alone felt this pang : the stricken Senate of Bordeaux—alas !—felt this untimely chance, flourishing while you were its chief, declining as your strength failed, and at your death falling into the power of Valentinus. Alas, my Maximus, why were you reft from us, and from the joy of children and grandchildren, the flower and fruit of your race? And yet you do have joy of these, if any share of presage dwells among the shades, and if it is granted them to know of those delights which one day are to be. Longer also this enjoyment of delights is held to be—to have foreseen awhile that which you now partake.

XVI.—Veria Liceria, Wife of Arborius, my Sister's Son

You also, Veria—whether I think of you as my nephew's wife or as my daughter—take the last

cuius si probitas, si forma et fama fidesque
   morigerae uxoris lanificaeque manus
nunc laudanda forent, procul et de manibus imis   5
   accersenda foret vox [1] proavi Eusebii.
qui quoniam functo iam pridem conditus aevo
   transcripsit partes in mea verba suas,
accipe funereas, neptis defleta, querellas,
   coniunx Arborii commemoranda mei,   10
cui parva ingentis luctus solacia linquens
   destituis natos, quo magis excrucias.
at tibi dilecti ne desit cura mariti,
   iuncta colis thalamo nunc monumenta tuo.
hic, ubi primus hymen, sedes ibi maesta sepulcri :   15
   nupta magis dici quam tumulata potes.

XVII.—Pomponius Maximus Herculanus Sororis Filius

   Nec germana genitum te
   modulamine nenia tristi
   tacitum sine honore relinquat,
   super indole cuius adulti
   magnae bona copia laudis.   5
   verum memorare magis quam
   functum laudare decebit.
   decus hoc matrisque meumque
   in tempore puberis aevi
   vis perculit invida fati.   10
   eheu quem, Maxime, fructum,
   facunde et musice et acer,
   mentem bonus, ingenio ingens,
   volucer pede, corpore pulcher,
   lingua catus, ore canorus.   15

---

[1] *Mommsen* : uxor est, *V, Peiper.*

tribute of my verse. If your uprightness, beauty,
faithfulness as a duteous wife, and skill in spinning
wool were to be praised here, then should we have
to summon from far back and from the inmost
place of souls, the voice of Eusebius your great-
grandfather. But since he is dead and buried
long ago, and has bequeathed to me the task of
speaking in his stead, receive these sad com-
plaints, lamented daughter, whom, as the wife of
my Arborius, I must not leave unsung. To him
you leave behind your children, small comforts to
assuage o'ermastering grief, and thereby increase
his pain the more. But that the tender thoughts
of your loved husband may not fail you, the
tomb, now your abode, is built hard by your bridal
chamber. And where the glad marriage-song first
was raised, there stands your mournful sepulchre.
So may we say that you are wedded rather than
buried here.

XVII.—Pomponius Maximus Herculanus, my Sister's Son

Nor may my dirge leave you unhonoured and
unsung in strains of sorrow, son of my own sister,
upon whose already ripened powers a full measure
of high praise was lavished. Yet will it be fitter
here to commemorate rather than to praise the dead.
Him who was both his mother's pride and mine
Fate's envious power laid low in the season of
his youth. Alas, for thy fruit, my Maximus, so
eloquent, so skilled in arts, so quick, so kind in
heart, so gifted in mind, so fleet of foot, so graceful,
clever of tongue as tuneful of voice! Take as the

cape munera tristia patrum,
lacrimabilis orsa querellae,
quae funereo modulatu
tibi maestus avunculus offert.

XVIII.—Fl. Sanctus Maritus Pudentillae quae Soror Sabinae meae

Qui ioca laetitiamque colis, qui tristia damnas
   nec metuis quemquam nec metuendus agis,
qui nullum insidiis captas nec lite lacessis,
   sed iustam et clemens vitam agis et sapiens,
tranquillos manes supremaque mitia Sancti   5
   ore pio et verbis advenerare bonis.
militiam nullo qui turbine sedulus egit,
   praeside laetatus quo Rutupinus ager,
octoginta annos cuius tranquilla senectus
   nullo mutavit deteriore die.   10
ergo precare favens, ut qualia tempora vitae,
   talia et ad manes otia Sanctus agat.

XIX.—Namia Pudentilla Adfinis

Tuque Pudentillam verbis adfare supremis,
   quae famae curam, quae probitatis habes.
nobilis haec, frugi, proba, laeta, pudica, decora,
   coniugium Sancti iugiter haec habuit.
inviolata tuens castae praeconia vitae   5
   rexit opes proprias otia agente viro:
non ideo exprobrans aut fronte obducta marito,
   quod gereret totam femina sola domum.

---

[1] *Militia* here, as not uncommonly, indicates civil and not military service: the still-surviving Roman fortress at Rich-

sad offerings ordained by our fathers, this effort to
raise a tearful lament, cast in a woeful strain which
in his grief your uncle presents to you.

XVIII.—Flavius Sanctus, Husband of Pudentilla, the Sister of my Wife Sabina

You, Sir, who love jests and merriment, you who
hate all moroseness, neither fearing any man nor
causing any man to fear, who entrap no man by
trickery nor vex him at the law, but mildly and
wisely live an upright life, come with reverent lips
and words of good omen to do honour to the peace-
ful shade and the remains of kindly Sanctus. His
service[1] he performed diligently without tumult;
with him for governor the Rutupian land rejoiced;
his eighty years a peaceful old age marred not with
any day of decline. Therefore be this your pro-
pitious prayer, that Sanctus may enjoy such peace
among the shades as he found in the season of his
life.

XIX.—Namia Pudentilla, my Sister-in-Law

You also, Lady, who think highly of a good name
and upright life, speak a word of last farewell to
Pudentilla. Well-born, thrifty, and upright, cheerful,
modest, and fair, she shared without a break the
wedded life of Sanctus. Keeping unstained the
praises due to a modest life, she managed her own
property, while her lord lived at ease: but for all
that she did not taunt her husband nor look black
upon him because he left a woman to manage the

borough (Rutupiae) was in the command of the "Count of
the Saxon Shore," but *Rutupinus ager* here denotes Britain.

83

heu nimium iuvenis, sed laeta superstite nato
    atque viro, patiens fata suprema obiit :   10
unanimis nostrae et quondam germana Sabinae
    et mihi inoffenso nomine dicta soror.
nunc etiam manes placidos pia cura retractat
    atque Pudentillam fantis honore colit.

XX.—LUCANUS TALISIUS EORUM FILIUS

NEC iam tu, matris spes unica, ephebe Talisi,
    consobrine meus, inmemoratus eris,
ereptus primis aevi florentis in annis,
    iam tamen et coniunx, iam properate pater.
festinasse putes fatum, ne funus acerbum   5
    diceret hoc genitor tam cito factus avus.

XXI.—ATTUSIA LUCANA TALISIA ET MINUCIUS REGULUS ADFINES

NOTITIA exilis nobis, Attusia, tecum,
    cumque tuo plane coniuge nulla fuit.
verum tu nostrae soror es germana Sabinae,
    adfinis quoque tu, Regule, nomen habes.
sortitos igitur tam cara vocabula nobis   5
    stringamus maesti carminis obsequio.
quamvis Santonica procul in tellure iacentes
    pervenit ad manes exequialis honor.

whole house alone. Alas! Too young, yet happy
that her husband and her son still lived, she met
her final doom and died. She was of one heart
and one in blood with my Sabina, and by me was
she called sister unreproved. Now also my loving
thoughts busy themselves with her peaceful shade,
and voice these words of tribute to my Pudentilla.

XX.—LUCANUS TALISIUS, THEIR SON

You, too, in turn shall not pass unregarded, young
Talisius, my nephew and your mother's only hope.
Though you were snatched from us in the first years
of your prime, yet you were already wed, already
early made a father: and we may think Fate
hastened that event, that being so quickly made a
grandfather, your own sire might not declare your
death to be untimely.

XXI.—ATTUSIA LUCANA TALISIA AND MINUCIUS REGULUS, MY SISTER AND BROTHER-IN-LAW

THOUGH slight was my acquaintance with you, At-
tusia, and though I had none at all with him who
was your husband, yet you are own sister of my wife
Sabina, and you also, Regulus, rank as my brother-in-
law. Wherefore, since ye have names which are so
dear to me, let me touch you with the homage of
my sorrowing verse. For although ye be buried far
from here in the soil of Saintes, yet the last homage
can find its way to the souls of the departed.

XXII.—Severus Censor Iulianus Consocer

Desinite, o veteres, Calpurnia nomina, Frugi
    ut proprium hoc vestrae gentis habere decus.
nec solus semper censor Cato nec sibi solus
    iustus Aristides his placeant titulis.
nam sapiens quicumque fuit verumque fidemque   5
    qui coluit, comitem se tibi, Censor, agat.
tu gravis et comis cum iustitiaque remissus,
    austeris doctus iungere temperiem.
tu non adscito tibi me nec sanguine iuncto
    optasti nostras consociare domos.   10
nempe aliqua in nobis morum simulacra tuorum
    effigies nostri praebuit ingenii ;
aut iam Fortunae sic se vertigo rotabat,
    ut pondus fatis tam bona vota darent.
si quid aput manes sentis, fovet hoc tibi mentem,   15
    quod fieri optaras, id voluisse deum.

XXIII.—Paulinus et Dryadia Filii Paulini et Megentirae Sororis Filiae.

Qui nomen vultumque patris, Pauline, gerebas,
    amissi specimen qui genitoris eras ;
propter quem luctus miserae decedere matris
    coeperat, offerret cum tua forma patrem,

---

[1] Father of Thalassius, who married a daughter of Ausonius (Ausonia ?), the widow of Euromius.

86

XXII.—Severus Censor Julianus,[1] Joint Father-in-Law

Ye ancients of the Calpurnian name, cease to think
Frugi[2] the peculiar glory of your clan. No more let
Cato vaunt himself as the one and only "Censor,"
nor Aristides pride himself as sole owner of the
title of "The Just." For any man who has been
wise and who has followed honour and good faith
would rank you, Censor, as his peer. Stern and
yet kindly, just and merciful withal, you had the
art to blend mildness with severity. Though I
was unacquainted with you and unallied in blood,
yet you desired to join our houses in alliance.
Doubtless you pictured my nature to yourself in
such a form as to reflect some image of your own
character; or at that time Fortune so turned her
wheel that such a worthy wish weighed down
the balance of Destiny. If you feel aught at all
amidst the shades, the thought must cheer you,
that God has willed that which you had hoped
might be.

XXIII.—Paulinus and Dryadia, Children of Paulinus and Megentira, my Sister's Daughter

You who bore at once your father's name and looks,
Paulinus, who were a very copy of your lost sire;
because of whom your hapless mother's sorrow for
his loss had begun to pass away, whilst your face
offered her a picture of your father and mirrored,

---

[2] *sc.* Lucius Calpurnius Piso, " whose virtue and upright-
ness were such that he was named Frugi (the Honourable) in
distinction from all others " (Cic. *Tusc.* III. xviii. 16 f.).

redderet et mores et moribus adderet illud,   5
   Paulinus caruit quo pater, eloquium :
eriperis laetis et pubescentibus annis
   crudaque adhuc matris pectora sollicitas.
flemus enim et raptam thalami de sede sororem,
   heu non maturo funere, Dryadiam.   10
flemus, ego in primis, qui matris avunculus, ac vos
   natorum tamquam diligo progeniem.
illa manus inter genetricis et oscula patris
   occidit, Hispana tu regione procul.
quam tener et primo nove flos decerperis aevo,   15
   nondum purpureas cinctus ephebe genas !
quattuor ediderat nunc functa puerpera partus,
   funera set tumulis iam geminata dedit.
Sit satis hoc, Pauline pater ; divisio facta est :[1]
   debetur matri cetera progenies.   20

XXIV.—Paulinus Sororis Gener

Qui laetum ingenium, mores qui diligit aequos
   quique fidem sancta cum pietate colit,
Paulini manes mecum veneratus amicis
   inroret lacrimis annua liba ferens.
aequaevus, Pauline, mihi natamque sororis   5
   indeptus thalamo : sic mihi paene gener.
stirpis Aquitanae mater tibi : nam genitori
   Cossio Vasatum, municipale genus.

---

[1] cp. Corpus Inscr. Graec. Pars xxxiv. No. 6791 (found at Bordeaux) :

   Λείψανα Λουκίλλης διδυματόκου ἐνθάδε κεῖτε (sic),
   ἧς μεμέρισται (sic) βρέφη, ζωὸν πατρί, θάτερον αὐτῇ.

too, his character, adding to character that gift which your father Paulinus lacked, the gift of eloquence; you—you are hurried hence in the bright years of early youth and grieve your mother's still bleeding heart. For we mourn also your sister Dryadia, torn from her bridal bed—alas!—by an untimely death. We mourn for you, and I not least; for I am your mother's uncle, and love you as the offspring of my own children. Your sister died amid her mother's and her father's kisses, you, far off in the land of Spain. O fresh and tender flower, so early plucked while yet your spring was young, a lad whose rosy cheeks were yet unfringed with down! Four children had your mother borne in travail, but of these she has surrendered two already to the grave.

[19] Paulinus, be content with these;[1] for they make up your fair share as father, and your remaining offspring are their mother's due.

XXIV.—Paulinus, my Sister's Son-in-Law

Whoso loves a cheerful soul and an unruffled temper, or who reverences good faith linked with pure affection, let him now join with me in honouring Paulinus' shade, bringing the yearly offering due and friendship's rain of tears. You were of one age with me, Paulinus, and had won my sister's daughter for your bride, thus becoming almost my son-in-law. Your mother's people were of Aquitaine, while your father was of Cossio Vasatum (Bazas), sprung of its

---

[1] Paulinus, the father, was already dead: see ll. 1-6.

scrinia praefecti meritus, rationibus inde
    praepositus Libycis praemia opima capis.   10
nam correcturae tibi Tarraco Hibera tribunal
    praebuit, adfectans esse clienta tibi.
tu socrum pro matre colens adfinis haberi
    non poteras, nati cum fruerere loco.
inter concordes vixisti fidus amicos,   15
    duodeviginti functus Olympiadas.

XXV.—Aemilia Dryadia Matertera

Te quoque Dryadiam materteram
    flebilibus modulis
germana genitus, prope filius,
    ore pio veneror.
quam thalamo taedisque iugalibus   5
    invida mors rapuit;
mutavitque torum feretri vice
    exequialis honor.
discebas in me, matertera
    mater uti fieres;   10
unde modo hoc maestum tibi defero
    filius officium.

XXVI.—Iulia Cataphronia Amita

Quin et funereis amitam inpertire querellis,
    Musa, Cataphroniam.
innuba devotae quae virginitatis amorem
    parcaque anus coluit:

---

[1] *i.e.* Paulinus was *magister scriniorum.* For the three
scrinia (departments for receiving petitions, etc.) of the
Western Empire see the *Notitia Dignitatum,* Occidens, xvii.
(Seeck, pp. 161 f.).

[2] *i.e.* as *rationalis* or *procurator.*

burgesses. When you had gained the presidency
of the Bureaux,[1] and had been set over the Ex-
chequer[2] for Libya, rich the prizes which you
gained. For the Spanish province of Tarraco (Tarra-
gona) offered you its *corrector's*[3] court, and anxiously
sought to have you for its patron. You could not
be regarded as a son-in-law—you who adored your
wife's mother as your own, and were treated as a
son by her. A loyal friend, you lived among others
of like heart, and died after a span of eighteen
Olympiads.

XXV.—Aemilia Dryadia, my Aunt

To you also, Dryadia my aunt, in mournful strains
I, whom your sister bare, almost your son,—do re-
verence with loving lips. Death, jealous of your
happiness, hurried you from your bridal-chamber and
the light of the nuptial torches; and funeral cere-
monies changed your bridal-couch for a bier. You
learned, my aunt, to be a mother to me; therefore
now I, a son, offer you this sad token of my love.

XXVI.—Julia Cataphronia, my Paternal Aunt

Nay, and on Cataphronia, too, who was my aunt,
bestow your sad lament, my Muse. Unwed and
vowed to virginity, she cherished that love, and
lived to old age in thrift. Generous as a mother,

---

[3] The *corrector*, originally a commissioner appointed to
remedy abuses (see Pauly-Wissowa, *Real-Encycl.* iv. 1646),
was in the time of Ausonius practically equivalent to the
praeses or civil governor: cp. *Dig.* i. xviii. 10. According
to Fleury the corregidors of modern Spain answer in function
as in title to the Roman *correctores*.

et mihi, quod potuit, quamvis de paupere summa,   5
   mater uti, adtribuit.
ergo commemorata have maestumque vocata
   pro genetrice vale.

XXVII.—Iulia Veneria Amita

Et amita Veneria properiter obiit :
cui brevia melea modifica recino :
cinis ut placidulus ab opere vigeat,
celeripes adeat loca tacita Erebi.

XXVIII.—Iulia Idalia Consobrina

Parva etiam fuit Idalia,
nomine praedita quae Paphiae
et speciem meruit Veneris ;
quae genita est mihi paene soror.
filia nam fuit haec amitae,   5
quam celebrat sub honore pio
nenia carmine funereo.

XXIX.—Aemilia Melania Soror

Aemilia et, vix nota mihi soror, accipe questus,
   debent quos cineri maesta elegea tuo.
coniunxit nostras aequaeva infantia cunas,
   uno quamvis tu consule maior eras.
invida set nimium Lachesis properata peregit   5
   tempora et ad manes funera acerba dedit.
praemissa ergo vale manesque verere parentum,
   qui maiore aevo quique minore venit.

she bestowed on me all that she could out of her slender funds.

7 Therefore I now call you to remembrance as a mother and utter the sad cry, "Hail and farewell."

XXVII.—Julia Veneria, my Paternal Aunt

My aunt Veneria also died an early death, and to her I now chant these short, measured lines. May her poor ashes rest in peace and repose from toil, and swift be her passage to the silent realms of Erebus.

XXVIII.—Julia Idalia, my Cousin

Little Idalia, too, is gone, who received the title of the Paphian queen, and herself won Venus' beauty; who by birth was well-nigh my sister. For this was the child of my aunt, whom my dirge now honours with the loving homage of a mournful strain.

XXIX.—Aemilia Melania, my Sister

Though I scarce knew you, Aemilia, my sister, receive this lament which my sad strains owe to your ashes. When we were infants almost of one age we shared one cradle, though you were the elder by one year. But Lachesis, too jealous, hurried on your final hour and sent you to the shades—an untimely death. Since, therefore, you are gone before me, take my farewell and do honour to our parents' shades—his who in riper, and hers who in earlier years is come to rejoin you.

XXX.—Pomponia Urbica Consocrus Uxor Iuliani Censoris

Ut generis clari, veterum sic femina morum,
  Urbica, Censoris nobilitata toro;
ingenitis pollens virtutibus auctaque et illis,
  quas docuit coniunx, quas pater et genetrix—
quas habuit Tanaquil, quas Pythagorea Theano   5
  quaeque sine exemplo in nece functa viri.
et tibi si fatum sic permutare dedisset,
  viveret hoc nostro tempore Censor adhuc.
set neque tu viduo longum cruciata sub aevo
  protinus optato fine secuta virum.   10
annua nunc maestis ferimus tibi iusta querellis
  cum genero et natis consocer Ausonius.

---

[1] Wife of the elder Tarquin, remarkable for her high spirit and for skill in augury.

PARENTALIA

XXX.—Pomponia Urbica, Joint Mother-in-Law, Wife of Julianus Censor

Urbica, famed both for illustrious birth and old-time virtues, and renowned as Censor's wife, rich as was the store of your natural qualities, you have added those besides which your spouse taught you, and your father and your mother—those qualities which Tanaquil[1] possessed, and Theano the Pythagorean,[2] and those which perished without copy when your husband died. And had Fate suffered you so to exchange, Censor would still be living in these our days. Yet not for long did you suffer grief in your widowed state, but welcomed death and straightway followed your husband to the shades. Now I, Ausonius, your fellow parent-in-law, with my son-in-law[3] and his children, bring you your yearly due with sad lament.

[2] A female disciple or, according to some, the wife of Pythagoras, famous both for wisdom and virtue.

[3] *sc.* Thalassius, son of Julianus Censor and Urbica, who had married a daughter (Ausonia?) of Ausonius.

LIBER V

COMMEMORATIO PROFESSORUM
BURDIGALENSIUM

Praefatio

Vos etiam, quos nulla mihi cognatio iunxit,
  set fama et carae relligio patriae,
et studium in libris et sedula cura docendi,
  commemorabo viros morte obita celebres.
fors erit, ut nostros manes sic adserat olim,   5
  exemplo cupiet qui pius esse meo.

I.—Tiberius Victor Minervius Orator

Primus Burdigalae columen dicere, Minervi,
  alter rhetoricae Quintiliane togae.
inlustres quondam quo praeceptore fuerunt
  Constantinopolis, Roma, dehinc patria,
non equidem certans cum maiestate duarum,   5
  solo set potior nomine, quod patria :
adserat usque licet Fabium Calagurris alumnum,
  non sit Burdigalae dum cathedra inferior.
mille foro dedit hic iuvenes, bis mille senatus
  adiecit numero purpureisque togis ;   10

---

¹ According to Jerome (*Chron.*, Olymp. 283), Minervius
flourished at Rome in 358 A.D.

BOOK V

POEMS COMMEMORATING
THE PROFESSORS OF BORDEAUX

Preface

Your memories, too, I will recall as famous men now dead, whom no kinship linked with me, but renown, and the love of our dear country, and zeal of learning, and the industrious toil of teaching. Perchance one day another in the same way may make my shade his theme, and after my example will seek to do a pious deed.

I.—Tiberius Victor Minervius, the Orator

You shall be named first, Minervius, chief ornament of Bordeaux, a second Quintilian to adorn the rhetorician's gown. Your teaching in its day made glorious Constantinople, Rome,[1] and lastly our native town; which, though it cannot vie with that pair in dignity, yet for its name alone is more acceptable, because it is our native place: let Calagurris[2] make every claim to Fabius as her son, if the chair of Bordeaux receive no less degree. A thousand pupils has Minervius given to the courts, and twice a thousand to the Senate's ranks and to the purple robes. I, too,

[2] Calahorra, in Spain, the birthplace of M. Fabius Quintilianus.

me quoque : set quoniam multa est praetexta, silebo
   teque canam de te, non ab honore meo.
sive panegyricis placeat contendere libris,
   in Panathenaicis tu numerandus eris;
seu libeat fictas ludorum evolvere lites,   15
   ancipitem palmam Quintilianus habet.
dicendi torrens tibi copia, quae tamen aurum,
   non etiam luteam volveret inluviem.
et Demosthenicum, quod ter primum ille vocavit,
   in te sic viguit, cedat ut ipse tibi.   20
anne et divini bona naturalia doni
   adiciam, memori quam fueris animo,
audita ut vel lecta semel ceu fixa teneres,
   auribus et libris esset ut una fides?
vidimus et quondam tabulae certamine longo   25
   omnes, qui fuerant, te numerasse bolos,
alternis vicibus quot praecipitante rotatu
   fundunt excisi per cava buxa gradus:
narrantem fido per singula puncta recursu,
   quae data, per longas quae revocata moras.   30
nullo felle tibi mens livida, tum sale multo
   lingua dicax blandis et sine lite iocis.
mensa nitens, quam non censoria regula culpet
   nec nolit Frugi Piso vocare suam:
nonnumquam pollens natalibus et dape festa,   35
   non tamen angustas ut tenuaret opes.

---

[1] *i.e.* with Isocrates as author of the two great orations
Panegyricus and *Panathenaicus*.

[2] This was *action* : *cp.* Cic. *de Orat.* iii. 56; Quintilian,
xi. 3.

was of that number; but since my consulship is so
great a theme, I will refrain, and praise you for your-
self and not through my distinctions. Should pane-
gyric be the field of rivalry, then must you be classed
with the orator of the *Panathenaicus*; [1] or if the test
be to develop the mock law-suits of our schools,
Quintilian must look to his laurels. Your speech was
like a torrent in full spate, yet one which whirled
down pure gold without muddy sediment. As for
that art [2] in Demosthenes which that great man
thrice over called the orator's chief virtue, it was
so strong in you that the master himself gives place
to you. Shall I speak also of your natural gifts and
that divine blessing, your memory, which was so
prodigious that you retained what you had heard or
read over once as though it were engraven on your
mind, and that your ear was as retentive as a book?
Once, after a long contested game, [3] I have seen you
tell over all the throws made by either side when
the dice were tipped out with a sharp spin over the
fillets cut out in the hollowed boxwood of the dice-
box; and recount move by move, without mistake,
which pieces had been lost, which won back, through
long stretches of the game. No malice ever black-
ened your heart: your tongue, though free and full
of wit, indulged only in kindly jests that held no
sting. Your table showed that refinement with
which a censor's code could find no fault: Piso the
Frugal would not blush to call it his. Sometimes,
as on birthdays or some other feast, it was furnished
with greater luxury, but never so lavishly as to

[3] A board-game, such as backgammon or tric-trac, in
which the moves were determined by casting dice. The
dice-box was grooved or filleted to prevent any manipulation
of the dice.

quamquam heredis egens, bis sex quinquennia functus,
    fletus es a nobis ut pater et iuvenis.
Et nunc, sive aliquid post fata extrema superfit,
    vivis adhuc aevi, quod periit, meminens: 40
sive nihil superest nec habent longa otia sensus,
    tu tibi vixisti: nos tua fama iuvat.

II.—LATINUS ALCIMUS ALETHIUS RHETOR

NEC me nepotes impii silentii
    reum ciebunt, Alcime,
minusque dignum, non et oblitum ferent
    tuae ministrum memoriae,
opponit unum quem viris prioribus   5
    aetas recentis temporis.
palmae forensis et camenarum decus,
    exemplar unum in litteris,
quas aut Athenis docta coluit Graecia,
    aut Roma per Latium colit.   10
moresne fabor et tenorem regulae
    ad usque vitae terminum?
quod laude clarus, quod operatus litteris
    omnem refugisti ambitum?
te nemo gravior vel fuit comis magis   15
    aut liberalis indigis,
danda salute, si forum res posceret;
    studio docendi, si scholam.
vivent per omnem posterorum memoriam,
    quos tu sacrae famae dabas   20
et Iulianum tu magis famae dabis
    quam sceptra, quae tenuit brevi.

---

[1] *i.e.* as for one very dear (*pater*) and also as one who has
died untimely (*iuvenis*).

diminish your slender means. And when you died after six decades, although you left no heir, you were mourned by me as a father and a youth.[1]

[39] And now, if anything survives after Fate has struck her final blow, you are living yet and not unmindful of your days gone by; or, if nothing at all remains, and death's long repose knows no feeling, you have lived your own life: we take pleasure in your fame.

II.—LATINUS ALCIMUS ALETHIUS, THE RHETORICIAN

NOR shall Posterity arraign me on the charge of unduteous silence touching you, Alcimus, and say I was too unworthy and unheedful to be entrusted with the memory of one whom our later age matches alone with the men of olden time. In legal eloquence you were supreme, you were the Muses' pride, and our one model in those letters which learned Greece fostered at Athens, or which Rome fosters throughout the Latin world. Shall I speak of your character and of the rule of life maintained to your life's end? Or of the brilliance of your renown, and the devotion to learning which made you wholly shun ambition? No man was more dignified than you, yet none was more agreeable or more generous to the needy in undertaking the defence if legal aid was needed, or in zealously teaching some pupil in the schools. Those upon whom you bestowed glorious renown will live in the memory of all succeeding ages, and your works will bestow upon Julian [2] greater renown than will the sceptre which he held so short a time. Your

---

[2] Apparently Alcimus had written a history or panegyric on the Emperor Julian: it is not extant.

Sallustio plus conferent libri tui,
　　quam consulatus addidit.
morum tuorum, decoris et facundiae　　　　　25
　　formam dedisti filiis.
Ignosce nostri laesus obsequio stili :
　　amoris hoc crimen tui est,
quod digna nequiens promere officium colo,
　　iniuriose sedulus.　　　　　　　　　　30
quiesce placidus et caduci corporis
　　damnum repende gloria.

III.—Luciolus Rhetor

Rhetora Luciolum, condiscipulum atque magistrum
　　collegamque dehinc, nenia maesta refer,
facundum doctumque virum, seu lege metrorum
　　condita seu prosis solveret orsa modis.
eripuit patri Lachesis quem funere acerbo　　　5
　　linquentem natos sexu in utroque duos :
nequaquam meritis cuius responderit heres
　　obscurus, quamvis nunc tua fama iuvet.
Mitis amice, bonus frater, fidissime coniunx,
　　nate pius, genitor : paenitet, ut fueris.　　10
comis convivis, numquam inclamare clientes,
　　ad famulos numquam tristia verba loqui.
ut placidos mores, tranquillos sic cole manes
　　et cape ab Ausonio munus, amice, vale.

IV.—Attius Patera [Pater] Rhetor

Aetate quamquam viceris dictos prius,
　　Patera, fandi nobilis ;

histories will throw more lustre on Sallust's[1] name than he ever gained through his consulship. So in your virtues, graces, and eloquence you have set a pattern to your sons.

[27] If my pen, seeking to please, only offends, yet pardon me: 'tis the love I bear you is guilty, if, though I cannot voice aught worthy, I seek to pay my homage, harmfully zealous. Calm be your rest, and with renown outweigh the frail body's loss.

III.—LUCIOLUS, THE RHETORICIAN

OF Luciolus the rhetorician, my fellow-pupil, my tutor, and afterwards my colleague, tell now, sad Dirge—a man eloquent and skilful, whether he poured forth utterances shaped to the laws of verse, or to the rhythms of prose. Him Lachesis brought to an untimely end and reft from his father, leaving two children, one of either sex : yet can your heir by no means live up to the standard of your worth, for all the aid your high repute still lends his obscurity to-day.

[9] Ah, gentle friend, kind brother, husband most faithful, loving son and father, what a grief that you are gone ! Courteous to your guests, you were never one to browbeat your dependents or to speak harshly to your servants. So gentle was your nature : may your shade enjoy the same repose ! Take as a tribute from Ausonius, friend, my "farewell."

IV.—ATTIUS PATERA, THE ELDER, THE RHETORICIAN

PATERA, renowned speaker, although in years you outpassed the men named earlier, yet, seeing that

---

[1] This Sallust was prefect of Gaul and colleague of Julian in the consulate of 363 A.D.

tamen, quod aevo floruisti proximo
    iuvenisque te vidi senem,
honore maestae non carebis neniae,   5
    doctor potentum rhetorum.
tu Baiocassi stirpe Druidarum satus,
    si fama non fallit fidem,
Beleni sacratum ducis e templo genus,
    et inde vobis nomina :   10
tibi Paterae : sic ministros nuncupant
    Apollinares mystici.
fratri patrique nomen a Phoebo datum
    natoque de Delphis tuo.
doctrina nulli tanta in illo tempore   15
    cursusque tot fandi et rotae :
memor, disertus, lucida facundia,
    canore, cultu praeditus,
salibus modestus felle nullo perlitis,
    vini cibique abstemius,   20
laetus, pudicus, pulcher, in senio quoque
    aquilae ut senectus aut equi.

V.—Attius Tiro Delphidius Rhetor

Facunde, docte, lingua et ingenio celer,
    iocis amoene, Delphidi,
subtextus esto flebili threno patris,
    laudi ut subibas aemulus.
tu paene ab ipsis orsus incunabulis   5
    dei poeta nobilis,
sertum coronae praeferens Olympiae,
    puer celebrasti Iovem :

---

[1] A Celtic god identified with Apollo. Tertullian (*Apol.*
24) regards him as specially connected with Noricum : in-
scriptions relating to this god are found mostly in the region

your prime was in the age next before my own, and
that in my youth I saw you in your old age, you
shall not lack the tribute of my sad dirge, teacher
of mighty rhetoricians. If report does not lie,
you were sprung from the stock of the Druids of
Bayeux, and traced your hallowed line from the
temple of Belenus ; [1] and hence the names borne by
your family : you are called Patera ; so the mystic
votaries call the servants of Apollo. Your father
and your brother were named after Phoebus, [2] and
your own son after Delphi. [3] In that age there was
none who had such knowledge as you, such swift
and rolling eloquence. Sound in memory as in
learning, you had the gift of clear expression cast
in sonorous and well-chosen phrase ; your wit was
chastened and without a spice of bitterness : sparing
of food and wine, cheerful, modest, comely in per-
son, even in age you were as an eagle or a steed
grown old.

V.—ATTIUS TIRO DELPHIDIUS, A RHETORICIAN

ELOQUENT, learned, quick in word and wit, genial
in humour, Delphidius, even as you rose to rival
your father in renown, so must your praises follow
hard upon the tearful lament that I have made
for him. Almost in the cradle itself, you began
to be the poet of a famous god ; a boy, wearing
on your brow the garland of the Olympian crown,
you sang Jove's praises : next, pressing onward

of Aquileia. See Ihm, *s.v.* Belenus, in Pauly-Wissowa, *Real-
Encyclopädie*, iii. cols. 199 ff.
 [2] *sc.* Phoebicius : see *Prof.* x.
 [3] *sc.* Delphidius : see the following poem. Jerome (*Chron.*)
dates his prime at 358.

mox inde cursim more torrentis freti
    epos ligasti metricum,   10
ut nullus aequa lege liber carminum
    orationem texeret.
celebrata varie cuius eloquentia
    domi forisque claruit:
seu tu cohortis praesulem praetoriae   15
    provinciarum aut iudices
coleres, tuendis additus clientibus
    famae et salutis sauciis.
felix, quietis si maneres litteris
    opus Camenarum colens   20
nec odia magnis concitata litibus
    armaret ultor impetus
nec inquieto temporis tyrannici
    palatio te adtolleres.
dum spem remotam semper arcessis tibi,   25
    fastidiosus obviae,
tuumque mavis esse quam fati bonum,
    desiderasti plurima,
vagus per omnes dignitatum formulas
    meritusque plura quam gerens.   30
unde insecuto criminum motu gravi
    donatus aerumnis patris,
mox inde rhetor, nec docendi pertinax,
    curam fefellisti patrum,
minus malorum munere expertus dei,   35
    medio quod aevi raptus es,
errore quod non deviantis filiae
    poenaque laesus coniugis.

---

[1] In 358 Delphidius conducted the impeachment of Nu-
merian, governor of Gallia Narbonnensis, before Julian. The
scene between Julian and Delphidius is related by Ammianus
Marcellinus, xviii. 1.

like a raging flood, you strung together an epic
all in verse more rapidly than any man free from
the handicap of prosody could shape as much in
prose. In divers fields your eloquence achieved
renown, until its fame stood as high abroad as
here at home; now when you appeared before the
prefect of the pretorian cohort, and now in the
presence of the provincial judges when you were
briefed to defend the threatened honour or the life
of the accused. How happy had you been had you
pursued the Muses' tasks amid the peaceful toil of
letters; had not the impulse of revenge armed the
hatred which great lawsuits[1] breed; or had you
never sought to climb up to the unrestful Palace in
the days of tyranny![2] While you ever conjured up
far-distant hope, disdaining that which lay in your
way, and preferred success to be your work rather
than Fate's, you lost full much, wandering through
all the empty titles of distinction and deserving
greater prizes than you won. Hence arose the
crushing charges which ensued, though your father's
sorrow won your pardon. Thereafter you became
a rhetorician; but lack of diligence in teaching dis-
appointed the hopes of your pupil's fathers. It was
by the grace of God you suffered no worse ill, but
were carried off in middle age and spared the pain
of your daughter's perversity and the execution of
your wife.[3]

[2] The reference is apparently to the revolt of Procopius
against Valens in 365.

[3] Euchrotia, the wife of Delphidius, became a follower of
Priscillian, and was executed along with other members of
the sect under Clemens Maximus, the British pretender.
(Sulpicius Severus, *Sacra Hist.* ii. 65.)

AUSONIUS

VI.—Alethio Minervio Filio Rhetori

O flos iuvenum
spes laeta patris
nec certa tuae
data res patriae,
rhetor Alethi:　5
tu primaevis
doctor in annis:
tempore, quo te
discere adultum
non turpe foret,　10
praetextate,
iam genitori
conlatus eras
postque Paterae
et praeceptor.　15
ille superbae
moenia Romae
fama et meritis
inclitus auxit:
maior utroque　20
tu Burdigalae
laetus patriae
clara cohortis
vexilla regens,
cuncta habuisti　25
commoda fati,
non sine morsu
gravis invidiae:
omnia praecox
fortuna tibi　30
dedit et rapuit:
et rhetoricam
floris adulti
fruge carentem,
et conubium　35
nobile soceris
sine pace patris,
et divitias
utriusque sine
herede domus.　40
solstitialis
velut herba solet
ostentatus
raptusque simul,
pubere in aevo　45
deseruisti
vota tuorum,
non mansuris
ornate bonis.
quam fatiloquo　50
dicte profatu
versus Horati:
" Nil est ab omni
parte beatum."

---

¹ The military terms are metaphorical : *cohors* (*cp. Parent.*
XIV. 2) is the band of youths who were pupils and under the
leadership of Minervius.

THE PROFESSORS OF BORDEAUX

VI.—Alethius Minervius, Son of the Above, a Rhetorician

O flower of our youths and your father's fair hope, though not your country's abiding possession, Alethius the Rhetorician! In earliest years you were a teacher: at an age when it would have been no disgrace for you, a stripling, to have been learning still, ere you were come to manhood's estate, you were already held even a master equal to your father, and, afterwards, to Patera. He, with the brilliance of his renown and gifts, enriched the walls of haughty Rome: you, greater than either, were content to lead on the bright banners of a company[1] in your native town, Bordeaux. You had every blessing Fate can give, but withal felt the tooth of her cruel jealousy. For Fortune, too early ripe, gave you every gift and then snatched them away— your rhetoric, denied the fruit of mature age; your brilliant marriage marred by your father's restlessness; the wealth of your line and your wife's left without heir. Even as the grass of midsummer, you were but displayed[2] and snatched away at once, frustrating your friends' hopes, and were enriched with goods that would not endure. With what prophetic utterance is that verse of Horace[3] fraught:

"Nothing there is that is wholly blessed."

[2] *cp.* Virgil, *Aen.* VI. 869 (of Marcellus).
[3] *Odes*, II. xvi. 27 f.

AUSONIUS

VII.—Leontius Grammaticus Cognomento Lascivus [1]

Qui colis laetos hilarosque mores,
qui dies festos, ioca, vota, ludum,
annuum functi memora Leonti
    nomine threnum.

iste, Lascivus patiens vocari,   5
nomen indignum probitate vitae
abnuit numquam, quia gratum ad aures
    esset amicas.

litteris tantum titulum adsecutus,
quantus exili satis est cathedrae,   10
posset insertus numero ut videri
    grammaticorum.

Tu meae semper socius iuventae,
pluribus quamvis cumulatus annis,
nunc quoque in nostris recales medullis,   15
    blande Leonti!

et iuvat tristi celebrare cura
flebilem cantum memoris querellae:
munus ingratum tibi debitumque
    carmine nostro.   20

VIII.—Grammaticis Graecis Burdigalensibus

Romulum post hos prius an Corinthi,
anne Sperchei pariterque nati
Atticas musas memorem Menesthei
    grammaticorum?

---

[1] A fragmentary inscription found in the ruins of a Roman villa at Lupiac (thought to be the *fundus Lucaniacus* of Ausonius) shows the remains of verses to this same Leontius

THE PROFESSORS OF BORDEAUX

VII.—Leontius the Grammarian, Surnamed
Lascivus

You who love a glad and cheerful soul, you who
observe festal days with their jests, their prayers,
their shows, forget not to recall year by year the
name of Leontius with a dirge. Enduring to be
called Lascivus (Wanton), though the name was a
libel on his upright life, he never forbade its use,
because he knew it amused his friends' ears. In
letters he had attained a high enough degree to
qualify him for his humble chair, and to give him
some claim to be enrolled as a grammarian.

[13] You were the constant companion of my youth,
although you bare a heavier load of years, and still
to-day you have a warm place in my heart, kindly
Leontius. I take sad pleasure in the task of honour-
ing your memory with the mournful strain of this
complaint: it is a task unpleasing, but one that my
verse owes to you.

VIII.—To the Greek Grammarians of Bordeaux

" After these shall I recall Romulus first, or " [1]
Corinthius, or Spercheus and likewise Menestheus,
his son, those grammarians of the Attic Muses? All

---

[1] = Horace, *Od.* i. xii. 33.

Lascivus : see Dezeimeris, *Compte Rendu . . . de l'Acad. de
Bordeaux*, 1868–9, and Peiper's apparatus.

sedulum cunctis studium docendi, 5
fructus exilis tenuisque sermo :
set, quia nostro docuere in aevo,
commemorandi.

tertius horum mihi non magister,
ceteri primis docuere in annis, 10
ne forem vocum rudis aut loquendi
sic ¹ sine cultu :

obstitit nostrae quia, credo, mentis
tardior sensus neque disciplinis
adpulit Graecis puerilis aevi 15
noxius error.

Vos levis caespes tegat et sepulcri
tecta defendant cineres opertos
ac meae vocis titulus supremum
reddat honorem. 20

IX.—Iucundo Grammatico Burdigalensi Fratri
Leonti

Et te, quem cathedram temere usurpasse locuntur
nomen grammatici nec meruisse putant,
voce ciebo tamen, simplex, bone, amice, sodalis,
Iucunde, hoc ipso care magis studio :
quod, quamvis impar, nomen tam nobile amasti, 5
es meritos inter commemorande viros.

¹ *Peiper* : set, *V.*

these were patient, earnest teachers, although small their profit and scant their praise; yet, since they were teachers in my time, I owe a tribute to their memory. The third of these was not my tutor; the others taught me in my earliest years not to be unpolished in my speech and quite without refinement in my tongue. For a dullness of my brain, as I suppose, hindered my progress, and some mischievous perversity of boyhood estranged me from learning Greek.

[17] May the turf lie light upon you, may the roof of the tomb that holds you keep your ashes safe, and may the epitaph I now pronounce pay you the last tribute.

IX.—To Jucundus, the Grammarian of Bordeaux, the Brother of Leontius

Although men say you had rashly assumed your chair, and think you did not deserve to be called a grammarian, yet my voice shall hail you, Jucundus, so simple and so kind, my friend and my companion, whom I love the better for this aim of yours: since you loved so honourable a title, although unequal to it, I must commemorate you here among men of worth.

AUSONIUS

X.—Grammaticis Latinis Burdigalensibus Philologis
[Macrino Sucuroni Concordio Phoebicio [1]]
Ammonio Anastasio Grammatico Pictaviorum

Nunc ut quemque mihi
flebilis officii
relligiosus honor
suggeret, expediam,
qui, quamvis humili   5
stirpe, loco ac merito,
ingeniis hominum
Burdigalae rudibus
introtulere tamen
grammatices studium. 10

    Sit macrinus in his :
huic mea principio
credita pueries ;
et libertina
sucuro progenie,   15
sobrius et puerorum
utilis ingeniis.
et tu concordi,
qui profugus patria
mutasti sterilem   20
urbe alia cathedram.

nec reticebo senem
nomine phoebicium,
qui Beleni aedituus
nil opis inde tulit ;
set tamen, ut placitum,
stirpe satus Druidum
gentis Aremoricae,
Burdigalae cathedram
nati opera obtinuit :
permaneat series.

    ammonium [et recinam [2]—]
relligiosum etenim
commemorare meae
grammaticum patriae—
qui rudibus pueris
prima elementa dabat,
doctrina exiguus,
moribus inplacidis :
proinde, ut erat meritum,
famam habuit tenuem.

---

[1] Omitted in *V*: restored (but in a different order) by
Scaliger, and (in the above order) by Schenkl. Peiper omits
all but the name of Anastasius from the title.

[2] In *V* the name of Ammonius is omitted from the text:
it was replaced as the first half of l. 35 by Schenkl and
Peiper. The result is not good ; and a full stop is here sub-
stituted at the end of l. 31 for Peiper's semicolon, and l. 35

X.—To the Latin Grammarians, Scholars of
Bordeaux, Macrinus, Sucuro, Concordius,
Phoebicius, Ammonius, and Anastasius,
Grammarian of Poictiers

Now, as the pious homage of my mournful task
shall present each one, I will tell of those who,
though of humble birth and rank and merit, in-
stilled into the uncultured minds of the people of
Bordeaux the love of letters.

[11] Let Macrinus be named amongst these: to him
I was entrusted first when a boy; and Sucuro,
the freedman's son, temperate and well-suited to
form youthful minds. You too, Concordius, were
another such, you who, fleeing your country, took in
exchange a chair of little profit in a foreign town.
Nor must I leave unmentioned the old man Phoe-
bicius,[1] who, though the keeper of Belenus' temple,
got no profit thereby. Yet he, sprung, as rumour
goes, from the stock of the Druids of Armorica
(Brittany), obtained a chair at Bordeaux by his son's
help: long may his line endure!

[35] I will sing of Ammonius also—for, indeed, it is
a solemn duty to commemorate a grammarian of my
own native place—who used to teach raw lads their
alphabet:[2] he had scant learning and was of an
ungentle nature, and therefore—as was his due—
was held in slight repute.

---

[1] *cp. Prof.* IV. 13. For Belenus see note on *id.* l. 9.
[2] Or perhaps the elements of Latin are meant.

---

is placed between ll. 31 and 32 (whence it was possibly
omitted through homoeoteleuton with l. 32).

For the order of the verses (which is much confused) in
the MS., see the editions of Peiper or Schenkl.

The latter half of l. 35 is supplied by the Translator.

Pange et ANASTASIO
flebile, Musa, melum
et memora tenuem
nenia, grammaticum.   45
Burdigalae hunc genitum
transtulit ambitio
Pictonicaeque dedit.
pauper ibi et tenuem

victum habitumque colens,
gloriolam exilem   51
et patriae et cathedrae
perdidit in senio.
set tamen hunc noster
commemoravit honos,   55
ne pariter tumulus
nomen et ossa tegat.

XI.—HERCULANO SORORIS FILIO GRAMMATICO BURDIGALENSI

HERCULANE, qui, profectus gremio de nostro et schola,
spem magis, quam rem fruendam praebuisti avunculo,
particeps scholae et cathedrae paene sucessor meae,
lubricae nisi te iuventae praecipitem flexus daret,
Pythagorei non tenentem tramitis rectam viam :   5
esto placidus et quietis manibus sedem fove,
iam mihi cognata dudum inter memoratus nomina.

XII.—THALASSO GRAMMATICO LATINO BURDIGALENSI

OFFICIUM nomenque tuum, primaeve Thalasse,
    parvulus audivi, vix etiam memini.
qua forma aut merito fueris, qua stirpe parentum,
    aetas nil de te posterior celebrat.

---

[1] Pythagoras symbolised man's choice in life by the letter
Y (cp. Technopaegn. XIII. 9), the two arms representing the

[42] For Anastasius also shape a mournful lay, my Muse; and you, my dirge, recall that poor grammarian. He was born at Bordeaux, but ambition transferred him to Poictiers. There he lived a poor man, stinted alike in food and dress, and in his old age lost the faint glimmer of renown which his country and his chair had shed on him. Howbeit, I have here paid a tribute to his name, that the tomb should not swallow up his name with his bones.

XI.—To Herculanus, my Nephew, Grammarian of Bordeaux

Herculanus, though you came from my bosom and my class, you have repaid your uncle with promise rather than with fruit. You shared in the work of my class, and might have succeeded to my chair, had not the swerving steps of slippery youth caused you to fall headlong, through not keeping to the right path traced out by Pythagoras.[1] May you have rest, and may your spirit dwell in peace in its last home— you whose name I recalled a while ago amongst my relatives.[2]

XII.—To Thalassus, Latin Grammarian of Bordeaux

Of your rank and name, Thalassus, youthful teacher, I heard as a little boy, scarce even do I recall them. Of your person or attainments, of the family whence you were sprung, a later age proclaims nought concerning you. Only report used

paths of Vice and Virtue. It is in youth that a man must make his choice between these two divergent ways.

[2] See *Parent.* XVII.

grammaticum iuvenem tantum te fama ferebat,　5
　　tum quoque tam tenuis, quam modo nulla manet.
set quicumque tamen, nostro quia doctor in aevo
　　vixisti, hoc nostrum munus habeto, vale.

XIII.—Citario Siculo Syracusano Grammatico Burdigalensi Graeco

Et, Citari dilecte, mihi memorabere, dignus
　　grammaticos inter qui celebrere bonos.
esset Aristarchi tibi gloria Zenodotique
　　Graiorum, antiquus si sequeretur honos.
carminibus, quae prima tuis sunt condita in annis,　5
　　concedit Cei musa Simonidei.
urbe satus Sicula nostram peregrinus adisti
　　excultam studiis quam propere edideras.
coniugium nanctus cito nobilis et locupletis,
　　invidia fati non genitor moreris.　　　　　10
at nos defunctum memori celebramus honore,
　　fovimus ut vivum munere amicitiae.

XIV.—Censorio Attico Agricio Rhetori

Eloquii merito primis aequande, fuisti,
　　Agrici, positus posteriore loco :
aevo qui quoniam genitus functusque recenti,
　　dilatus nobis, non et omissus eras.
quocumque in numero, tristi memorabere threno :　5
　　unus honos tumuli, serus et ante datus.

to tell that you became a grammarian in your youth, but even this was then so slight that it no longer lingers now. Yet, be you who you were, because you lived and taught in my lifetime, take this my offering, "farewell!"

XIII.—To Citarius, the Sicilian of Syracuse, Greek Grammarian at Bordeaux

You also shall be recalled by me, beloved Citarius, for you deserve to be praised amongst good grammarians. If the custom of past ages still obtained, you would have the renown of Aristarchus and Zenodotus among the Greeks. Even the Muse of Simonides of Ceos yields place to the odes which you composed in your early years. Born in a Sicilian town, you came a stranger to our city, but quickly made it the home of culture with your learning. Here you soon found a wife well-born and rich; but Fate grudged you the gift of children ere your death. But, now that you are gone, we honour you with the tribute of our remembrance, even as we cheered you, while you lived, with the gift of our friendship.

XIV.—To Censorius Atticus Agricius, the Rhetorician

For mastery in eloquence worthy to be ranked equal with the foremost, here, Agricius, you have been set in a lower place: since you were born and died in later years, I had delayed to mention you, yet had not also forgotten you. But be your place where it may, my sad lament shall recall your memory: early or late, homage paid to the dead

tam generis tibi celsus apex, quam gloria fandi,
  gloria Athenaei cognita sede loci :
Nazario et claro quondam delata Paterae
  egregie multos excoluit iuvenes.   10
coniuge nunc natisque superstitibus generoque
  maiorum manes et monumenta foves.

XV. — Nepotiano Grammatico Eidem Rhetori

  Facete, comis, animo iuvenali senex,
    cui felle nullo, melle multo mens madens
    aevum per omne nil amarum miscuit,
    medella nostri, Nepotiane, pectoris,
    tam seriorum quam iocorum particeps,   5
    taciturne, Amyclas qui silendo viceris :
    te fabulantem non Ulixes linqueret,
    liquit canentes qui melodas virgines :
    probe et pudice, parce, frugi, abstemie,
    facunde, nulli rhetorum cedens stilo   10
    et disputator ad Cleanthen Stoicum :
    Scaurum Probumque corde callens intimo
    et Epirote Cinea memor magis :
    sodalis et convictor, hospes iugiter :

---

[1] An orator and rhetorician who delivered a panegyric
(which is still extant) in praise of Constantine I. in 321 A.D.
  [2] This Amyclae lay between Cajeta and Tarracina, in
Latium. It was forbidden for any citizen to announce the
approach of an enemy. *cp.* Virgil, *Aen.* x. 564.

is all one. The nobility of your birth was not less lofty than the renown of your eloquence—renown, no stranger to your chair here in this second Athens: bestowed on Nazarius[1] and famous Patera in former days, it trained to highest perfection many a youth. Now you have left a wife, children, and a son-in-law here on this earth and cheer the shades of your ancestors in their tombs.

XV.—To Nepotianus, Grammarian and Rhetorician

Witty and cheerful, an old man with a heart of youth, whose soul, steeped in honey with no drop of gall, never throughout all your life instilled aught of bitterness, balm of my heart, Nepotianus, taking your share in grave and gay alike: your lips once closed, you could surpass Amyclae[2] in silence; when once you began to discourse, even Ulysses could not leave you—he who left the tuneful Sirens at their song. Honourable and pure, sparing, frugal, temperate, eloquent, you were second to no orator in style, while in argument you were the equal of Cleanthes the Stoic.[3] Scaurus and Probus[4] you knew off by heart, and in memory were a match for Cineas of Epirus.[5] You were my comrade, companion, and my guest continually: and not my guest alone, but the

---

[3] *c.* 300–220 B.C., successor to Zeno as head of the Stoic school. His *Hymn to Zeus* (? quoted by St. Paul) is extant.
[4] See *Praef.* I. notes 5 and 6.
[5] Friend and agent of Pyrrhus. When on an embassy in Rome after the battle of Heraclea (280 B.C.), he was able to address any of the senators or equites by name after being once introduced. See Pliny, *N.H.* vii. 24.

parum quod hospes, mentis agitator meae.   15
consilia nullus mente tam pura dedit
vel altiore conditu texit data.
honore gesti praesidatus inclitus,
decies novenas functus annorum vices,
duos relinquens liberos morte oppetis,   20
dolore multo tam tuorum quam meo.

XVI.—Aemilius Magnus Arborius Rhetor Tolosae

Inter cognatos iam fletus, avuncule, manes
  inter rhetoricos nunc memorandus eris.
illud opus pietas, istud reverenda virorum
  nomina pro patriae relligione habeant.
bis meritum duplici celebremus honore parentem   5
  Arborium, Arborio patre et avo Argicio.
Stemma tibi patris Haeduici, Tarbellica Maurae
  matris origo fuit : ambo genus procerum.
nobilis et dotata uxor, domus et schola, cultae
  principum amicitiae contigerunt iuveni,   10
dum Constantini fratres opulenta Tolosa
  exilii specie sepositos cohibet.
Byzanti inde arcem Thressaeque Propontidis urbem
  Constantinopolim fama tui pepulit.
illic dives opum doctoque ibi Caesare honorus   15
  occumbis patribus, Magne, superstitibus.

---

[1] *cp.* xxiv. 9 f. He gave the best advice and, like a lawyer or doctor, treated the matter as confidential.

[2] *cp. Parent.* iii. 1–2, 8.

[3] There is no other reference to this fact.

awakener of my mind. None gave advice out of a
heart more sincere, or concealed it, when given,
with deeper secrecy.[1] When you had been dis-
tinguished by your appointment as governor, and
had lived through the changes of ninety years, you
met your end leaving two children, to your kins-
folk's great sorrow as to mine.

XVI.—Aemilius Magnus Arborius, the Rhetorician
of Toulouse

Though mourned already among my departed
relatives, you must be mentioned here, my uncle,
among rhetoricians. Let love of kindred claim
that work; but be this a tribute to the names of
famous men, inspired by devotion to my native
land. As doubly earned, let me pay this double
meed of praise to my father [2] Arborius, son of Ar-
borius, and grandson of Argicius. Your father was
of Aeduan stock, while your mother, Maura, sprang
from Aquae Tarbellae (Dax): both were of high de-
scent. A wife, noble-born and well-portioned, a home,
a professorial chair, with the friendship of the great
which you gained—all these you attained while still
young, while wealthy Toulouse held the brothers of
Constantine secluded there in nominal exile.[3] From
there your renown forced its way to the strong-
hold of Byzantium, and to that city of the Thracian
Propontis, Constantinople. In that place, full of
wealth and famed as the tutor of a Caesar [4] there,
you died, Magnus, while your parents were yet

[4] This prince is identified with Constantine, born in
316 A.D. and proclaimed Caesar in 317 A.D. This Aemilius
Arborius is perhaps referred to in *Gratiarum Actio*, c. vii.

in patriam sed te sedem ac monumenta tuorum
    principis Augusti restituit pietas.
hinc renovat causam lacrimis et flebile munus
    annuus ingrata relligione dies.   20

XVII.—Exuperius Rhetor Tolosae

Exuperi, memorande mihi, facunde sine arte,
incessu gravis et verbis ingentibus, ore
pulcher et ad summam motuque habituque venusto:
copia cui fandi longe pulcherrima, quam si
auditu tenus acciperes, deflata placeret,   5
discussam scires solidi nihil edere sensus.
Palladiae primum toga te venerata Tolosae
mox pepulit levitate pari.   Narbo inde recepit.
illic Dalmatio genitos, fatalia regum
nomina, tum pueros, grandi mercede docendi   10
formasti rhetor metam prope puberis aevi.
Caesareum qui mox indepti nomen honorem
praesidis Hispanumque tibi tribuere tribunal.
decedens placidos mores tranquillaque vitae
tempora praedives finisti sede Cadurca.   15
sed patriae te iura vocant et origo parentum.
Burdigalae ut rursum nomen de rhetore reddas.

---

[1] *i.e.* his eloquence was "full of sound and fury, signifying
nothing"; or like that of the Professor of Rhetoric in *Le
Bourgeois Gentilhomme.*

alive. Howbeit, with loving care our prince Augustus restored your body to your native place and to the tomb of your family. So year by year this day brings round a cause for tears and this mournful task of joyless devotion.

XVII.—Exuperius of Toulouse, the Rhetorician

Now must I renew your memory, Exuperius, an orator without help of rules, solemn of gait, majestic in speech, handsome in features and, in a word, admirable in gesture and deportment. Your eloquence was matchless in its fluency, and if judged only by the ear, would please through mere force of sound, but if closely examined would be found to contain no solid thought.[1] At first the councillors of Toulouse, that home of Pallas, received you with adoration, but soon drove you as lightly away. Then Narbo harboured you : there, taking a high fee for your teaching, you trained in rhetoric the sons of Dalmatius [2]—royal but tragic names—from boyhood up to the beginning of manhood. When in due time they assumed the title of Caesar, they bestowed upon you the dignity of a governorship and a tribunal in Spain. Passing away, exceeding rich, you brought your unruffled nature and your peaceful years to a close in your abode at Cadurca (Cahors). But your country's claims and the birthplace of your family summon you to bequeath your title of rhetorician to Bordeaux.

[2] *sc.* Dalmatius and Anaballianus, who were both killed in a military revolt after the death of Constantine, in 337 A.D.

AUSONIUS

XVIII.—Marcello Marcelli Filio Grammatico Narbonensi

Nec te Marcello genitum, Marcelle, silebo,
  aspera quem genetrix urbe, domo pepulit:
sed fortuna potens cito reddidit omnia et auxit:
  amissam primum Narbo dedit patriam.
nobilis hic hospes Clarentius indole motus   5
  egregia natam coniugio adtribuit.
mox schola et auditor multus praetextaque pubes
  grammatici nomen divitiasque dedit.
sed numquam iugem cursum fortuna secundat,
  praesertim pravi nancta virum ingenii.   10
verum oneranda mihi non sunt, memoranda recepi
  fata; sat est dictum cuncta perisse simul:
non tamen et nomen, quo te non fraudo, receptum
  inter grammaticos praetenuis meriti.

XIX.—Sedatus Rhetor Tolosanus

Relligio est, tacitum si te, Sedate, relinquam,
  quamvis docendi munus indepte es foris.
communis patria est tecum mihi: sorte potentis
  fati Tolosam nanctus es sedem scholae.
illic coniugium natique opulensque senectus   5
  et fama, magno qualis est par rhetori.
quamvis externa tamen a regione reducit
  te patria et civem morte obita repetit,

THE PROFESSORS OF BORDEAUX

XVIII.—To Marcellus, Son of Marcellus, the Grammarian of Narbonne

I WILL not pass you by without a word, Marcellus, son of Marcellus. The harshness of your mother drove you from your home and your city, but all-powerful Fortune soon restored all you had lost and added more. For firstly, in Narbo you found the country you had lost; and here Clarentius, a stranger of high birth, was led by your noble nature to give you his daughter to wife. And in due time your classes and lectures, thronged with crowds of boys, brought you the title of grammarian and wealth. But Fortune never favours a career of un-varying success, especially when she finds a man of a crooked nature. Howbeit, 'tis not for me to make heavier your destiny: my task is to recall it. It is enough to say that you lost all at one stroke; yet not your title also, whereof I do not rob you, but give you a place amongst grammarians of very scant deserving.

XIX.—Sedatus, the Rhetorician of Toulouse

IT were a thing unholy to leave you unmentioned, Sedatus, although it was abroad that you obtained your post as teacher. We had one native place, you and I; but the hazards of all-powerful Destiny gave you a chair at Toulouse. There you found a wife, and children, and riches for your old age, with such renown as is the due of a great rhetorician. Yet from that land, however far, your native place now brings you home, and after death claims you again

cumque vagantem operam divisae impenderis urbi,
    arbitrium de te sumit origo suum.   10
et tua nunc suboles morem sectata parentis
    Narbonem ac Romam nobilitat studiis;
sed [quid conquerimur?   Longum post tempus et
      illos[1]]
    fama, velit nolit, Burdigalam referet.

XX.—STAPHYLIUS RHETOR CIVIS AUSCIUS

HACTENUS observata mihi lex commemorandi
    cives, sive domi seu docuere foris.
externum sed fas coniungere civibus unum
    te, Staphyli, genitum stirpe Novem populis.
tu mihi, quod genitor, quod avunculus, unus
      utrumque,   5
    alter ut Ausonius, alter ut Arborius.
grammatice ad Scaurum atque Probum, promptissime
      rhetor,
    historiam callens Livii et Herodoti.
omnis doctrinae ratio tibi cognita, quantam
    condit sescentis Varro voluminibus.   10
aurea mens, vox suada tibi, tum sermo quietus:
    nec cunctator erat, nec properator erat.
pulchra senecta, nitens habitus, procul ira dolorque;
    et placidae vitae congrua meta fuit.

[1] Suppl. *Translator.*

as its citizen. You may have strayed away and
spent your pains on a distant city, but the country
of your birth resumes its right to you. And now
your sons are following their father's example, and
adding to the renown of Narbo and of Rome with
their learning. But why do we complain? After
long years, will they or nill they, Fame will bring
them also back to Bordeaux.

XX.—Staphylius, the Rhetorician, a Native of Ausci [1]

So far I have kept to the rule of commemorating
my fellow-countrymen, whether they taught in our
city or abroad. Yet it is no sin to couple with my
countrymen a single stranger such as you, Staphylius,
a son of Novem Populi. You were to me a father
and an uncle, both in one, like a second Ausonius,
like a second Arborius. As a grammarian you
rivalled Scaurus and Probus; as a rhetorician, most
ready; in history you knew all Livy and Herodotus.
You knew every branch of learning and all the lore
which Varro stored in his innumerable tomes. Your
heart was golden, your tongue persuasive and your
speech unflurried; no hesitating was there and yet
no hurrying. In old age you were comely and dis-
tinguished in appearance; anger and grief were
strangers to you, and your peaceful life had a be-
fitting close.

[1] Now Auch.

XXI.—Crispus et Urbicus Grammatici Latini et
Graeci

Tu quoque in aevum, Crispe, futurum
maesti venies commemoratus
    munere threni.

qui primaevos fandique rudes
elementorum prima docebas   5
    signa novorum :

creditus olim fervere mero,
ut Vergilii Flaccique locis [1]
    aemula ferres.

Et tibi Latiis posthabite orsis,   10
Urbice, Grais celebris, carmen
    sic ἐλελείσω.

nam tu Crispo coniuncte tuo
prosa solebas et versa loqui
    impete eodem,   15

priscos ut [mox] heroas olim
carmine Homeri commemoratos
    fando referres :

dulcem in paucis ut Plistheniden,
et torrentis ceu Dulichii   20
    ninguida dicta,

et mellitae nectare vocis
dulcia fatu verba canentem
    Nestora regem.

Ambo loqui faciles, ambo omnia carmina docti, 25
    callentes mython plasmata et historiam,
liberti ambo genus, sed quos meruisse deceret
    nancisci, ut cluerent patribus ingenuis.

[1] So *V*: iocis, *Peiper* (after *Heinsius*) ; but what are " Ver-
gilii . . . ioca " ?

THE PROFESSORS OF BORDEAUX

XXI.—Crispus and Urbicus, Greek and Latin Grammarians

Your name also, Crispus, shall be kept in memory by this sad lament which I offer you, and go down to future ages—you who used to teach the youngest boys, unskilled in speech, the simple signs of their new task, the alphabet: at times it was thought that you used to prime yourself with wine in order to produce verse rivalling passages of Vergil and of Flaccus.

[10] For you also, Urbicus, held of less account for Latin themes, though famous for your Greek, thus will I raise a chant of grief. For in the company of your friend Crispus you would pour out a flood of words in prose and verse with equal ease and with such eloquence as to remind us of those heroes sung by old Homer [1]—that son of Pleisthenes, so sweet but terse, and the impetuous lord of Dulichium [2] whose words were as flakes of snow, and Nestor the king, whose melodious speech was sweet of utterance with the nectar of his honeyed lips.

[25] Both ready speakers, both learned in all the lore of poësy, and skilled alike in mythic fictions and in history, you were both freedmen by birth, but in your natures such as might well have deserved to be called the sons of free-born fathers.

---

[1] *cp.* Γ 214, 222 and Λ 248 f.
[2] *sc.* Menelaus and Ulysses.

AUSONIUS

XXII.—Victorio Subdoctori sive Proscholo

Victori studiose, memor, celer, ignoratis
  adsidue in libris nec nisi operta legens,
exesas tineis opicasque evolvere chartas
  maior quam promptis cura tibi in studiis.
quod ius[1] pontificum, quae foedera, stemma quod olim
  ante Numam fuerit sacrifici Curibus: 6
quid Castor cunctis de regibus ambiguis, quid
  coniugis e libris ediderit Rhodope:
quod ius pontificum, veterum quae scita Quiritum
  quae consulta patrum, quid Draco quidve Solon 10
sanxerit et Locris dederit quae iura Zaleucus,
  sub Iove quae Minos, quae Themis ante Iovem,
nota tibi potius, quam Tullius et Maro nostri
  et quidquid Latia conditur historia.
fors istos etiam tibi lectio longa dedisset,   15
  supremum Lachesis ni celerasset iter.
exili nostrae fucatus honore cathedrae,
  libato tenuis nomine grammatici:
longinquis posthac Cumae defunctus in oris,
  ad quas de Siculo litore transieras.   20
sed modo nobilium memoratus in agmine gaude,
  pervenit ad manes si pia cura tuos.

---

[1] *V*: Peiper alters to *quidvis, pontificum* etc.; but the
MS. reading is supported by Quintilian, viii. 2: "at ob-
scuritas fit etiam verbis ab usu remotis: ut si commentarios
(= ius) quis pontificum, et vetustissima foedera, et exoletos
scrutatus auctores id ipsum petat . . ."

---

[1] The chief town of the Sabines in early days and the
birthplace of Numa, who was credited with seven books on
priestly lore (Livy xl. 29). Quintilian (*cp.* note on text,
l. 5) cites such hieratic works (*commentarii*), early treaties,
and obsolete authors as examples of obscurity and objects of
pedantic study.

THE PROFESSORS OF BORDEAUX

XXII.—To Victorius, Assistant-Teacher or Usher

Scholarly Victorius, gifted with memory and a quick brain, how patiently you used to pore over books which no one read, and study only abstruse lore! You liked better to unroll worm-eaten and outlandish scrolls than to give yourself to more familiar pursuits. What was the code of the pontifices, what the treaties, what the pedigree of the sacrificial priest at Cures[1] long before Numa's days, what Castor[2] had to say on all the shadowy kings, what Rhodope published out of her husband's books, what the code of the priests, what the resolutions of the old Quirites, what the decrees of the Senate, what measures Draco or what Solon passed, and what laws Zaleucus[3] gave the Locrians, what Minos under the reign of Jove, what Themis even before Jove's time—all these were better known to you than our Tully or Maro, and all the stores of Roman history. Maybe continued reading would have brought them also within your ken, had not Lachesis hurried on the date of your last journey. Your post here in our city had brought you only a faint tincture of renown, and given you but a slight foretaste of the title of grammarian, when you died on the coast of far-off Cumae whither you had crossed over from Sicily. But now that I have numbered you in a company of famous men, rejoice—if this my pious tribute reaches your shade.

[2] According to Suidas, Castor was either a Rhodian, a Galatian, or a Massilian. It was probably in his Χρονικὰ Ἀγνοήματα that he dealt with the early Roman kings. Since he is quoted by Apollodorus, his date is not later than c. 150 B.C. Of Rhodope (his wife?) nothing is known.

[3] c. 660 B.C. His code was regarded by the Greeks as the earliest written code which they possessed.

XXIII.—Dynamio Burdigalensi qui in Hispania Docuit et Obiit

Set neque te maesta, Dynami, fraudabo querella,
    municipem patriae causidicumque meae,
crimine adulterii quem saucia fama fugavit,
    parvula quem latebris fovit Hilerda suis,
quem locupletavit coniunx Hispana latentem;   5
    namque ibi mutato nomine rhetor eras,
rhetor Flavini cognomine dissimulatus,
    ne posset profugum prodere culpa suum.
reddiderat quamvis patriae te sera voluntas,
    mox residem rursum traxit Hilerda domus.   10
Qualiscumque tuae fuerit fuga famaque vitae,
    iungeris antiqua tu mihi amicitia,
officiumque meum, sensus si manibus ullus,
    accipe iam serum morte obita, Dynami.
diversis quamvis iaceas defunctus in oris,   15
    commemorat maestis te pia cura elegis.

XXIV.—Acilio Glabrioni Grammatico Iun. Burdigalensi

Doctrinae vitaeque pari brevitate caducum,
    Glabrio, te maestis commemorabo elegis,
stemmate nobilium deductum nomen avorum,
    Glabrio Acilini,[1] Dardana progenies.
tu quondam puero conpar mihi, discipulus mox,   5
    meque dehinc facto rhetore grammaticus,

---

[1] *Heinsius, Peiper* : Aquilinus, *V.*

XXIII.—To Dynamius of Bordeaux, who Taught and Died in Spain

From you also, Dynamius, I will not withhold my sad complaint—from you, my fellow-citizen and a pleader here ; who fled the country with a good name tarnished by a charge of adultery, to whom tiny Lerida gave a snug hiding-place, whom a Spanish wife enriched while you lay hid ; for there, under a changed name, you were a rhetorician—a rhetorician disguised under the name of Flavinus for fear the story of your slip should betray you as the runaway. And though of your own accord you came back later to your native place, your home in Lerida soon drew you back to live at ease.

[11] Whatever may have been the nature of your flight, and whatever your repute, old friendship links you and me together ; and therefore, if the shades can feel at all, accept this friendly service, Dynamius, albeit offered this long while after your death. Though you have ceased to be and lie buried in a distant land, my reverent care dedicates this sad plaint to your memory.

XXIV.—To Acilius Glabrio the Younger, of Bordeaux, a Grammarian

Fallen with short span alike of learning and of years, you will I commemorate in mournful verse, Glabrio—a name drawn from a line of famous ancestors—Glabrio, son of Acilinus, offspring of Dardanus. In old days we were boys together ; then you became my pupil, and next, when I was made

inque foro tutela reis et cultor in agris,
   digne, diu partis qui fruerere bonis:
commode, laete, benigne, abstemie, tam bone dandis
   semper consiliis, quam taciturne datis,   10
tam decus omne tuis quam mox dolor, omnia acerbo
   funere praereptus, Glabrio, destituis:
uxore et natis, genitore et matre relictis,
   eheu quam multis perdite nominibus!
flete diu nobis, numquam satis, accipe acerbum,   15
   Glabrio, in aeternum commemorate, vale.

XXV.—Coronis

Quos legis a prima deductos menide libri,
   doctores patriae scito fuisse meae,
grammatici in studio vel rhetoris aut in utroque,
   quos memorasse mihi morte obita satis est.
viventum inlecebra est laudatio: nomina tantum   5
   voce ciere suis sufficiet tumulis.
ergo, qui nostrae legis otia tristia chartae,
   eloquium ne tu quaere, set officium,
quo claris doctisque viris pia cura parentat,
   dum decora egregiae commeminit patriae.   10

---

[1] The *grammaticus* taught Greek and Latin mainly from the linguistic side (grammar, syntax, metre, antiquities). The *rhetor* gave more advanced instruction, but was chiefly concerned with training in declamation and all subjects subsidiary to it.

[2] *i.e.* as husband, father, and son.

rhetorician, you became grammarian.[1] In the courts you were the bulwark of the accused; in the country you farmed your estate, and deserved long to enjoy the fruits you earned. Obliging, cheerful, kindly, temperate, you were always as ready to give advice as silent when you had given it. At once all the pride of your kin as presently their sorrow, you leave all desolate, my Glabrio, reft from us by untimely death: wife, children, father, mother, left—alas, under how many names were you lost to them![2] Long mourned by me, though never mourned enough, your name is here recorded for all time; and so, friend Glabrio, receive my sorrowful farewell!

XXV.—Conclusion

Know that these men, of whom you read in order after the exordium[3] of my book, were once teachers in my native place, some of grammar, some of rhetoric, and some of both. They are dead, and it is enough that I have recalled their memories. For the living praise is a lure: to but cry their names[4] will satisfy those within the tomb. Wherefore, do you, who in my pages read these mournful trifles, not look for pomp of words but for the affection wherewith my reverent care makes offering to famous and learned men, while it recalls the glories of my splendid native land.

[3] From μῆνις ("wrath")—the first word in the *Iliad* and the title of the first Book.

[4] *cp. Parent.*, Preface in Verse, 10 f., *Epitaph* xiii. 3-4. To call aloud upon the dead was a recognised funerary rite: see Virgil, *Aen.* vi. 507: magna Manes ter voce vocavi; *id.* iii. 67: magna supremum voce ciemus.

XXVI.—Poeta

Valete, manes inclitorum rhetorum :
    valete, doctores probi,
historia si quos vel poeticus stilus
    forumve fecit nobiles,
medicae vel artis dogma vel Platonicum   5
    dedit perenni gloriae :
et si qua functis cura viventum placet
    iuvatque honor superstitum :
accipite maestum carminis cultum mei
    textum querella flebili.   10
sedem sepulcri servet immotus cinis,
    memoria vivat nominum,
dum remeat illud, iudicis dono dei,
    commune cunctis saeculum.

THE PROFESSORS OF BORDEAUX

XXVI.—The Poet

Fare ye well, shades of famous rhetoricians: fare ye well, worthy teachers, whether it were history, or poetry, or eloquence in the courts that made you famous; or whether medicine or Plato's system won you undying renown. And if any care of the living please the dead, and if the tribute of their survivors please them, then take the sad homage of my verse, a fabric of tears and sighs. Undisturbed may your ashes keep their place within the tomb, may the memory of your names live on until that other age return [1] in which, by grace of God our judge, we all shall share!

---

[1] Ausonius apparently regards "the world to come" as a Golden Age which is to come *back* to man. Doubtless he had in mind Virgil, *Ecl.* iv. 6 : redeunt Saturnia regna.

LIBER VI

EPITAPHIA HEROUM QUI BELLO TROICO INTERFUERUNT

Ausonius Lectori Suo Salutem.

AD rem pertinere existimavi, ut vel vanum opusculum materiae congruentis absolverem et libello, qui commemorationem habet eorum, qui vel peregrini [Burdigalae vel[1]] Burdigalenses peregre docuerunt, Epitaphia subnecterem [scilicet titulos sepulcrales[2]] heroum, qui bello Troico interfuerunt. quae antiqua cum aput philologum quendam repperissem, Latino sermone converti, non ut inservirem ordinis persequendi [studio[3]], set ut cohercerem libere nec aberrarem.

I.—AGAMEMNONI

REX regum Atrides, fraternae coniugis ultor,
  oppetii manibus coniugis ipse meae.
quid prodest Helenes raptum punisse dolentem,
  vindicem adulterii cum Clytemestra necet?

---

[1] Suppl. *Vinetus.*   [2] A gloss.   [3] Suggested by *Peiper.*

---

[1] The *Peplos* of "Aristotle" (a collection of sixty-seven couplets commemorating Greek and Trojan heroes) contains the originals of many, but by no means all, of these pieces. Nos. xxvii.–xxxv. have no connection with the Trojan

BOOK VI

EPITAPHS ON THE HEROES WHO TOOK PART IN THE TROJAN WAR[1]

PREFACE

Ausonius to the Reader, greeting.

I have thought it to the purpose to finish off this little work and to append it—for however trifling it may be, it is kindred in substance—to my little book commemorating the Professors of Bordeaux, whether they were strangers teaching at Bordeaux or fellow-countrymen teaching abroad. It is the *Epitaphs* [that is to say, funerary inscriptions] *on the Heroes who took part in the Trojan War.* It consists, indeed, of ancient poems which I found in the possession of some scholar and turned into Latin, on such terms as not to follow the strict letter of the original slavishly, but to paraphrase it freely, though without missing the point.

I.—FOR AGAMEMNON.[2]

I, THE son of Atreus, the king of kings, the avenger of my brother's wife, met my end at my own wife's hands. What, then, avails it that in my grief I punished Helen's ravisher, since Clytemnaestra slays the chastiser of adultery?

War, and were probably thrust into their present place by an editor who, after the death of Ausonius, introduced his unpublished work into the published collection wherever it seemed to fit in more or less appropriately. See *Introduction.*

[2] cp. *Pepl.* 1.

II.—Menelao

FELIX o Menelae, deum cui debita sedes
  decretumque piis manibus Elysium,
Tyndareo dilecte gener, dilecte Tonanti,
  coniugii vindex, ultor adulterii,
aeterno pollens aevo aeternaque iuventa,   5
  nec leti passus tempora nec senii.

III.—Aiaci

AIACIS tumulo pariter tegor obruta Virtus,
  inlacrimans bustis funeris ipsa mei,
incomptas lacerata comas, quod pravus Atrides
  cedere me instructis compulit insidiis.
iam dabo purpureum claro de sanguine florem,   5
  testantem gemitu crimina iudicii.

IV.—Achilli

NON una Aeaciden tellus habet : ossa teguntur
  litore Sigeo, crinem Larisa cremavit.
pars tumulis [secreta iacet, pars] classe [relata est ;[1]]
  orbe set in toto [redivivum ostendet Homerus[2]].

V.—Ulixi

CONDITUR hoc tumulo Laerta natus Ulixes :
  perlege Odyssean omnia nosse volens.

     [1] Suppl. *Translator.*   [2] Suppl. *Heinsius.*

---

     [1] *cp. Pepl.* 3.
     [2] *cp.* Hesiod, *W. and D.* 169.
     [3] Tyndareus was the reputed and Zeus (Juppiter) the
actual father of Helen : *cp. Epigr.* lxvi. 4.
     [4] *Pepl.* 7 = *Anth. Pal.* vii. 145.

EPITAPHS

II.—For Menelaus [1]

O HAPPY Menelaus, who hast the allotted dwelling-place of gods,[2] and Elysium, ordained for pious souls! Beloved of Tyndareus, beloved of the Thunderer as their son-in-law,[3] champion of wedlock, avenger of adultery, strong in unending life, unending youth, you have endured no day of death, no day of eld.

III.—For Ajax [4]

AT Ajax' tomb I, Valour, lie o'erwhelmed along with him. Here, over the mound which marks my obsequies, I weep with hair all torn and towsled, because the mean son of Atreus forced me to yield to his calculated wiles. Now will I make to spring from this noble blood a ruddy flower [5] that with a word of woe bears witness to that unrighteous judgment.[6]

IV.—For Achilles

NOT one the land which holds the son of Aeacus: his bones are buried on the Sigean shore, and at Larissa were his tresses burned. Part of him lies hidden in the tomb, part was borne home by the fleet; but in the whole world Homer shall show him living once again.

V.—For Ulysses [7]

BENEATH this mound lies buried Laërtes' son, Ulysses. If you would learn all his story, read through the *Odyssey.*

[5] The hyacinth, on which was supposed to appear the Greek interjection aἴ (alas !). *cp.* Ovid, *Metam.* x. 215, for the parallel story of Hyacinthus.

[6] *sc.* the judgment which assigned the arms of Achilles to Ulysses and not to Ajax.   [7] *Pepl.* 12.

AUSONIUS

VI.—Diomedi

Conditur hic genitore bono melior Diomedes,
crimen ob uxoris pulsus dotalibus Argis,
Argyripam clarosque viris qui condidit Arpos,
clarior urbe nova patriae quam sede vetusta.

VII.—Antilocho

Consiliis belloque bonus, quae copula rara est,
    carus et Atridis, carus et Aeacidis :
praemia virtutis simul et pietatis adeptus,
    servato Antilochus Nestore patre obii.
non hic ordo fuit : set iustius ille superstes,   5
    Troia capi sine quo perfida non poterat.

VIII.—Nestori

Hoc tegor in tumulo quarti iam prodigus aevi
    Nestor, consilio clarus et eloquio.
obiecit sese cuius pro morte peremptus
    filius et nati vulnere vivo pater.
eheu cur fatis disponere sic placet aevum,   5
    tam longum ut nobis, tam breve ut Antilocho ?

---

[1] *Pepl.* 14.
[2] Aegiale, daughter of Adrastus. She was incited by
Aphrodite to unfaithfulness.

EPITAPHS

VI.—For Diomedes [1]

Here lies buried Diomedes, nobler son of a noble father, banished through his wife's sin [2] from Argos, the city of her dowry, who founded Argyripa and Arpi,[3] famed for heroes, and gained greater fame from his new city than from the ancient seat whence he was sprung.

VII.—For Antilochus [4]

Good both in council and in field—rare is the union—and dear to the sons of Atreus and of Aeacus alike, I am that Antilochus who died to gain the double meed of valour and of piety in saving my father, Nestor. Such was not Nature's order; yet it was fitter that he survived without whom false Troy could not be taken.

VIII.—For Nestor [5]

Here in this tomb I lie, my fourth lifetime wholly spent at last, Nestor, famed for wisdom and for eloquence. To save me from death, my son exposed himself and died; and it was by my son's wounds I lived. Alas, why was it Fate's pleasure so to order our lives, giving me so long, giving Antilochus so short a span?

[3] *cp.* Virgil, *Aen.* xi. 246, 250: Arpi was the later name for Argyripa in Apulia.
[4] *Pepl.* 11.　　[5] *cp. Anth. Pal.* vii. 144.

IX.—Pyrrho

Orbe tegor medio, maior virtute paterna,
  quod puer et regis Pyrrhus opima tuli.
Impius ante aras quem fraude peremit Orestes,
  quid mirum, caesa iam genetrice furens.

X.—Euryalo

Nec me non dignum titulo Pleuronia credit,
  quae[1] communis erat cum Diomede domus,
Euryalo et Sthenelo: nam tertius hoc ego regnum
  possedi, de quo nunc satis est tumulus.

XI.—Guneo

Gunea pontus habet, tumulus sine corpore nomen.
  fama homines inter, caelum animus repetit.
cuncta elementa duci tanto commune sepulcrum.
  quae? caelum et tellus et mare et ora virum.

XII.—Protesilao

Fatale adscriptum nomen mihi Protesilao;
  nam primus Danaum bello obii Phrygio,
audaci ingressus Sigeia litora saltu,
  captus pellacis Lartiadae insidiis.

---

[1] *Translator*: cui, *Peiper* and *MS*.

---

[1] Pyrrhus was slain by Orestes at Delphi, where the supposed centre of the earth was marked by a conical stone, the *Omphalos*: *cp*. Paus. x. xvi. 3.

EPITAPHS

IX.—For Pyrrhus

At the world's centre[1] I am buried, greater in prowess than my father, seeing that while yet a boy I, Pyrrhus, won a king's[2] own spoils.

[3] Orestes slew me before the altar, adding sacrilege to treachery—what wonder, when he was raving from his mother's murder?

X.—For Euryalus[3]

I, too, am not unworthy of an epitaph; so Pleuronia holds, which was the common home of Euryalus and Sthenelus with Diomede. I was the third who held that realm, wherein a grave alone contents me now.

XI.—For Gunes[4]

The sea holds Gunes; this tomb, his name but not his body. His fame dwells amongst men; his spirit is returned above. All elements unite to form one tomb for so great a leader. Which? Heaven, earth, and sea, and the breath of men.

XII.—For Protesilaus

Ominous the name assigned me—Protesilaus; for first of the Danaans I perished[5] in the Trojan War when, boldly leaping, I invaded the Sigean shore—tricked by the wiles of Laërtes' deceitful son. He

---

[2] *sc.* Priam: see Virgil, *Aen.* ii. 533 ff.
[3] *cp. Pepl.* 35.   [4] *Pepl.* 32.
[5] The derivation here suggested is from πρῶτος and λαός: *i.e.* he was the first of the people (to perish).

qui, ne Troianae premeret pede litora terrae,   5
   ipse super proprium desiluit clipeum.
quid queror ? hoc letum iam tum mea fata canebant,
   tale mihi nomen cum pater inposuit.

XIII.—Deiphobo

Proditus ad poenam sceleratae fraude Lacaenae
   et deformato corpore Deiphobus
non habeo tumulum, nisi quem mihi voce vocantis
   et pius Aeneas et Maro conposuit.

XIV.—Hectori

Hectoris hic tumulus, cum quo sua Troia sepulta est :
   conduntur pariter, qui periere simul.

XV.—Astyanacti

Flos Asiae tantaque unus de gente superstes,
parvulus, Argivis set iam de patre timendus,
hic iaceo Astyanax, Scaeis deiectus ab altis.
pro dolor !   Iliaci Neptunia moenia muri
viderunt aliquid crudelius Hectore tracto.   5

XVI.—Sarpedoni

Sarpedon Lycius, genitus Iove, numine patris
   sperabam caelum, set tegor hoc tumulo
sanguineis fletus lacrimis : pro ferrea fata,
   et patitur luctum, qui prohibere potest.

---

[1] *sc.* Virgil (see *Aen.* vi. 505–6).
[2] *cp. Anth. Pal.* vii. 139.
[3] See Π 459.

leaped down upon his shield lest his should be the
first foot to touch Trojan soil. Yet why do I com-
plain? My Fates sang of this doom even at the
time when my father laid upon me such a name.

XIII.—For Deïphobus

Betrayed to vengeance by the accursed Spartan
woman's treachery I, Deïphobus, mangled in body,
have no other tomb but that which pious Aeneas and
Maro[1] have made for me by calling on my name.

XIV.—For Hector[2]

This is the grave of Hector, and with him is buried
the Troy he loved: along with him are laid those
who perished together with him.

XV.—For Astyanax

The flower of Asia and the one poor little hope of
so great a line, but already dreaded by the Argives
for my father's sake, I, Astyanax, lie here, hurled
down from the high Scaean gate. Alack! Now
have the walls of Ilium, which Neptune built, seen a
deed more cruel than the haling of Hector's corpse.

XVI.—For Sarpedon

I am Lycian Sarpedon, the seed of Jove: in virtue
of my father's godhead I hoped for heaven; yet I
am buried in this tomb though bewailed with tears
of blood.[3] Ah, iron-hearted Fates! He[4] also suffers
grief who can prevent it.

[4] sc. Jove, who could have saved Sarpedon and so have
escaped from sorrow himself.

XVII.—Nasti et Amphimacho

Nastes Amphimachusque, Nomionis inclita proles,
    ductores quondam, pulvis et umbra sumus.

XVIII.—Troilo

Hectore prostrato nec dis nec viribus aequis
    congressus saevo Troilus Aeacidae,
raptatus bigis fratris coniungor honori,
    cuius ob exemplum nec mihi poena gravis.

XIX.—Polydoro

Cede procul myrtumque istam fuge, nescius hospes :
    telorum seges est sanguine adulta meo.
confixus iaculis et ab ipsa caede sepultus
    condor in hoc tumulo bis Polydorus ego.
scit pius Aeneas et tu, rex impie, quod me   5
    Thracia poena premit, Troia cura tegit.

XX.—Euphemo

Euphemum Ciconum ductorem Troia tellus
    condidit hastati Martis ad effigiem.
nec satis est titulum saxo incidisse sepulcri ;
    insuper et frontem mole onerant statuae.
ocius ista ruunt, quae sic cumulata locantur :   5
    maior ubi est cultus, magna ruina subest.

---

¹ *cp.* B 871.   ² *cp.* Virgil, *Aen.* v. 809, i. 474–5.

EPITAPHS

XVII.—For Nastes and Amphimachus

Nastes and Amphimachus, Nomion's famous seed,[1] once champions, we are dust and shades.

XVIII.—For Troïlus

Though Hector was laid low, and though in strength of arm and heavenly aid ill-matched, I, Troïlus, met the fierce son of Aeacus face to face, and, dragged to death by my own steeds,[2] am linked in glory with my brother, whose example made my sufferings light.

XIX.—For Polydorus

Begone far hence, unconscious stranger, and avoid that myrtle-tree : 'tis grown from darts and nourished with my blood. Pierced through with spears and almost buried in my very slaying, I, Polydorus, lie twice interred beneath this mound. Pious Aeneas[3] knows my story, and you also, impious king ; for as it was Thracian cruelty that crushed me, so it was Trojan piety that buried me.

XX.—For Euphemus

Euphemus, leader of the Cicones, was laid in Trojan soil hard by the statue of spear-bearing Mars. No epitaph graven on his tombstone suffices, but statues also pile their weight upon him. Those monuments fall the sooner which are heaped up so high, and where magnificence is too great, great ruin lurks beneath.

[3] For the story of Polydorus, see Virgil, *Aen.* iii. 22 ff.

XXI.—Hippothoo et Pyleo in Horto Sepultis

Hippothoum Pyleumque tenet gremio infima tellus:
  caulibus et malvis terga superna virent.
nec vexat cineres horti cultura quietos,
  dum parcente manu molle holus excolitur.

XXII.—Ennomo et Chromio

Ennomus hic Chromiusque iacent: quis Mysia regnum,
  quis pater Alcinous Oceanusque atavus.
nobilitas quid tanta iuvat? quo clarius istis
  est genus, hoc mortis condicio gravior.

XXIII.—Priamo

Hic Priami non est tumulus nec condor in ista
  sede: caput Danai deripuere meum.
ast ego cum lacerum sine nomine funus haberem,
  confugi ad cineres Hectoreos genitor.
illic et natos Troiamque Asiamque sepultam   5
  inveni et nostrum quidquid ubique iacet.

XXIV.—Item Priamo

Qui tumulum Priami quaerit, legat Hectoris ante.
  ille meus, nato quem prius ipse dedi.

XXIVa.—[Hectori]

Hectoris et patriae simul est commune sepulcrum,
  amborum quoniam iuncta ruina fuit.

EPITAPHS

XXI.—For Hippothoüs and Pyleus Buried in a Garden

Hippothoüs and Pyleus[1] lie buried in this ignoble soil, and over their bodies mallows and cabbages grow green. And yet the tilling of the garden troubles not their peaceful ashes, if these soft herbs are tilled by no rude hands.

XXII.—For Ennomus and Chromius

Ennomus and Chromius[2] lie here : Mysia was their kingdom, Alcinoüs their father, Ocean their ancestor. What profits them so illustrious a descent? The brighter their ancestry, the heavier their lot when dead.

XXIII.—For Priam

Here is not Priam's tomb, nor am I buried in this place : the Danaans despoiled me of my head. A mangled, nameless end was mine, and so I, his sire, fled for shelter to Hector's ashes. There I found my sons, and Troy and Asia buried together, and whatsoever of mine lies scattered everywhere.

XXIV.—For Priam Again

He who seeks Priam's tomb must find Hector's first. That tomb is mine which I first gave my son.

XXIVa.—For Hector

Here in one common grave lie Hector and his country, for in their fall both were united.

---

[1] cp. B 842.   [2] cp. B 858.

AUSONIUS

XXV.—Hecubae

Quae regina fui, quae claro nata Dymante,
    quae Priami coniunx, Hectora quae genui,
hic Hecuba iniectis perii superobruta saxis,
    set rabie linguae me tamen ulta prius.
fidite ne regnis et prole et stirpe parentum,   5
    quicumque hoc nostrum σῆμα κυνὸς legitis.

XXVI.—Polyxenae

Troas Achilleo coniuncta Polyxena busto
    malueram nullo caespite functa tegi.
non bene discordes tumulos miscetis, Achivi:
    hoc violare magis, quam sepelire fuit.

XXVII.—De Niobe in Sipylo Monte iuxta Fontem Sepulta

Thebarum regina fui, Sipyleia cautes
    quae modo sum: laesi numina Letoidum.
bis septem natis genetrix laeta atque superba,
    tot duxi mater funera, quot genui.
nec satis hoc divis: duro circumdata saxo   5
    amisi humani corporis effigiem;
set dolor obstructis quamquam vitalibus haeret
    perpetuasque rigat fonte pio lacrimas.
pro facinus! tantaene animis caelestibus irae?
    durat adhuc luctus, matris imago perit.   10

EPITAPHS

XXV.—For Hecuba

I who was a queen, I, famous Dymas' child, I,
Priam's wife, I who bare Hector, I, Hecuba, perished
here, o'erwhelmed with showers of stones, though
not before the fury of my tongue had avenged me.
Put not your trust in royal state, nor motherhood,
nor lofty birth, ye who read this my Cynosema.[1]

XXVI.—For Polyxena

I am Polyxena of Troy, mated with Achilles in the
tomb: would rather I had died without a sod to
cover me. You do not well, Achaeans, to unite
enemies in the grave: this was to violate, rather than
to bury me.

XXVII.—On Niobe Buried on Mount Sipylus
near a Fountain

A queen of Thebes was I, who am now a crag
of Sipylus for my offence against the godhead of
Leto's offspring. Happy and proud to have borne
twice seven children, I buried as many as I bare.
Yet even this did not content the gods: hard stone
encased me round until I lost all shape of human
form. But though my vital parts are crusted o'er,
grief clings to them and pours forth a perpetual
stream of pitying tears. Ah, cruel deed! Do
heavenly spirits hate so bitterly? A mother's grief
lasts on, her shape passes away.

---

[1] *sc.* "this epitaph on my tomb." Hecuba was changed
into a dog.

XXVIII.— In Diogenis Cynici Sepulcro in quo pro Titulo Canis Signum est

Dic, canis, hic cuius tumulus?—Canis.—At canis hic
  quis?—
  Diogenes.—Obiit?—Non obiit, set abiit.—
Diogenes, cui pera penus, cui dolia sedes,
  ad manes abiit?—Cerberus inde vetat.—
Et quonam?—Clari flagrat qua stella Leonis,   5
  additus est iustae nunc canis Erigonae.

XXIX.—Item Diogenis

Pera, polenta, tribon, baculus, scyphus, arta supellex
  ista fuit Cynici : set putat hanc nimiam.
namque cavis manibus cernens potare bubulcum :
  cur, scyphe, te, dixit, gesto supervacuum.

XXX.—Item

Effigiem, rex Croese, tuam, ditissime regum,
  vidit aput manes Diogenes Cynicus.
nil, inquit, tibi, Croese, tuum ; superant mihi cuncta.
  nudus eram : sic sum.   nil habui : hoc habeo.
rex ait : Haud egui, cum tu, mendice, carebas   5
  omnibus ; et careo, si modo non egeo?

---

[1] This epitaph is a close imitation of *Anth. Pal.* vii. 64.
[2] Properly a store-jar (of earthenware) = Gk. πίθος.

XXVIII.—On the Tomb of Diogenes the Cynic, upon which there was a Figure of a Dog instead of Epitaph

"Tell me, dog, whose tomb is this?"[1] "It is a dog's." "But what dog was that?" "Diogenes." "And is he passed away?" "Not passed away, but gone away." "What, has that Diogenes gone to the shades, whose wealth was his wallet and whose house a cask?"[2] "Cerberus will not let him in." "Where is he gone, then?" "Where the bright star of Leo burns he has been installed now as watch-dog for righteous Erigone."[3]

XXIX.—Another Epitaph on Diogenes[4]

A haversack, some barley-meal, a cloak, a stick, a cup—these were the Cynic's scanty furniture; but now he thinks this over much. For, seeing a bumpkin drink from his hollowed hands, quoth he: "Why do I carry you about, you useless cup?"

XXX.—Another Epitaph[5]

King Croesus, wealthiest of kings, Diogenes the Cynic saw your form amongst the shades. Said he: "Now you have nothing, Croesus, that was yours; while I still have all that I had. Bare was I: so am I now. I had nothing: and that I still have." The king replied: "I wanted for nothing when you, you beggar, lacked everything; and do I lack if I need nothing now?"

[3] Daughter of Icarius, who hanged herself through grief for her father's death.
[4] *Anth. Pal.* xvi. 333.   [5] *Anth. Pal.* ix. 145.

XXXI.—In Tumulo Hominis Felicis

Sparge mero cineres bene olentis et unguine nardi,
    hospes, et adde rosis balsama puniceis.
perpetuum mihi ver agit inlacrimabilis urna
    et commutavi saecula, non obii.
nulla mihi veteris perierunt gaudia vitae,   5
    seu meminisse putes omnia, sive nihil.

XXXII.—De Nomine Cuiusdam Lucii Sculpto
in Marmore

Una quidem, geminis fulget set dissita punctis
    littera, praenomen sic [L:] nota sola facit.
post .M. incisum est : puto sic [Λ\] : non tota
    videtur :
    dissiluit saxi fragmine laesus apex.
nec quisquam, marius seu marcius anne metellus   5
    hic iaceat, certis noverit indiciis.
truncatis convulsa iacent elementa figuris,
    omnia confusis interiere notis.
miremur periisse homines ?   monumenta fatiscunt ;
    mors etiam saxis nominibusque venit.   10

XXXIII.—Iussu Augusti Equo Admirabili

Phosphore, clamosi spatiosa per aequora circi
    septenas solitus victor obire vias,
inproperanter agens primos a carcere cursus,
    fortis praegressis ut potereris equis,
promptum et veloces erat anticipare quadrigas :   5
    victores etiam vincere laus potior.

EPITAPHS

XXXI.—On the Tomb of a Happy Man

Sprinkle my ashes with pure wine and fragrant oil of spikenard; bring balsam too, O stranger, with crimson roses. Unending spring pervades my tearless urn: I have but changed my state, and have not died. I have not lost a single joy of my old life, whether you think that I remember all or none.

XXXII.—On the Name of a certain Lucius Engraved on Marble

One letter shows up clearly, marked off with a double stop, and that single sign forms the *praenomen* thus: L: Next M is graved—somehow thus, I think, Μ; for the broken top is flaked away where the stone is cracked, and the whole letter cannot be seen. No one can know for certain whether a Marius, or Marcius, or Metellus lies here. With their forms mutilated, all the letters are confused, and when the characters are jumbled all their meaning is lost. Are we to wonder that man perishes? His monuments decay, and death comes even to his marbles and his names.

XXXIII.—On a Wonderful Horse: Written by Order of the Emperor

Phosphorus, who used victoriously to cover the seven circuits over the broad track in the uproarious circus, cantering leisurely over the first lap after the start, and saving your mettle to come up with the horses who led, easy was it for you to outpace swift four-horsed chariots also: to win a race against

hunc titulum vani solacia sume sepulcri
  et gradere Elysios praepes ad alipedes.
Pegasus hinc dexter currat tibi, laevus Arion
  funis eat, quartum det tibi Castor equum.   10

XXXIV.—De Sepulcro [Cari] Vacuo

Me sibi et uxori et natis commune sepulcrum
  constituit seras Carus ad exequias.
iamque diu monumenta vacant sitque ista querella
  longior et veniat ordine quisque suo,
nascendi qui lege datus, placidumque per aevum   5
  condatur, natu qui prior, ille prior.

XXXV.—In Tumulum Sedecennis Matronae

Omnia quae longo vitae cupiuntur in aevo,
ante quater plenum consumpsit Anicia lustrum.
infans lactavit, pubes et virgo adolevit.
nupsit, concepit, peperit, iam mater obivit.
quis mortem accuset? quis non accuset in ista?   5
aetatis meritis anus est, aetate puella.

winners is higher praise. Take, then, this epitaph—
poor consolation!—for your tomb, and gallop nimble-
hoofed to join the wing-hoofed steeds of Elysium.
Hereafter let Pegasus run on your right and Arion
be your left-wheeler; and let Castor find you the
fourth horse!

XXXIV.—ON THE EMPTY TOMB [OF CARUS]

CARUS has built me as one sepulchre for himself,
his wife, and children, when at length they die.
Long now their resting-places have lain empty, and
may that complaint grow yet older: let each come
in the order fixed by the law of birth, and through
peaceful years let him who is the earlier born be laid
to rest the earlier.

XXXV.—FOR THE TOMB OF A MARRIED LADY OF SIXTEEN

ANICIA has spent all those treasures which are the
hope of a long life before her second decade reached
its full. While a mere baby she gave suck; while
yet a girl she was mature; she married, she con-
ceived, she bare her child, and now has died a
matron. Who can blame death? And yet who can
not blame him in this case? In age's gains she is a
crone; in age itself, a girl.

LIBER VII

[ECLOGARUM LIBER]

I.—Ausonius Drepanio Filio

"Cui dono lepidum novum libellum?"[1]
Veronensis ait poeta quondam
inventoque dedit statim Nepoti.
at nos inlepidum, rudem libellum,
burras, quisquilias ineptiasque,   5
credemus gremio cui fovendum?
inveni, trepidae silete nugae,
nec doctum minus et magis benignum,
quam quem Gallia praebuit Catullo.
hoc nullus mihi carior meorum,   10
quem pluris faciunt novem sorores,
quam cunctos alios Marone dempto.
"Pacatum haut dubie, poeta, dicis?"
ipse est.   intrepide volate, versus,
et nidum in gremio fovete tuto.   15
hic vos diligere, hic volet tueri;
ignoscenda teget, probata tradet:
post hunc iudicium timete nullum.   vale.

II.—Ex Graeco Pythagoricum de Ambiguitate Eligendae Vitae

Quod vitae sectabor iter, si plena tumultu
sunt fora, si curis domus anxia, si peregrinos

---

[1] Catullus i. 1.

BOOK VII

THE ECLOGUES

I.—Ausonius to his Son Drepanius

"To whom do I give my pretty, new book?"
quoth the poet of Verona long ago, and, straight-
way finding Nepos, presented it to him. But this
ugly, rough little book—junk, trash, and drivelling
—to whose bosom shall I commit it to be cherished?
I have it! (Peace, my anxious trifles!) 'Tis one
not less learned and more generous than he with
whom Gaul [1] furnished Catullus. No one of my own
kin is dearer to me than he, and the Nine Sisters
esteem him more than all other poets saving Maro.
"No doubt, sir Poet, it is Pacatus whom you mean?"
The very man! Take wing without a fear, my verses,
and nestle safely in his bosom. He will be ready to
fondle you, he to guard you; he will hide away your
shortcomings, will pass on what he approves: after
him, fear ye no critic! Farewell.

II.—From the Greek.[2] A Pythagorean Reflection on the Difficulty of Choosing one's Lot in Life

What path in life shall I pursue? The courts are
full of uproar; the home is vexed with cares; home

---

[1] *sc.* Transpadane Gaul, of which Nepos was a native.
[2] *cp. Anth. Pal.* ix. 359.

cura domus sequitur, mercantem si nova semper
damna manent, cessare vetat si turpis egestas;
si vexat labor agricolam, mare naufragus horror   5
infamat, poenaeque graves in caelibe vita
et gravior cautis custodia vana maritis;
sanguineum si Martis opus, si turpia lucra
faenoris et velox inopes usura trucidat?
omne aevum curae, cunctis sua displicet aetas.   10
sensus abest parvis lactantibus, et puerorum
dura rudimenta, et iuvenum temeraria pubes.
adflictat fortuna viros per bella, per aequor,
irasque insidiasque catenatosque labores [1]
mutandos semper gravioribus. ipsa senectus   15
expectata diu votisque optata malignis
obicit innumeris corpus lacerabile morbis.
spernimus in commune omnes praesentia; quosdam
constat nolle deos fieri.   Iuturna reclamat:
"quo vitam dedit aeternam? cur mortis adempta est 20
condicio?"   sic Caucasea sub rupe Prometheus
testatur Saturnigenam nec nomine cessat
incusare Iovem, data sit quod vita perennis.
respice et ad cultus animi.   sic nempe pudicum
perdidit Hippolytum non felix cura pudoris.   25
e contra inlecebris maculosam degere vitam
quem iuvat, adspiciat poenas et crimina regum,
Tereos incesti vel mollis Sardanapalli.
perfidiam vitare monent tria Punica bella;
set prohibet servare fidem deleta Saguntos.   30

---

[1] *cp.* Martial, *Epigr.* I. xv. 7.

troubles follow us abroad; the merchant always has fresh losses to expect, and the dread of base poverty forbids his rest; the husbandman is worn out with toil; frightful shipwreck lends the sea a grim name; the unwedded life has its sore troubles, but sorer is the futile watch and ward which jealous husbands keep; to serve Mars is a bloody trade; the tarnished gains of interest and swift-mounting usury slaughter the needy. Every stage of life has its troubles, and no man is content with his own age: the infant at the breast lacks understanding; boys have hard lessons to afflict them, and youths the rash folly of their kind. Hazards still plague the full-grown man, of war or sea, or anger, or deceit, or the long chain of toils to be exchanged for ever heavier. Old age itself, long looked-for and desired with mean-hearted prayers, exposes the poor body to be torn by diseases beyond number. With one accord we all scorn our present lot: some ('tis well known) care not to become as gods. Juturna cries out in protest[1]: "Wherefore did Jove give me eternal life? Why has the lot of death been taken from me?" Likewise Prometheus, beneath the Caucasian crags, calls upon Saturn's son and ceases not to chide Jove by name, because an endless life was given him. Consider, too, the affections of the mind. Thus, mark you, chaste Hippolytus was destroyed by disastrous care for his own chastity. And on the other hand, he who delights to spend a life stained with loose pleasures, should consider how sinful kings are punished, as incestuous Tereus or effeminate Sardanapalus. Faithlessness the three Punic Wars warn us to avoid, yet the destruction of Saguntum forbids

---

[1] *Aen.* xii. 879.

vive et amicitias semper cole.—Crimen ob istud
Pythagoreorum periit schola docta sophorum.—
hoc metuens igitur nullas cole.—Crimen ob istud
Timon Palladiis olim lapidatus Athenis.
dissidet ambiguis semper mens obvia votis,   35
nec voluisse homini satis est: optata recusat.
esse in honore placet, mox paenitet: et dominari
ut possint, servire volunt.   idem auctus honore
invidiae obicitur.   pernox est cura disertis;
set rudis ornatu vitae caret.   esto patronus,   40
et defende reos: set gratia rara clientis.
esto cliens: gravis imperiis persona patroni.
exercent hunc vota patrum: mox aspera curis
sollicitudo subit.   contemnitur orba senectus
et captatoris praeda est heredis egenus.   45
vitam parcus agas: avidi lacerabere fama,
et largitorem gravius censura notabit.
cuncta tibi adversis contraria casibus.   ergo
optima Graiorum sententia: quippe homini aiunt
non nasci esse bonum aut natum cito morte potiri. 50
   [Haec[1] quidem Pythagorica est apophasis secun-
dum tale quod subiectum est distichon:

> πρῶτον μὲν μὴ φῦναι ἐν ἀνθρώποισιν ἄριστον,
> δεύτερον ὅττι τάχιστα πύλας Ἀίδαο περῆσαι.[2]

---

[1] All that follows l. 50 is found only in P^1 and its depen-
dent MSS.
[2] cp. Theognis, 425, 427:

> πάντων μὲν μὴ φῦναι ἐπιχθονίοισιν ἄριστον
> . . . .
> φύντα δ᾽ ὅπως ὤκιστα πύλας Ἀίδαο περῆσαι.

---

[1] sc. the brotherhood bound together by vows founded by
Pythagoras at Croton.   The populace became suspicious of
this society and massacred the members.

us to keep faith. Live your life and always practise friendship : that was the very charge which destroyed the learned college of the Pythagorean sages.[1] Fearing this end, then, make no friendships : that was the very charge on which Timon was stoned of old in Athens, dear to Pallas. Conflicting wishes ever beset and distract our hearts, nor is it enough for a man that things are as he wished ; for what he once longed to have, he now refuses. His heart is set on rank and dignities, but presently he regrets his wish : he is content to obey, that he may command one day : he rises to high station, and straightway is exposed to envy. Learning costs sleepless nights of toil ; yet ignorance lacks all that makes life fair. Become a pleader and defend the accused : you will find it rare to get a thankful client. Well, be a client then : you cannot bear your patron's domineering ways. A man prays earnestly to become a father : soon, harsh cares and anxieties steal upon him. Yet, on the other hand, childless old age is scorned ; and he who lacks heirs is the fortune-hunter's prey. Should you live sparingly, people will tear your character to rags for a miser. Be prodigal, and you will incur a heavier charge. All paths in life confront you with unfavourable issues. Therefore the opinion of the Greeks is wisest ; for they say that it is good for a man not to be born at all, or, being born, to die quickly.

[51] [Such,[2] at least, is the Pythagorean pronouncement as expressed in the following couplet :

"The first and greatest boon is never to be born :
　The next, to pass through Hades' gates without delay."

[2] The following refutation of the Pythagorean view of life appears to have been added by a critic who took his Christianity more seriously than did Ausonius.

Contra sed alterius sectator dogmatis ista   55
    quid doceat reprobans, subdita disce legens:
" Ergo nihil quoniam vita est quod amemus in ista,
nec tamen incassum fas est nos credere natos,
auctorem vitae si iustum credimus esse,
vita alia est nobis illi vivendo paranda,   60
cum quo post istam possimus vivere vitam.
illi equidem stygias properent descendere ad umbras,
Pythagoreorum stolidum qui dogma secuti
non nasci sese quam natos vivere malint."]

III.—De Viro Bono Πυθαγορικη Αποφασις

Vir bonus et sapiens, qualem vix repperit unum
milibus e cunctis hominum consultus Apollo,
iudex ipse sui totum se explorat ad unguem.
quid proceres vanique levis quid opinio volgi

    *   *   *   *   *   *

securus, mundi instar habens, teres atque rotundus, 5
externae ne quid labis per levia sidat.[1]
ille, dies quam longus erit sub sidere Cancri
quantaque nox tropico se porrigit in Capricorno,
cogitat et iusto trutinae se examine pendit,
ne quid hiet, ne quid protuberet, angulus aequis   10
partibus ut coeat, nil ut deliret amussis,

---

[1] *cp.* Hor. *Sat.* II. vii. 86.

⁵⁵ But on the other hand, read what follows now, and learn what a follower of another system teaches to refute this.

⁵⁷ " Therefore, since we have nothing in this life to love, and yet it is wrong for us to believe that we were born in vain, if we believe the Giver of our life is true, 'tis for another life we must prepare by living for Him, that after this life we may be able to live with Him. Let those, indeed, make haste to go down to the Stygian shades, who, following the foolish doctrine of the Pythagoreans, would rather not be born than, when once born, to live."]

III.—On the Good Man: a Pythagorean Sentence

The upright man and wise—Apollo, when invoked,[1] could scarce find one such amongst all the thousands of mankind—sits in judgment on himself and searches out his whole self to a hair's breadth. What the great think, or what the fickle opinion of the empty-headed mob, . . . he cares not, but, after the fashion of the globe, keeps himself rounded and compact, too smooth for any blemish from without to settle upon him. However long the day may be when the Crab is in the ascendant, however long the night under the tropic of Capricorn, he reflects and weighs himself by the test of a just balance : there must be no hollows, no projections ; the angle must be formed of equal lines, and the rule not

---

[1] Chaerephon consulted the Delphic Oracle as to who was the wisest of men. The Pythia replied :—

ἀνδρῶν ἁπάντων Σωκράτης σοφώτατος.

See Diog. Laërt. ii. v. 18.

sit solidum, quodcumque subest, nec inania subter
indicet admotus digitis pellentibus ictus,
non prius in dulcem declinans lumina somnum,
omnia quam longi reputaverit acta diei :   15
quae praetergressus, quid gestum in tempore, quid
    non ?
cur isti facto decus afuit aut ratio illi ?
quid mihi praeteritum ? cur haec sententia sedit,
quam melius mutare fuit ? miseratus egentem
cur aliquem fracta persensi mente dolorem ?   20
quid volui, quod nolle bonum foret ? utile honesto
cur malus antetuli ? num dicto aut denique voltu
perstrictus quisquam ? cur me natura magis quam
disciplina trahit ? sic dicta et facta per omnia
ingrediens ortoque a vespere cuncta revolvens   25
offensus pravis dat palmam et praemia rectis.

IV.—ΝΑΙ ΚΑΙ ΟΥ ΠΥΘΑΓΟΡΙΚΟΝ

Est et Non cuncti monosyllaba nota frequentant.
his demptis nil est, hominum quod sermo volutet.
omnia in his et ab his sunt omnia, sive negoti
sive oti quidquam est, seu turbida sive quieta.
alterutro pariter nonnumquam, saepe seorsis   5
obsistunt studiis, ut mores ingeniumque
ut faciles vel difficiles contentio nancta est.
si consentitur, mora nulla intervenit " Est Est,"
sin controversum, dissensio subiciet " Non."
hinc fora dissultant clamoribus, hinc furiosi   10

deviate a jot; the underlying metal must be sound, and no tap of the finger reveal flaws beneath. He suffers not sweet sleep to weigh down his eyelids until he has pondered over all things done in the long day's course; what he has left undone, what he has done at the right, what at the wrong moment; why this action fell short in virtue, or that in sound reason. What have I left undone? Why has this opinion become settled which it was better to have changed? When I have taken pity on the poor, why have I felt deeply grieved and brokenhearted? What have I wished which it would have been well not to wish? Why have I perversely preferred expediency to honour? Have I by word or even by look wounded any man? Why has nature more power over me than self-control?

[24] Thus he goes into all his words and acts, and turning all over when evening is come, he condemns the bad and gives the palm and prize to the good.

IV.—THE PYTHAGOREAN "YEA" AND "NAY"

"YES" and "no": all the world constantly uses these familiar monosyllables. Take these away and you leave nothing for the tongue of man to discuss. In them is all, and all from them; be it a matter of business or pleasure, of bustle or repose. Sometimes two parties both use one word or the other at the same time, but often they are opposed, according as men easy or contentious in character and temperament are engaged in discussion. If both agree, forthwith "Yea, yea" breaks in; but if they dispute, then disagreement will throw in a "Nay." From these arises the uproar which splits the air of the

iurgia sunt circi, cuneati hinc lata theatri
seditio, et tales agitat quoque curia lites.
coniugia et nati cum patribus ista quietis
verba serunt studiis salva pietate loquentes.
hinc etiam placidis schola consona disciplinis   15
dogmaticas agitat placido certamine lites,
hinc omnis certat dialectica turba sophorum.
estne dies? est ergo dies!   non convenit istuc;
nam facibus multis aut fulgeribus quotiens lux
est nocturna homini, non est lux ista diei.   20
est et Non igitur, quotiens lucem esse fatendum est,
set non esse diem.   mille hinc certamina surgunt,
hinc rauco, multi quoque talia commeditantes
murmure concluso rabiosa silentia rodunt.

    Qualis vita hominum, duo quam monosyllaba
      versant!   25

V.—DE AETATIBUS ANIMANTIUM.   HESIODION

TER binos deciesque novem super exit in annos
iusta senescentum quos implet vita virorum.
hos novies superat vivendo garrula cornix
et quater egreditur cornicis saecula cervus.
alipedem cervum ter vincit corvus et illum   5
multiplicat novies Phoenix, reparabilis ales.

---

¹ A sample of the word-splitting practised in the rhetorical
schools.   In l. 18 there is a play on the two meanings of *dies*,
light (daylight) and day.   *cp.* Quintilian v. viii. 7: dies est,
nox non est.

courts, from these the feuds of the maddened Circus and the wide-spread partizanship which fills the tiers of the theatre, from these the debates which occupy the Senate. Wives, children, fathers, bandy these two words in peaceful debate without unnatural quarrelling. They are the instruments with which the schools fit for peaceful learning wage their harmless war of philosophic strife. On them the whole throng of rhetoricians depends in its wordy contests: " You grant that it is light?[1] Yes? Then it is day!" " No, the point is not granted; for whenever many torches or lightning-flashes give us light by night, yes, it is light; but that is not the light of day." It is a case of " yes " and " no " then; for we are bound to say: " Yes, it is light," and " No, it is not day." There you have the source of countless squabbles: that is why some—nay, many—pondering on such things, smother their gruff protests and bite their lips in raging silence.

[25] What a thing is the life of man which two monosyllables toss about!

V.—On the Ages of Living Things: a Fragment from Hesiod [2]

Three times two and nine times ten complete the tale of years whereto the life of men who live to fulness of old age attains. Nine times the chattering crow passes this limit in her span of life, while the stag passes through four times the lifetime of the crow. Thrice the raven outstrips the swift-footed stag in length of years; while that bird which renews its life, the Phoenix, multiplies ninefold the raven's years.

[2] From the *Precepts of Chiron*, fr. 3 (Loeb ed.) = Rzach (1913), fr. 171, quoted by Plutarch, *Mor.* p. 415 c.

quem nos perpetuo decies praevertimus aevo,
Nymphae Hamadryades, quarum longissima vita est.
 Haec cohibet finis vivacia fata animantum.
cetera secreti novit deus arbiter aevi,[1]   10
tempora quae Stilbon volvat, quae saecula Phaenon,
quos Pyrois habeat, quos Iuppiter igne benigno
circuitus, quali properet Venus alma recursu,
qui Phoeben, quanti maneant Titana labores,
donec consumpto, magnus qui dicitur, anno,   15
rursus in anticum veniant vaga sidera cursum,
qualia dispositi steterunt ab origine mundi.

VI.—De Ratione Librae

Miraris quicumque manere ingentia mundi
corpora, sublimi caeli circumdata gyro,
et tantae nullam moli intercedere labem,
accipe, quod mirere magis.   tenuissima tantis
principia et nostros non admittentia visus :   5
parvarum serie constant conexa atomorum ;
set solidum in parvis nullique secabile segmen.
unde vigor viresque manent aeternaque rerum
mobilitas nulloque umquam superabilis aevo.
divinis humana licet conponere.   sic est   10

---

[1] The following seven lines are found only in *V*. Though detached by Peiper from the preceding verses, and numbered by him as a separate fragment, it is possible that the connection is genuine : such a passage would have formed a characteristic transition from the *Precepts of Chiron* to the *Astronomy* in the Hesiodic corpus.

But we, the Hamadryad Nymphs, the longest-lived of living things, pass through ten lifetimes of the Phoenix in continuous span.

⁹ This limit bounds the lives of living creatures. As for the rest, God, the disposer of all hidden time, knows what periods Stilbon[1] and what ages Phaenon[2] have to roll, what orbits Pyroïs[3] and the benignant fires of Jupiter must yet fulfil, or in what revolutions kindly Venus hastens on her way, or how long are the toils that yet await Phoebe (the Moon) and Titan (the Sun), before that which they call the Great Year[4] reaches its close, and the wandering stars come back again in their ancient courses as they stood at the beginning of the ordered universe.

VI.—On the Nature of the Pound or Balance

Whoso you are who wonder that the vast heavenly bodies still endure, hung round about the lofty circle of the firmament, and that no decay creeps in upon their mighty mass, hearken, that you may wonder yet the more. First-beginnings of utmost fineness and which baffle our sight, are in these great bodies: they hold close together, closely linked in a group of tiny atoms; but in these tiny atoms is a solid particle which cannot be parted. Hence comes it that their strength and power endure, and that these motions are not overcome by any lapse of time. We may compare things human with divine.

[1] The Glittering One (Mercury).
[2] The Shining One (Saturn).   [3] The Fiery One (Mars).
[4] *i.e.* the Cycle of Ages (Shelley's "the world's Great Age"), at the close of which all things will return to their primitive state and a new Cycle begin. *cp.* Virgil, *Ecl.* iv. 4 ff.

as solidus, quoniam bis sex de partibus aequis
constat et in minimis paribus tamen una manet vis.
nam si quid numero minuatur, summa vacillat
convulsaeque ruunt labefacto corpore partes.
ut, medium si quis vellat de fornice saxum,   15
incumbunt cui cuncta, simul devexa sequentur
cetera communemque trahent a vertice lapsum;
non aliter libra est.   si defuit uncia, totus
non erit as nomenque deunx iam cassus habebit.
nec dextans retinet nomen sextante remoto,   20
et dodrans quadrante satus auctore carebit
divulsusque triens prohibet persistere bessem.
iam quincunx tibi nullus erit, si gramma [1] revellas.
et semis cui semis erit pereuntibus assis
partibus? et cuius librae pars septima septunx?   25
libra igitur, totum si nulla in parte vacillet.
ponderis et numeri morumque operumque et aquarum
libra: nec est modulus, quem non hoc nomine signes.
telluris, medio quae pendet in aere, libra est [2]
et solis lunaeque vias sua libra cohercet.   30

---

[1] *Peiper* (apparatus) : prama, *V*, *Peiper* (text).
[2] *cp.* Ovid, *Met.* i. 12 : nec circumfuso pendebat in aëre
tellus Ponderibus librata suis.

---

[1] The wedge-like stones of which an arch is constructed.
[2] A *gramma* has the weight of two obols (one-third of a
drachm).
[3] Ausonius here passes from the *as* or *libra* (the even-
balanced pound) to *libra* in the sense of "balance."   Thus
the earth is balanced (*cp.* note on text, l. 29) in mid-air,
while sun and moon, day and night balance each other.   The
reference to the Caledonian tide is to be understood in the

In the same way the pound is a solid whole, for it consists of twelve equal parts, and in these equal parts, small though they are, one virtue always abides. For if aught is subtracted from their sum, the total is impaired, the parts are thrown out of place and fall because the frame is ruined. As, if we were to wrench out from an arch the keystone upon which all the voussoirs [1] bear, the rest will follow suit and come to the ground, their general downfall caused by the topmost stone ; even so is it with the pound. If one ounce is wanting, it will no longer be a pound, but being short in weight will be called *deunx* (eleven-twelfths). The *dextans* (five-sixths), too, does not retain that name if a *sextans* (one-sixth) be taken from it, and the *dodrans* (three-quarters) will be left without the author of its being if we subtract the *quadrans* (one-fourth). So, too, the *bessis* (two-thirds) cannot endure once the *triens* (one-third) is torn from it. Take away one scruple,[2] and you will have no *quincunx* (five-twelfths) left you. And how can the *semis* (one-half) be a half if the fractions of the pound thus waste away ? And of what pound will the *septunx* (seven-twelfths) stand for seven parts ? That is a pound, then, which is impaired in no single part. Weight and number, character, tasks, and waters—all have a *libra* [3] : there is no form of regulation which you may not mark with this name. There is a *libra* of the earth, which hangs in mid-air, and a *libra* of their own controls the paths

light of Pliny, who (*N.H.* ii. 27) quotes Pytheas of Marseilles as stating that in Britain the tide rises 80 cubits above the level of the land. This phenomenon, too, is to be explained on the theory of a natural poise or balance. The *libra* (l. 33) of the poet's character is doubtless the good influence of his friend which keeps him " upright."

Libra dii somnique pares determinat horas,[1]
libra Caledonios sine litore continet aestus:
tu quoque certa mane morum mihi libra meorum.

VII.—DE RATIONE PUERPERII MATURI

OMNIA, quae vario rerum metimur in actu,
astrorum dominatus agit; terrenaque tantum
membra homini: e superis fortuna et spiritus auris
septeno moderanda choro: set praesidet ollis
sortitus regimen nitidae Sol aureus aethrae.   5
nec sola in nobis moderatur tempora vitae,
dum breve solliciti spatium producimus aevi:
creditur occultosque satus et tempora vitae
materno ducenda utero formare videndo
et nondum exortae leges conponere vitae.   10
namque ubi conceptus genitali insederit arvo,
haut dubium Solem cuicumque insistere signo.
qui cum vicini stationem ceperit astri,
contiguos nullum transfundit lumen in ortus.
ast ubi conversis post menstrua tempora habenis   15
scandit purpureo iam tertia sidera curru,
obliqua exilem demittit linea lucem,
adspirans tenues per inertia pondera motus.
quarta in sede viget primi indulgentia Solis,

---

[1] *cp.* Virgil, *Georg.* i. 208: Libra die somnique pares ubi
fecerit horas. (The reference is to the constellation, "the
Balance.")

of the Sun and Moon. *Libra* measures out equal hours of day and night, a *libra* curbs the Caledonian tides unaided by the shore : do thou also remain the sure *libra* of my character.

VII.—On the Nature of Timely Childbirth [1]

THE sovereign influence of the stars directs all things which we calculate in Nature's manifold activities; it is the limbs of man alone that are of clay : his lot, his life coming from the realms above, must be controlled by the company of the Seven Planets. But chief among them is the golden Sun, to whom the governance of the bright upper air has been allotted. And it is not the seasons of our life alone which he guides in us, while we spin out the short span of our troubled years : it is believed that by his glance are formed in the womb those hidden seeds from which there spring the seasons of that life we are to spend, and those laws laid down which are to govern the life not yet begun. For when conception first takes place, the Sun must needs stand in some planetary house, whichever it may be. And when he has begun to occupy the mansion of the star next in order, he casts no beam of light upon things begotten in the house near by. But when, after a month's space, he wheels his course and in his glowing car climbs up now into the third constellation, he sheds down upon them a slanting ray of feeble light, breathing some slight stir into the sluggish mass. In his fourth station the

[1] The source of this poem is the *De Die Natali* of Censorinus (written A.D. 238) : the theory advanced is there alleged to be Chaldaean.

suadet et infusus teneros coalescere fetus.   20
fulgore et trigono aspectus [1] vitale coruscat,
clarum et lene micans, quinti qui cardine signi
incutit attonitam vegetato infante parentem.
nam sexto vis nulla loco, quia nulla tuendi
aequati lateris signatur regula Phoebo. [2]   25
ast ubi signiferae media in regione cohortis
septimus accepit limes rutilantia flammis
recto castra situ : turgentis foedera partus
iam plena sub luce videt, nec fulgura parci
luminis intendens toto fovet igne coronae.   30
hinc illud, quod legitimos Lucina labores
praevenit et gravidos sentit subrepere nixus
ante expectatum festina puerpera votum ;
quod nisi, septeno cum lumina fudit ab astro,
impulerit tardi claustra obluctantia partus,   35
posterior nequeat, possit prior : an quia sexto
aemulus octavi conspectus inutilis astri
nescit conpariles laterum formare figuras ?
set nono incumbens signo cunctantia matrum
vota levat, trigono vires sociante sequenti.   40
at si difficilis rursum trahit Ilithyia,
tetragono absolvet dubiarum vincla morarum.

---

[1] *Translator* : fulgor tetrigono aspectus, *V* : fulgor tetra-
gono, *Peiper* (after *Vinetus*) ; but the sun's aspect is triangular
when in the fifth sign.   For the quantity of the reading in
the text, *cp.* l. 40 trigŏnō.
[2] *cp.* Censorinus viii. 10 : ceterum a loco sexto conspectus
omni caret efficientia ; eius enim linea (= regula) nullius
polygoni efficit latus.

Sun first makes strong influence felt, and, streaming in, causes the soft foetus to solidify. And with its fire his triangular aspect [1] flashes an enlivening glow, beaming bright and mild — that aspect which at the threshold of the fifth sign beats upon the mother, astonished at the quickened life within her. For in the sixth House the Sun has no power at all, because for Phoebus no line of sight is marked forming a side of any equal-sided figure. But when he has accomplished half his progress through the starry company, and moved his blazing camp across the frontiers of the seventh House, then he looks upon the ever-growing embryo with a direct aspect and in full flood of light; then he pours down his beams upon it without stint and warms it with all the heat of his fiery crown. And the reason why Lucina sometimes comes before the appointed hour of travail, and why she who is with child feels the pangs of labour stealing over her before the time awaited with prayers, is that, had he not shaken the reluctant bars restraining birth at the time when he poured his light from the place of the seventh sign, the Sun could not afterwards effect what he could have done before. Or can this be the cause, that the ineffective glance of the eighth planet, as of the sixth, cannot form any equal-sided figure? But when he occupies the ninth sign, he brings relief to the long-drawn prayers of mothers, the resultant triangle [1] joining its power with his. Yet if perverse Ilithyia tarries once again, he will break through the bonds of hesitation and delay when he passes on to assume his quadrilateral aspect (in the tenth sign).

----

[1] See the diagram on p. 398.

AUSONIUS

VIII.—De Nominibus Septem Dierum

Nomina, quae septem vertentibus apta diebus
annus habet, totidem errantes fecere planetae,
quos indefessa volvens vertigine mundus
signorum obliqua iubet in statione vagari.
primum supremumque diem radiatus habet Sol.　　5
proxima fraternae succedit Luna coronae.
tertius adsequitur Titania lumina Mavors.
Mercurius quarti sibi vindicat astra diei.
illustrant quintam Iovis aurea sidera zonam.
sexta salutigerum sequitur Venus alma parentem.　10
cuncta supergrediens Saturni septima lux est.
octavum instaurat revolubilis orbita Solem.

IX.—Monosticha de Mensibus

Primus Romanas ordiris, Iane, kalendas.
　　Februa vicino mense Numa instituit.
Martius antiqui primordia protulit anni.
　　fetiferum Aprilem vindicat alma Venus.
maiorum dictus patrum de nomine Maius.　　5
　　Iunius aetatis proximus est titulo.
nomine Caesareo Quintilem Iulius auget.
　　Augustus nomen Caesareum sequitur.
autumnum, Pomona, tuum September opimat.
　　triticeo October faenore ditat agros.　　10
sidera praecipitas pelago, intempeste November.
　　tu genialem hiemem, feste December, agis.

---

[1] A feast of purification held on February 15th : see Ovid,
Fasti, ii. 19.
[2] The months of January and February were instituted
by Numa.　　[3] *cp.* Suet. *Julius*, 76.

182

THE ECLOGUES

VIII.—On the Names of the Seven Days

The names borne by the seven days recurring throughout the year, are given by as many planets, which the firmament rolls along in unwearied revolutions, bidding them roam amid the stars which stand athwart them. The first day and the last the ray-crowned Sun holds for his own. The Moon next succeeds to her brother's crown. Mars, following these Titan lights, is counted third. Mercury claims for his own the stars of the fourth day. The golden star of Jupiter illumines the fifth zone; and in the sixth place kindly Venus follows the health-bringing father of the gods. The seventh day is Saturn's, and comes last of all; for on the eighth the circling orbit restores the Sun once more.

IX.—Single Lines on each Month

Thou, Janus, beginnest the first calends of the Roman year. Numa established the Februa [1] in the next month. The month of Mars brought in the opening of the old-style year. [2] Kindly Venus claims April, month of fertility. May was so called to celebrate our ancestors (*maiores*). June is the title of the next period in the year. Julius enriched Quintilis with a Caesar's name. [3] August follows Caesar's name. [4] September brings Autumn, thy season, O Pomona, with wealth of fruits. October enriches the fields with usury of grain. Thou hurlest the stars headlong into the sea, unwholesome November. Thou spendest cheerful winter, festal December.

[4] First so called in B.C. 8 in honour of Augustus (Octavian). It was previously known as Sextilis, the sixth month of the (old-style) year.

AUSONIUS

X.—ITEM DISTICHA

IANE nove, primo qui das tua nomina mensi,
    Iane bifrons, spectas tempora bina simul.
post superum cultus vicino Februa mense
    dat Numa cognatis manibus inferias.
Martius et generis Romani praesul et anni,   5
    prima dabas Latiis tempora consulibus.
Aeneadum genetrix vicino nomen Aprili
    das Venus : est Marti namque Aphrodita comes.
Maia dea, an maior Maium te fecerit aetas,
    ambigo ; sed mensi est auctor uterque bonus.   10
Iunius hunc sequitur duplici celebrandus honore,
    seu nomen Iuno sive Iuventa dedit.
inde Dionaeo praefulgens Iulius astro
    aestatis mediae tempora certa tenet.
Augustus sequitur cognatum a Caesare nomen,   15
    ordine sic anni proximus, ut generis.
nectuntur post hos numerumque ex ordine signant :
    September, Bacchi munere praela rigans,
et qui sementis per tempora faenore laetus
    October cupidi spem fovet agricolae,   20
quique salo mergens sollemnia signa November
    praecipitat, caelo mox reditura suo.
concludens numerum genialia festa December
    finit, ut a bruma mox novus annus eat.

---

¹ *i.e.* the comet which appeared during Caesar's funerary
games (see Suet. *Julius*, §88) ; it was so called from Dione,

THE ECLOGUES

X.—Couplets on the Same Subject

Young Janus, who givest thy name to the first month of the year, twy-faced Janus, thou dost behold two seasons at one time. After worship of the gods, Numa ordains Februa in the next month, a feast of offerings to the shades of kinsfolk. Martian, leader both of the Roman race and year, thou wast wont to bring in the beginning of the Latin consulate. Mother of the sons of Aeneas, thou, Venus, givest thy name to April, the month which follows next; for Aphrodite keeps Mars company. I am in doubt whether the goddess Maia or generations passed (*maiores*) named thee May, but either is a good patron for a month. June follows next with double title to renown, whether it was Juno or Juventa who lent her name. Then July, brilliant with Dione's star,[1] occupies the fixed season of midsummer. Augustus' month follows that named after his kinsman Julius, next in the year's order even as he in race. Next comes a string of months marked by successive numbers: September, who soaks the presses with Bacchus' gift; October, gladdened with the seasons' usury for seedling grain, who flatters the grasping farmer's hopes; November, who casts headlong her appointed stars, and plunges them in the brine, soon to return to heaven their home. December closes the list and ends our cheerful feasts, that from winter a new year may presently go forth.

mother of Venus, the ancestress of the Julian line: *cp.* Virgil, *Ecl.* ix. 47 : ecce Dionaei processit Caesaris astrum.

XI.—De Tribus Menstruis Mensuum

Bis senas anno reparat Lucina kalendas
et totidem medias dat currere Iuppiter idus
nonarumque diem faciunt infra octo secundi.
haec sunt Romano tantum tria nomina mensi;
cetera per numeros sunt cognomenta dierum.   5

XII.—Quoteni Dies sint Mensuum Singulorum

Inplent tricenas per singula menstrua luces
Iunius Aprilisque et cum Septembre November.
unum ter denis cumulatius adde diebus
per septem menses, Iani Martisque kalendis
et quas Maius agit, quas Iulius Augustusque   5
et quas October positusque in fine December.
unus erit tantum duodetriginta dierum,
quem Numa praeposito voluit succedere Iano.
sic ter centenis decies accedere senos
quadrantemque et quinque dies sibi conputat annus. 10

XIII.—Quo Mense Quotae Nonae vel Idus sint

At nonas modo quarta aperit, modo sexta refert lux.
sexta refert Mai Octobris Martisque recursu
et qui solstitio sua tempora Iulius infert.
cetera pars mensum quartis est praedita nonis;
omnes vero idus octava luce recurrunt.   5

---

[1] In March, May, July and October the Ides were on the
15th, in other months on the 13th, so that Nones, being eight

THE ECLOGUES

XI.—On the Three Sacrificial Days of the Month

Twelve times a year Lucina renews the Calends, and as often do the Ides recur by Jove's gift at the mid-month, while eight successive days before [1] produce the Nones. The Roman month has these three names alone: all other days are known by numerals.

XII.—How many Days there are in each Month

June, April, and November, with September, each month of these has thirty days. For each of seven months add one besides to thrice ten days, one to the Calends of Janus and of Mars, and one to those which May, July, and August bring, and one to October and December, the last month of all. A single month remains with but eight and twenty days, that month which Numa caused to follow next to Janus, the leader of the year. Thus the year reckons its days to be three hundred and sixty-five, with one quarter day.

XIII.—On what Dates the Nones and Ides Fall in Various Months

Sometimes the fourth dawn after the Calends opens the Nones, sometimes the sixth brings them back. The sixth brings them back as May, October, March come round, and July, who intrudes his season on the solstice. The remaining months have their Nones on the fourth day; while the Ides always come round on the eighth day after Nones.

days earlier, fell on the 7th in the four months named, and on the 5th in other months.

AUSONIUS

XIV.—Quotae Kalendae sint Mensuum Singulorum

Post idus, quas quisque suas habet ordine mensis,
diversae numero redeunt variante kalendae,
dum [vertente anno[1]] rursumque iterumque vocantur,
ut tandem optati procedant temporis ortu.
ter senis unoque die genialia festa   5
porrigit, ut Ianum arcessat nova bruma morantem.
hoc numero mensisque Numae redit autumnique
principium referens Bacchi September alumnus.
Iulius et Maius positusque in fine December
Octoberque die revocatur tardius uno.   10
inde die redeunt minus uno quattuor ultra,
quos numero adiciam : Sextilis, Iunius atque
Aprilis, post quos paenultima meta November.
ter quinis unoque die, Iunonie Mavors,
ut redeas referasque exordia prima, cieris.   15
    Hoc numero ad plenum vertens reparabitur annus.

XV.—Ratio Dierum Anni Vertentis

Nonaginta dies et quattuor ac medium Sol
conficit, a tropico in tropicum dum permeat astrum,
octipedem in Cancrum Phrixeo ab Ariete pergens.
hoc spatio aestivi pulsusque et meta diei.

[1] Suppl. Mommsen.

---

[1] cp. Eclogue ix. 3.

THE ECLOGUES

XIV.—How many Days there are before the Calends of each Month

After the Ides, which each month reckons in its own way, the Calends return, varying with changing number, while, as the year rolls on, they are summoned again and yet once more, so that at length they may come forth at the rising of their desired season. For thrice six days and one the new-come winter prolongs feasts and cheer ere he summon lingering Janus. With the same tale of days Numa's month returns, and September, Bacchus' darling, who brings round the first days of Autumn. July, May, and December, the last of months, are recalled with October one day later. Then one day sooner return four months beside, which I will add to the list: Sextilis (August), June, and April, and after them November, the year's last goal but one. By thrice five days and one, thou son of Juno, Mars, art summoned to return and to bring back the year's first beginning.[1]

[16] This tale will bring the rolling year once more to its full strength.

XV.—A Computation of the Days in the Course of the Year

Ninety days and four and half a day the Sun wears out while he passes from tropic[2] to tropic star, journeying from Phrixus' Ram to the eight-clawed Crab. In this period lie the course and

---

[2] The Ram (indicating the vernal equinox) is here loosely called "tropic," because it marks the point at which the Sun passes from the southern to the northern hemisphere.

semidiemque duosque dies deciesque novenos   5
a Cancro in Chelas aequatae tempora noctis
atque dii cursu peragit Sol aureus altero,
autumni aestatisque simul confinia miscens.
unde autumnales transcurrens ordine menses
ad tropicum pergit signum gelidi Capricorni,   10
octo dies decies octonis insuper addens
quadrantemque dii, quinto qui protinus anno
mense Numae extremo nomen capit embolimaei.
inde ad Agenorei festinans cornua Tauri,
scandit Lanigeri tropicum Sol aureus astrum,   15
nonaginta dies decreto fine cohercens.
hic tibi circus erit semper vertentibus annis
ter centum ac senis decies et quinque diebus.

XVI.—In quo Mense quod Signum sit ad Cursum Solis

Principium Iani sancit tropicus Capricornus.
mense Numae in medio solidi stat sidus Aquari.
procedunt duplices in Martia tempora Pisces.
respicis Apriles, Aries Phryxeë, kalendas.
Maius Agenorei miratur cornua Tauri.   5
Iunius aequatos caelo videt ire Laconas.
solstitio ardentis Cancri fert Iulius astrum.
Augustum mensem Leo fervidus igne perurit.
sidere, Virgo, tuo Bacchum September opimat,
aequat et October sementis tempore Libram.   10
Scorpios hibernus praeceps iubet ire Novembrem.
terminat Arquitenens medio sua signa Decembri.

finish of the summer days. Ten times nine days and two and half a day, when hours of light and night are even, the golden Sun passes through in his second race from the Crab to the claws of the Scorpion, mingling the bounds of autumn and of summer. Then, traversing the autumn months in turn, he passes on to the tropic [1] star of chill Capricorn, adding further to his tale eight days and ten times eight with a fourth part of the day, which in each fourth year stands at the close of Numa's month and takes the name of "intercalary." Then, hastening toward the horns of Agenor's Bull, the golden Sun climbs up to the tropic star of the fleecy Ram, confining ninety days within ordained bounds. Here, then, you have the full round of the ever-circling years: three hundred and three score days and five.

XVI.—WHICH CONSTELLATION THE SUN PASSES THROUGH IN EACH MONTH

THE tropic star of Capricorn prescribes the opening of Janus's reign. In the midst of Numa's month stands the sign of stout Aquarius. The Fishes twain come forth in days of March. Thou, Ram of Phrixus, lookest back on April's calends. May marvels at the horns of Agenor's Bull. June sees the Spartan twins march in the heavens. July brings the star of the Crab which blazes at the solstice. The raging lion scorches the month of August with his fires. Beneath thy star, O Virgin, September loads the vines. October's seed-time balances the Scales. The wintry Scorpion bids November go headlong. The Archer ends his shining in mid-December.

[1] Tropic Stars are those which give their names to the two Tropics, *i.e.* Capricornus and Cancer.

AUSONIUS

XVII.—A Solistitio in Aequinoctium Ratio

Sol profectus a teporo veris aequinoctio
post semidiem postque totos nonaginta et quattuor
fervidis flagrans habenis pulsum aestivum conficit.
inde autumnus noctis horas librans aequo lumine
octo et octoginta goeris et super trihorio   5

     *   *   *   *   *   *

inde floridum reflexis ver revisit oreis
additis ad hos priores goeros geminis orbibus.

XVIII.—De Mensibus et Quattuor Anni Temporibus

Aeternos menses et tempora quattuor anni
quattuor ista tibi subiecta monosticha dicent.
Martius, Aprilis, Maius sunt tempora veris.
Iulius, Augustus nec non et Iunius aestas.
Septembri, Octobri autumnat totoque Novembri.   5
brumales Ianus, Februarius atque December.

XIX.—De Lustralibus Agonibus

Quattuor antiquos celebravit Achaia ludos.
  caelicolum duo sunt et duo festa hominum.
sacra Iovis Phoebique, Palaemonis Archemorique,
  serta quibus pinus, malus, oliva, apium.

---

[1] Some lines finishing with autumn and dealing with winter are missing.

THE ECLOGUES

XVII.—A Computation from the Solstice to the Equinox

THE Sun sets forth from the warm equinox of spring, and, all aglow upon his fiery car, finishes his course through summer after one half-day and after four and ninety days complete. Then autumn, balancing the hours of night with equal measure of light, for eight and eighty days and three hours besides . . . . [1] Then wheeling round his steeds, once more he [2] visits flowery spring, when he has added two circuits to these former days. [3]

XVIII.—On the Months and the Four Seasons of the Year

THESE four verses following will tell you the eternal months and the four seasons of the year. March, April, May, make up the season of spring. June, with July and August — these are summer months. In September, October, and all November, autumn reigns. The winter months are January, February, and December.

XIX.—On the Quinquennial Games [4]

FOUR gatherings for games did Greece celebrate of old. Two are festivals of gods and two of men. They are consecrate to Jove, Phoebus, Palaemon, and Archemorus, and their garlands are of pine, apple, olive-leaves, and parsley.

[2] Apparently the Sun.
[3] *i.e.* to the eighty-eight days of l. 5 : *cf.* above xv. 16.
[4] = *Anth. Pal.* ix. 357.

AUSONIUS

XX.—De Locis Agonum

Prima Iovi magno celebrantur Olympia Pisae.
Parnasus Clario sacravit Pythia Phoebo.
Isthmia Portuno bimari dicat alta Corinthos.
Archemori Nemeaea colunt funebria Thebae.

XXI.—De Auctoribus Agonum

Primus Olympiacae sacravit festa coronae
Iuppiter Argivi stadia ad longissima circi.
proximus Alcides Nemeum sacravit honorem.
haec quoque temporibus quinquennia sacra notandis,
Isthmia Neptuno data sunt et Pythia Phoebo   5
ancipiti cultu divorum hominumque sepultis.[1]

XXII.—Quod idem qui Sacri Agones sunt et Funebres Ludi Habeantur

Tantalidae Pelopi maestum dicat Elis honorem.
Archemori Nemeaea colunt quinquennia Thebae.
Isthmia defuncto celebrata Palaemone notum.
Pythia placando Delphi statuere draconi.

---

[1] Schenkl conjectures that ll. 4 and 6 should be placed at the beginning of xxii.

---

[1] = Opheltes, son of Lycurgus, king of Nemea. He was killed by a snake during the march of the Seven against Thebes.

THE ECLOGUES

XX.—On the Places where the Games are Held

FIRST in honour of great Jove the Olympian Games are held at Pisa. Parnassus consecrated the Pythia to Phoebus, lord of Claros. To Portumnus, god of twin seas, lofty Corinth dedicates the Isthmia. Thebes celebrates the Nemea in memory of the death of Archemorus.[1]

XXI.—On the Founders of the Games

JUPITER first hallowed the festival of the Olympian Games at the long race-course of the Grecian stadium. Next did the son of Alcaeus found the solemn Nemean rite. These festivals also are held at appointed seasons once in four years—the Isthmia, established by Neptune, and the Pythia by Phoebus, in honour of the dead worshipped both as human and divine.[2]

XXII.—To show that the Sacred Contests are also held as Funerary Games

To Pelops, son of Tantalus, Elis dedicates its tribute of woe. Thebes holds the Nemea each five years in honour of Archemorus. 'Tis known that the Isthmia commemorate Palaemon's end. The Delphians instituted their Pythian festival to appease the dragon slain by Phoebus.[3]

[2] The reference is to Melicertes, son of Athamas and Ino, with whom his mother leaped into the sea. He was transformed into a sea-god and known thenceforward as Palaemon (the Roman Portumnus : cp. xx. 3). He had therefore been both god and man.

[3] cp. Ovid, Metam. i. 446 f.

AUSONIUS

XXIII.—De Feriis Romanis

Nunc et Apollineos Tiberina per ostia ludos
  et Megalesiacae matris operta loquar
Vulcanique dies, autumni exordia primi,
  Quinquatrusque deae Pallados expediam
et medias idus Mai Augustique recursu,   5
  quas sibi Mercurius quasque Diana dicat;
matronae quae sacra colant pro laude virorum,
  Mavortis primi cum rediere dies.
festa Caprotinis memorabo celebria nonis,
  cum stola matronis dempta teget famulas.   10
quattuor illa etiam discretis partibus anni
  solstitia et luces nocte dieque pares.
nec Regifugium pulsis ex urbe tyrannis
  laetum Romanis fas reticere diem.
visne Opis ante sacrum vel Saturnalia dicam   15
  festaque servorum, cum famulantur eri?
et numquam certis redeuntia festa diebus,
  compita per vicos cum sua quisque colit?

---

  ¹ Established in 212 B.C.
  ² *sc.* Cybele. Her worship was introduced from Pessinus
in Phrygia in 202 B.C.
  ³ It was held on March 19th, *five* days after the Ides, in
honour of Minerva and Mars. It was celebrated especially
by all whose employment was under the patronage of Minerva
—*e.g.* the learned, schoolboys, and artizans.
  ⁴ The feast of Merchants, whose patron Mercury was, held
on May 15th.
  ⁵ On August 13th women whose prayers had been answered
made a torchlight procession to the grove of Diana at Aricia.
  ⁶ The Matronalia (March 1st), when prayers were offered
to Juno Lucina for a fruitful wedlock.

XXIII.—On the Roman Festivals

Now will I tell of the Games of Apollo held at
Tiber's mouth[1] and of the Mysteries of the Mega-
lesian mother,[2] and will recount Vulcan's festival
that heralds autumn's beginning, and the Quin-
quatrus,[3] the feast of the goddess Pallas, and the
mid-monthly Ides which come round with May and
August—the first is Mercury's festival,[4] the second
Diana[5] claims as her own—as also those rites[6]
which wedded women practise to bring their hus-
bands credit, when the first day of March is returned.
I will make mention also of the feast held on the
Nonae Caprotinae[7] when matrons doff their robes
to clothe their handmaidens, and of those seasons,
too, which separate the year into four parts, the
solstices and the equinoxes, when night and day
are equal. Nor dare I pass over in silence the Regi-
fugium,[8] that glad day for the Romans when they
drove their tyrants out. Or would you have me
speak first of the feast of Ops,[9] or of the Saturn
alia, the slaves' holiday, when masters turn servants?
And of those feasts which never come round on
fixed days, when each man worships at the cross-
ways[10] according to the district in which he lives?

[7] July 7th. The Romans, after their defeat by the Gauls,
were attacked by the Latins, who demanded the cession of a
number of Roman ladies. Female slaves took their place
disguised in matrons' dress, and made the enemy drunk.
Tutula, one of these slaves, then climbed a wild fig-tree
(*caprificus*) and gave the signal for the Romans to attack by
showing a torch.

[8] February 24th, when Tarquin was driven out.

[9] The Opalia, held on December 19th. Ops, the goddess
of fertility, was the consort of Saturn.

[10] The festival of the Lares, tutelary genii of cross-roads
(*compita*), was held four times a year.

aut duplicem cultum, quem Neptunalia dicunt,
    et quem de Conso consiliisque vocant?   20
festa haec navigiis, aut quae celebrata quadrigis
    iungunt Romanos finitimosque duces?
adiciam cultus peregrinaque sacra deorum,
    natalem Herculeum vel ratis Isiacae,
nec non lascivi Floralia laeta theatri,   25
    quae spectare volunt, qui voluisse negant?
nunc etiam veteres celebrantur Equirria ludi:
    prima haec Romanus nomina circus habet.
et Dionysiacos Latio cognomine ludos
    Roma colit, Liber quae sibi vota dicat.   30
Aediles etiam plebi aedilesque curules
    sacra Sigillorum nomine dicta colunt.
et gladiatores funebria proelia notum
    decertasse foro: nunc sibi harena suos
vindicat extremo qui iam sub fine Decembris   35
    falcigerum placant sanguine Caeligenam.

---

[1] The Neptunalia were held on July 23rd, the Consualia on August 21st. It was at the first celebration of the latter that the Sabine women were carried off, an event followed by the union of the Sabines and Romans. Consus was identified with Neptune the Horseman. Thus the two feasts being in honour of one god constituted a double act of worship (duplicem cultum).

[2] March 5th. Isis was worshipped as patroness of navigation and the inventor of sails.

[3] The Floralia, first instituted in 238 B.C., lasted from April 28th to May 3rd.

THE ECLOGUES

Or of those twin celebrations—that which they call Neptunalia,[1] and that which is named after Consus and good counsel? Of this festival which is celebrated with naval battles, or that with chariot-races, which unite the Romans and their neighbour-chiefs? Shall I tell also of the festivals and rites of strange gods introduced into Rome, of the birthday of Hercules or the day[2] of the Bark of Isis, and also of the merry rites of Flora[3] held in the licentious theatre—rites which they long to see who declare they never longed to see them? Now also the ancient games called Equiria[4] are held: 'tis the chief name known to the Roman circus. The Dionysiac Games Rome also keeps under a Latin name, the same which Liber claims as consecrate to himself.[5] The aediles also of the plebs and curule aediles observe the feast called Sigillaria.[6] And that gladiators once fought out funerary battles in the forum is well known[7]; now the arena claims as its own proper prey those who towards the end of December appease with their blood the sickle-bearing Son of Heaven.[8]

[4] Held three times a year, on February 27th, March 14th, October 15th. It took its name from the horse-races instituted by Romulus, which were held in the Campus Martius.

[5] The Liberalia, held on March 17th, when cakes (*liba*) of meal, honey, and oil were sold and burnt.

[6] The last days of the Saturnalia, when people gave little images (*sigillaria*) to one another.

[7] Gladiatorial shows, first exhibited in 264 B.C. at the funerary ceremonies of M. Junius Brutus, were at first confined to such occasions. Under Domitian these contests occupied ten days in December.

[8] Saturn or Cronos. For the origin of the sickle see Hesiod, *Theog.* 173 ff. There seems to be no other reference to gladiatorial combats at the Saturnalia.

AUSONIUS

XXIV —Monosticha de Aerumnis Herculis

Prima Cleonaei tolerata aerumna leonis.
proxima Lernaeam ferro et face contudit hydram.
mox Erymantheum vis tertia perculit aprum.
aeripedis quarto tulit aurea cornua cervi.
Stymphalidas pepulit volucres discrimine quinto.   5
Thraeiciam sexto spoliavit Amazona balteo.
septima in Augei stabulis inpensa laboris.
octava expulso numeratur adoria tauro.
in Diomedeis victoria nona quadrigis.
Geryone extincto decimam dat Hiberia palmam.   10
undecimo mala Hesperidum destricta triumpho.
Cerberus extremi suprema est meta laboris.

XXV.—Quinti Ciceronis hi Versus eo Pertinent ut quod Signum quo Tempore inlustre sit noverimus.   Quod superius quoque nostris Versibus expeditur

Flamina [1] verna cient obscuro lumine Pisces
curriculumque Aries aequat noctisque diique,
cornua quem condunt florum praenuntia Tauri,
aridaque aestatis Gemini primordia pandunt,
longaque iam munit praeclarus lumina Cancer,   5

    [1] *Wakefield* : flumina, *V*, *Peiper*.

---

    [1] = *Anth. Planud.* xvi. 92.
    [2] *sc.* the Nemean lion : Cleonae in Argolis is near Nemea.

THE ECLOGUES

XXIV.—Single Lines on each of the Toils of Hercules [1]

The first toil endured was that of the Cleonaean lion.[2] The next with sword and brand crushed the Lyrnaean hydra. The third exploit presently destroyed the boar of Erymanthus. Fourthly he carried off the golden antlers of the fleet-footed stag. In his fifth adventure he shot down the Stymphalian birds. Sixthly he despoiled the Thracian Amazon of her belt. His seventh labour was spent upon the stables of Augeas. The bull driven out of Crete [3] is counted his eighth glory. The team of Diomedes brought his ninth victory. Spain gives him his tenth palm for slaying Geryones. The plucked apples of the Hesperides made his eleventh triumph. Cerberus is the final goal of his last labour.

XXV.—These Verses of Quintus Cicero are intended to show us at what Season each Constellation is shining, a subject which I have also explained in a previous Poem [4]

The Fishes, showing a dim light, awaken the breezes of spring, and the Ram makes the cars of Night and Day run an even race. He is eclipsed by the horns of the Bull, the harbingers of flowers. The Twins bring in the dry opening of summer, the brilliant Crab establishes the lengthening days, and

---

[3] He *carried* it alive to Mycenae, where he let it go : it was afterwards killed by Theseus at Marathon.

[4] No other poetical work of Q. Cicero is known, and it is hard to see why it should be inserted in the works of Ausonius, if it was really by the brother of the orator. Ausonius' treatment of the subject is in *Ecl.* xvii.

languificosque Leo proflat ferus ore calores.
post modium quatiens Virgo fugat orta vaporem :
autumni reserat portas aequatque diurna
tempora nocturnis dispenso sidere Libra.
ecfetos[1] ramos denudat flamma Nepai,   10
pigra Sagittipotens iaculatur frigora terris,
bruma gelu glacians iubar exspirat Capricorni,
quam sequitur nebulas rorans liquor altus Aquari.
tanta supra circaque viget vis flammea[2] mundi.
at dextra laevaque ciet rota fulgida Solis   15
mobile curriculum et Lunae simulacra feruntur.

    *   *   *   *   *   *

squama sub aeterno conspectu torta Draconis
eminet. hunc infra fulgentes Arcera septem
magna quatit stellas : quam servans serus in alta
conditur oceani ripa cum luce Boötes.[3]   20

XXVI.—Hic Versus sine Auctore est.
Quo Die quid Demi de Corpore Oporteat

Ungues Mercurio, barbam Iove, Cypride crines.

Hoc sic Refellendum

Mercurius furtis probat ungues semper acutos
articulisque aciem non sinit imminui.

---

[1] *Riese* : et fetos, *V*.
[2] *Translator* : vigent umi flamina, *V* : vigent vi flamina,
Peiper (after *Riese*).   [3] *cp.* ε 275.

---

[1] *i.e.* of grain and fruits : Virgo is sometimes identified
with Demeter.

the fierce Lion breathes from his mouth enfeebling heat. Then the Virgin, brandishing her measure,[1] rises and drives moisture away. The constellation of the Scales, equally poised, opens the gates of Autumn and makes even the hours of night and day. Nepa's[2] fires strip the o'erteemed[3] branches of their leaves, the Archer rains shafts of numbing cold upon the earth, Winter, freezing with her frosty breath, sends forth Capricornus' ray, and after her comes Aquarius, whose pitcher from on high bedews the clouds. So great the fiery forces of the universe which strongly move above it and about. But on the right hand and the left the ever-moving chariot of the Sun speeds on with burning wheels, and the pale image of the Moon moves on its course . . . . the Dragon's scaly coils ever keep in sight. Below him twinkles the great Wain with its seven gleaming stars, while keeping watch over it, Boötes is slow to hide his light below Ocean's brink.

XXVI. — THIS LINE, WHICH IS ANONYMOUS, SHOWS WHAT SHOULD BE REMOVED FROM THE BODY ON CERTAIN DAYS

CLIP nails on Tuesday, beards on Wednesday, hair on Friday.[4]

THE ABOVE LINE MAY BE CONFUTED IN THE FOLLOWING WAY

MERCURY likes a thief's nails ever-sharpened, and suffers not the fingers to lose their points. His

---

[2] *sc.* the Scorpion. According to Festus, the name is African.   [3] *cp. Hamlet*, II. ii. 231.

[4] Mediaeval calendars usually add a note to each month on these and similar matters. See also Hesiod, *W. and D.* 724 f.

barba Iovi, crines Veneri decor: ergo necesse est,
    ut nolint demi, quo sibi uterque placent.
Mavors imberbos et calvos, Luna, adamasti: 5
    non prohibent comi tum caput atque genas.
Sol et Saturnus nil obstant unguibus: ergo
    non placitum divis tolle monostichium.

beard is Jove's, her hair is Venus' glory: therefore these needs must mislike the minishing of that in which they severally delight. Thou, Mars, lovest the beardless,[1] and thou, Moon, the bald: these do not forbid hair and cheeks to be trimmed. The Sun and Saturn have no scruples as to nails: therefore cancel that line of which gods disapprove.

[1] *i.e.* youths in their prime and fit for war. A persistent tradition denies the soldier a beard. Why the moon loves the bald is not clear, unless it be that the moon itself resembles a bald head.

LIBER VIII

[CUPIDO CRUCIATUR]

Ausonius Gregorio Filio Sal.

En umquam vidisti tabulam [1] pictam in pariete?
vidisti utique et meministi. Treveris quippe in tri-
clinio Zoili fucata est pictura haec: Cupidinem cruci
adfigunt mulieres amatrices, non istae de nostro sae-
culo, quae sponte peccant, sed illae heroicae, quae
sibi ignoscunt et plectunt deum. quarum partem in
lugentibus campis Maro noster enumerat. hanc ego
imaginem specie et argumento miratus sum. deinde
mirandi stuporem transtuli ad ineptiam poetandi.
mihi praeter lemma nihil placet; sed commendo tibi
errorem meum: naevos nostros et cicatrices amamus,
nec soli nostro vitio peccasse contenti, adfectamus ut
amentur. verum quid ego huic eclogae studiose
patrocinor? certus sum, quodcumque meum scieris,
amabis; quod magis spero, quam ut laudes. vale et
dilige parentem.

---

[1] *Vinetus* (*cp.* Plaut. *Men.* 143: dic mi, enunquam tu
vidisti tabulam pictam in pariete?). The MSS. have *nebulam*
which is senseless here, and is not supported by the supposed
parallel in *Epist.* ii. (aërius bratteae fucus aut picta nebula).

BOOK VIII

CUPID CRUCIFIED

AUSONIUS TO HIS SON GREGORIUS,[1] GREETING

"PRAY, have you ever seen a picture painted on a wall?" To be sure you have, and remember it. Well, at Trèves, in the dining-room of Zoïlus, this picture is painted: Cupid is being nailed to the cross by certain love-lorn women—not those lovers of our own day, who fall into sin of their own free-will, but those heroic lovers who excuse themselves and blame the gods. Some of these our own Virgil[2] recounts in his description of the Fields of Mourning. I was greatly struck by the art and the subject of this picture. Subsequently I translated my amazed admiration into insipid versification. Nothing in it satisfies me except the title; nevertheless I commit my failure to your care: we love our own warts and scars, and, not satisfied with erring by ourselves through our folly, seek to make others love them also. But why am I at such pains to plead the cause of this eclogue? I know well that you will welcome whatever you know to be mine; and it is for this I hope, more than for your praise. Farewell, and think kindly of your father.

[1] This person is unknown. The title "son" is one of endearment only, just as Theodosius (*Praef.* iii.) addresses Ausonius as "father."   [2] *Aen.* vi. 440 ff.

AUSONIUS

Cupido Cruciatur

Aeris in campis, memorat quos musa Maronis,[1]
myrteus amentes ubi lucus opacat amantes,[2]
orgia ducebant heroides et sua quaeque,
ut quondam occiderant, leti argumenta gerebant,
errantes silva in magna et sub luce maligna[3]   5
inter harundineasque comas gravidumque papaver
et tacitos sine labe lacus, sine murmure rivos:
quorum per ripas nebuloso lumine marcent
fleti, olim regum et puerorum nomina, flores[4]
mirator Narcissus et Oebalides Hyacinthus   10
et Crocus auricomans et murice pictus Adonis
et tragico scriptus gemitu Salaminius Aeas;
omnia quae lacrimis et amoribus anxia maestis
exercent memores obita iam morte dolores:
rursus in amissum revocant heroidas aevum.   15
fulmineos Semele decepta puerpera partus
deflet et ambustas lacerans per inania cunas
ventilat ignavum simulati fulguris ignem.
irrita dona querens, sexu gavisa virili,
maeret in antiquam Caenis revocata figuram.   20
vulnera siccat adhuc Procris Cephalique cruentam
diligit et percussa manum.   fert fumida testae
lumina Sestiaca praeceps de turre puella.
et de nimboso saltum Leucate minatur

---

[1] Virgil, *Aen.* vi. 887.   [2] *cp id.* vi. 440 ff.
[3] *id.* vi. 270.
[4] *cp.* Virgil, *Ecl.* iii. 106 f.: inscripti nomina regum Nascuntur flores.

---

[1] *cp. Epitaph.* iii. 5–6 and note.   The phrase might also be rendered "the theme of woeful tragedy."

CUPID CRUCIFIED

In the aerial fields, told of in Virgil's verse, where
groves of myrtle o'ershade lovers lorn, the heroines
were holding frantic rites, each one of them bearing
tokens of the death she died of old, and wandering
in a great wood, lit by scanty light, 'mid tufted
reeds, and full-blown poppies, and still meres with-
out a ripple, and unbabbling streams, along whose
banks flowers of woe hung drooping in the murky
light, bearing the names of kings and boys of old:
here was admiring Narcissus, Hyacinthus, son of
Oebalus, golden-headed Crocus, Adonis purple-
stained, and Aeas of Salamis inscribed with the
word of woe.[1] All things which, fraught with grief
or with the pangs of love, prolong the memory of
sorrow even when death is passed, call back again
the heroines to the lives which they have lost. Here
pregnant Semele, robbed of her hopes, bewails her
birthpangs amid the lightning, and in the void rends
a charred cradle and brandishes the harmless fire of
an imagined thunderbolt.   Bewailing the unavailing
gift of manhood in which she once rejoiced, Caenis[2]
grieves for her restoration to her former shape.
Procris[3] still staunches her wounds, and loves the
fatal hand of Cephalus which struck her down. The
maid of Sestos[4] carries her smoking earthen lamp
and casts herself headlong from her tower.   And
man-like Sappho, doomed to be slain by the shafts

---

[1] The girl Caenis was changed by Poseidon into a man
and made invulnerable. As a man he bore the name Caeneus.
[3] Daughter of Erechtheus and wife of Cephalus. In her
jealousy she hid in a thicket to spy on her husband while
hunting, and was speared by Cephalus, who supposed a wild
beast was lurking there.   [4] *sc.* Hero.

[mascula Lesbiacis Sappho peritura sagittis.[1]]   25
Harmoniae cultus Eriphyle maesta recusat,
infelix nato nec fortunata marito.
tota quoque aeriae Minoia fabula Cretae
picturarum instar tenui sub imagine vibrat:
Pasiphae nivei sequitur vestigia tauri,   30
licia fert glomerata manu deserta Ariadne,
respicit abiectas desperans Phaedra tabellas.
haec laqueum gerit, haec vanae simulacra coronae:
Daedaliae pudet hanc latebras subiisse iuvencae.
praereptas queritur per inania gaudia noctes   35
Laudamia duas, vivi functique mariti.
parte truces alia strictis mucronibus omnes
et Thisbe et Canace et Sidonis horret Elissa:
coniugis haec, haec patris et haec gerit hospitis ensem.
errat et ipsa, olim qualis per Latmia saxa   40
Endymioneos solita adfectare sopores,
cum face et astrigero diademate Luna bicornis.
centum aliae veterum recolentes vulnera amorum
dulcibus et maestis refovent tormenta querellis.

Quas inter medias furvae caliginis umbram   45
dispulit inconsultus Amor stridentibus alis.
agnovere omnes puerum memorique recursu
communem sensere reum, quamquam umida circum
nubila et auratis fulgentia cingula bullis

---

    [1] Suppl. *Ugoletus*: *cp.* Horace, *Ep.* I. xix. 28.

---

    [1] Bribed by Polynices with the necklace of Harmonia, she sent her husband to his death on the expedition of the Seven against Thebes. Amphiaraus, aware of this, charged his son Alcmaeon to avenge him.
    [2] The letter addressed to her stepson Hippolytus.

of love for Lesbian Phaon, threatens to leap from
cloud-wrapped Leucas. Sad Eriphyle[1] refuses the
necklace of Harmonia, unhappy in her son and
luckless in her husband. Here also the whole story
of Minos and aëry Crete glimmers like some faint-
limned pictured scene. Pasiphaë follows the foot-
steps of her snow-white bull, forlorn Ariadne carries
a ball of twine in her hand, hopeless Phaedra looks
back at the tablets[2] she has cast away. This wears
a halter, this the empty semblance of a crown, while
this hesitates in shame to enter her hiding-place
in the heifer wrought by Daedalus. Laodamia[3]
cries out on those two nights passed all too soon in
unreal joys, one with her living lord, one with her
dead. Elsewhere, fierce with drawn swords all,
stand Thisbe and Canace and Sidonian Elissa: this
carries her husband's blade, that her father's, and
the third her guest's. She also wanders here, even
as of old o'er Latmus' rocks when she was wont to
woo the slumbering Endymion,—twy-horned Luna
with her torch and starry diadem. A hundred
more besides, renewing the wounds of their old
passions, revive their pangs with plaints both sweet
and sad.

[45] Into the midst of these Love rashly broke
scattering the darkness of that murky gloom with
rustling wings. All recognized the boy, and as their
thoughts leapt back, they knew him for the one
transgressor against them all, though the damp
clouds obscured the sheen of his golden-studded

---

[3] Daughter of Acastus and wife of Protesilaus. She ob-
tained from the gods the favour that Protesilaus, to whom
she had been wedded only one day before he set forth to fall
at Troy, should be permitted to return for a few hours to
the earth : *see* Wordsworth's *Laodamia.*

et pharetram et rutilae fuscarent lampados ignem.　50
agnoscunt tamen et vanum vibrare vigorem
occipiunt hostemque unum loca non sua nanctum,
cum pigros ageret densa sub nocte volatus,
facta nube premunt: trepidantem et cassa parantem
suffugia in coetum mediae traxere catervae.　　55
eligitur maesto myrtus notissima luco,
invidiosa deum poenis.　cruciaverat illic
spreta olim memorem Veneris Proserpina Adonin.
huius in excelso suspensum stipite Amorem
devinctum post terga manus substrictaque plantis　60
vincula maerentem nullo moderamine poenae
adficiunt.　reus est sine crimine, iudice nullo
accusatur Amor.　se quisque absolvere gestit,
transferat ut proprias aliena in crimina culpas.
cunctae exprobrantes tolerati insignia leti　　65
expediunt: haec arma putant, haec ultio dulcis,
ut, quo quaeque perit, studeat punire dolorem.
haec laqueum tenet, haec speciem mucronis inanem
ingerit, illa cavos amnes rupemque fragosam
insanique metum pelagi et sine fluctibus aequor.　70
nonnullae flammas quatiunt trepidaeque minantur
stridentes nullo igne faces.　rescindit adultum
Myrrha uterum lacrimis lucentibus inque paventem
gemmea fletiferi iaculatur sucina trunci.
quaedam ignoscentum specie ludibria tantum　　75
sola volunt, stilus ut tenuis sub acumine puncti
eliciat tenerum, de quo rosa nata, cruorem
aut pubi admoveant petulantia lumina lychni.

belt, his quiver, and the flame of his glowing torch.
Yet they recognize him, and essay to wield their
phantom strength against him, and upon their one
foe, now lighted on a realm not his own where he
could ply his wings but feebly under the clogging
weight of night, gathering in a throng they press:
him trembling and vainly seeking to escape, they
dragged into the midst of the crowding band. A
myrtle-tree is chosen, well known in that sad grove
and hateful from the vengeance of the gods. Thereon
had Proserpine, once slighted, tormented Adonis,
mindful of his Venus. On the tall trunk of this Love
was hung up, his hands bound behind his back, his
feet tied fast; and though he weeps, they lay on him
no milder punishment. Love is found guilty without
charge, condemned without a judge. Each to ac-
quit herself of blame, seeks to lay her offences to
another's charge. All upbraid him, and prepare to use
on him the tokens of the death they once endured:
these are their choice weapons, this is vengeance
sweet—each eagerly to avenge her grief with that
which slew her. One holds a halter ready, another
advances the unreal phantom of a sword, another
displays yawning rivers, jagged rocks, the horrors
of the raging sea, and a deep that has no waves.
Some shake firebrands, and in frenzy menace him
with torches which crackle without fire. Myrrha,[1]
with glistening tears, rends open her ripe womb and
hurls at the trembling boy the drops of sparkling
amber which trickle from her stem. A few pretend
to pardon, but only seek to mock him and with
sharp-pointed bodkins draw his dainty blood from
which roses spring, or let their lamps' flame play

---

[1] See Ovid, *Metam.* x. 500 ff.

ipsa etiam simili genetrix obnoxia culpae
alma Venus tantos penetrat secura tumultus.   80
nec circumvento properans suffragia nato
terrorem ingeminat stimulisque accendit amaris
ancipites furias natique in crimina confert
dedecus ipsa suum, quod vincula caeca mariti
deprenso Mavorte tulit, quod pube pudenda   85
Hellespontiaci ridetur forma Priapi,
quod crudelis Eryx, quod semivir Hermaphroditus.
nec satis in verbis : roseo Venus aurea serto
maerentem pulsat puerum et graviora paventem.
olli purpureum mulcato corpore rorem   90
sutilis expressit crebro rosa verbere, quae iam
tincta prius traxit rutilum magis ignea fucum.
inde truces cecidere minae vindictaque maior
crimine visa suo, Venerem factura nocentem.
ipsae intercedunt heroides et sua quaeque   95
funera crudeli malunt adscribere fato.
tum grates pia mater agit cessisse dolentes
et condonatas puero dimittere culpas.
  Talia nocturnis olim simulacra figuris
exercent trepidam casso terrore quietem.   100
quae postquam multa perpessus nocte Cupido
effugit, pulsa tandem caligine somni
evolat ad superos portaque evadit eburna.

---

[1] See *Odyssey*.
[2] Son of Venus and Mercury (or Bacchus). He was born
at Lampsacus (hence called Hellespontine), and was the god
of gardens, the terror of birds and thieves.

wantonly upon his tender frame. His very mother, too, the lady Venus, as guilty of like shame, passes fearlessly through this frenzied throng. And hastening not to plead for her son entrapped, she redoubles his fear, and kindles their slackening rage with new bitterness. She lays to her son's charge her own disgrace because she endured the hidden bonds set by her husband,[1] when taken in the act with Mars, because Hellespontine Priapus[2] is laughed to scorn for his deformity, because Eryx[3] is cruel, and because Hermaphroditus[4] is of neither sex. But words were not enough: with her rosy wreath golden Venus scourged the boy who wept and feared yet harsher punishment. From his torn body the entwined roses drew forth a ruddy dew with many a stroke and, though already dyed before, took on a hue more fiery red. Thereat the fierce threats died away, and the punishment seemed too great for the offence, as like to leave the guilt on Venus' side. The heroines themselves intervene, each one preferring to blame Fate's cruelty for her death. Then the fond mother thanked them for laying by their griefs to forgive the boy and to pardon his offences.

[99] Such visions with their night-born shapes sometimes disturb his rest, disquieting it with idle fears. When these he has endured through a great part of the night, Cupid flees forth, banishing sleep's gloom at last, flits forth to the gods above, and passes forth by the gate of ivory.[5]

---

[3] Son of Venus and Butes. He used to challenge his guests to box with him, and so slew them. He was at last slain by Hercules.

[4] See *Epigr.* cii., ciii.   [5] *cp.* Virgil, *Aen.* vi. 895 f.

LIBER IX

DE BISSULA

AUSONIUS PAULO SUO S. D.

PERVINCIS tandem[1] et operta musarum mearum,
quae initiorum velabat obscuritas, quamquam non
profanus, irrumpis, Paule carissime. quamvis enim
te non eius vulgi existimem, quod Horatius[2] arcet
ingressu, tamen sua cuique sacra, neque idem Cereri,
quod Libero, etiam sub isdem cultoribus. poematia,
quae in alumnam meam luseram rudia et incohata ad
domesticae solacium cantilenae, cum sine metu
[laterent[3]] et arcana securitate fruerentur, proferre
ad lucem caligantia coegisti. verecundiae meae
scilicet spolium concupisti, aut, quantum tibi in me
iuris esset, ab invito indicari. ne tu Alexandri Mace-
donis pervicaciam supergressus, qui, fatalis iugi lora

---

[1] MS. used by *Accursius* : tamen, *Peiper.*
[2] *Odes*, III. i. 1. Odi profanum vulgus et arceo.
[3] Suppl. *Peiper* (in apparatus).

---

[1] It was fated that whosoever could untie the knot fasten-
ing the yoke to the chariot of Gordius, king of Gordium in

BOOK IX

BISSULA

You have your way at last, my dearest Paulus, and, though not uninitiate, are bursting into the secret chambers of my Muses, which the darkness proper to Mysteries once veiled. For though I do not regard you as one of that "common herd" which Horace prevents from entering, yet every god has his own rites, and Ceres is not approached in the same way as Liber, even by the same worshippers. The bits of poems which I had composed on my little maid, playfully and in rough, unfinished form, for the solace which a fire-side ditty gives (since they lay hid without misgiving and enjoyed the confidence of concealment)—these you have forced me to bring forth from their darkness into the light. You have set your mind, assuredly, on winning a triumph over my shyness, or on showing in my despite how great is your power over me. Indeed you have surpassed in persistence Alexander of Macedon, who, when he could not untie them, cut the thongs which fastened that fateful yoke [1]

Phrygia, should rule Asia. Alexander contented himself with cutting the knot with his sword.

cum solvere non posset, abscidit et Pythiae specum,
quo die fas non erat patere, penetravit.

Utere igitur ut tuis, pari iure, sed fiducia dispari :
quippe tua possunt populum non timere ; meis etiam
intra me erubesco.   vale.

I.—Praefatio

Ut voluisti, Paule, cunctos Bissulae versus habes,
lusimus quos in Suebae gratiam virgunculae,
otium magis foventes, quam studentes gloriae.
tu molestus flagitator lege molesta carmina.
tibi, quod intristi, exedendum est[1] : sic vetus verbum
    iubet,   5
compedes, quas ipse fecit, ipsus ut gestet faber.

II.—Ad Lectorem Huius Libelli

Carminis incompti tenuem lecture libellum,
    pone supercilium.
seria contractis expende poemata rugis :
    nos Thymelen sequimur.
Bissula in hoc scedio cantabitur, haut Erasinus :   5
    admoneo, ante bibas.
ieiunis nil scribo ; meum post pocula si quis
    legerit, hic sapiet.
sed magis hic sapiet, si dormiet et putet ista
    somnia missa sibi.   10

---

[1] *cp.* Terence, *Phorm.* 318: tute hoc intristi : tibi omnest
exedendum.

---

[1] Alexander, before setting out on his conquest of Persia,
went to consult the Oracle at Delphi.   As he arrived on a

218

and made his way into the cave of the Pythia[1] on a day when it was not permitted to be opened.

Make use of these verses, then, as freely, but not as confidently, as though they were your own: for your writings can face the public, mine make me blush even in private.   Farewell.

I.—The Preface

As you desired, Paulus, you have all the verses of my *Bissula*—playful verses which I have written in honour of a slip of a Swabian girl, rather amusing my idleness than aiming at renown.   Tiresome you have been, so read these tiresome poems which you demanded: you must eat up all the mess you have compounded; or, as the old saw bids:—

> " Let the smith who made them wear
> The shackles which he did prepare."

II.—To the Reader of this Little Book

You who propose to read this booklet of un-polished verse, smooth out your frown.   Weigh sober poems with a knitted brow: I follow Thymele.[2] Bissula shall be sung in this rough sketch, not Erasinus.[3]   I warn you fairly: drink before you read. This is no reading for a fasting saint; whoso shall read this book after a cup or two, he will be wise. But he will be wiser still to sleep and think this is a dream sent to him.

day when no response could be given, he dragged the Pythia into the temple; whereupon she exclaimed: " You are irre-sistible, my son."

[2] A famous dancer and mime, often mentioned by Martial and Juvenal.   [3] Unknown.

III.—Ubi Nata sit Bissula et Quomodo in Manus Domini Venerit

Bissula, trans gelidum stirpe et lare prosata Rhenum,
  conscia nascentis Bissula Danuvii,
capta manu, sed missa manu dominatur in eius
  deliciis, cuius bellica praeda fuit.
matre carens, nutricis egens, [quae] nescit herai   5
  imperium, [domini quae regit ipsa domum,] [1]
fortunae ac patriae quae nulla obprobria sensit,
  illico inexperto libera servitio,
sic Latiis mutata bonis, Germana maneret
  ut facies, oculos caerula, flava comas.   10
ambiguam modo lingua facit, modo forma puellam:
  haec Rheno genitam praedicat, haec Latio.

IV.—De Eadem Bissula

Delicium, blanditiae, ludus, amor, voluptas,
barbara, sed quae Latias vincis alumna pupas,
Bissula, nomen tenerae rusticulum puellae,
horridulum non solitis, sed domino venustum.

V.—Ad Pictorem de Bissulae Imagine

Bissula nec ceris nec fuco imitabilis ullo
naturale decus fictae non commodat arti.
sandyx et cerusa, alias simulate puellas:
temperiem hanc vultus nescit manus. ergo age, pictor,
puniceas confunde rosas et lilia misce,   5
quique erit ex illis color aeris, ipse sit oris.

---

[1] *Translator* (herai, *Ugoletus*): (egens) nescitere imperium,
T: nescit ere imperium, *M*: nescivit herae imperium,
nescivit . . . ere | . . . imperium |, *Peiper ed. princeps.*

BISSULA

III.—Where Bissula was born, and how she came into her Master's Hands

Bissula, born and bred beyond chilly Rhine, Bissula, privy to the secrets of the Danube's birth, a captive maid, a free girl made,[1] she queens it as the pet of him whose spoil of war she was. Lacking a mother, wanting a nurse, she who knows not a mistress' control, who herself rules her master's house, who for her lot and native land felt no disgrace, being straightway freed from slavery ere she felt it,—is not so changed by Roman blessings, but that she remains German in features, blue of eyes and fair of hair. A maid of either race now speech, now looks present her: the last declare her a daughter of the Rhine, the first a child of Latium.

IV.—On the same Bissula

Darling, delight, my pet, my love, my joy! Barbarian and adopted you may be, but you surpass your Roman sister-lasses. Bissula! 'Tis a clumsy little name for so delicate a girl, an uncouth little name to strangers; but to your master, charming.

V.—To a Painter: on Bissula's Portrait

Bissula, whom no wax nor any paint can imitate, adapts not her natural beauty to the shams of art. Vermilion and white, go picture other girls: the artist's skill cannot so blend you as to match this face. Away, then, painter, mingle crimson roses and lilies, and let that colour which they give the air be the very colour of her face.

[1] The play on *capta manu . . . missa manu* cannot be directly reproduced.

VI.—AD PICTOREM DE BISSULA PINGENDA

PINGERE si nostram, pictor, meditaris alumnam,
 aemula Cecropias ars imitetur apes.

*   *   *   *   *   *

MAP TO ILLUSTRATE THE *MOSELLE* OF AUSONIUS.

(*After H. de la Ville de Mirmont.*)

BISSULA

VI.—To a Painter : on Painting Bissula's Portrait

PAINTER, if you intend to paint my darling's face,
let your art imitate the Attic [1] bees.

*   *   *   *   *   *

[1] *sc.* the famous bees of Hymettus.   Doubtless the painter
was directed to ransack all the flowers for suitable colours.

NOTE.—Ancient names are shown in block characters, the
modern equivalents (in brackets) in ordinary type. The
route followed by Ausonius is shown thus —.—.—.
Starting E. of the Nahe at Bingen, the poet travelled *via*
Dumnissus and Berncastel to Neumagen, and then south-
westwards to Trèves.

The *Moselle* seems to have been written in 370–1 A.D., and
the journey described was probably taken in connection with
the expedition against the Alamanni of 368–9.

[*See p.* 224.

LIBER X

MOSELLA

Transieram celerem nebuloso flumine Navam,
addita miratus veteri nova moenia Vinco,
aequavit Latias ubi quondam Gallia Cannas
infletaeque iacent inopes super arva catervae.
unde iter ingrediens nemorosa per avia solum   5
et nulla humani spectans vestigia cultus
praetereo arentem sitientibus undique terris
Dumnissum riguasque perenni fonte Tabernas
arvaque Sauromatum nuper metata colonis:
et tandem primis Belgarum conspicor oris   10
Noiomagum, divi castra inclita Constantini.
purior hic campis aer Phoebusque sereno
lumine purpureum reserat iam sudus Olympum.
nec iam, consertis per mutua vincula ramis,
quaeritur exclusum viridi caligine caelum: 15

---

[1] For the date and occasion of this poem, see *Introduction*.

[2] Vincum, or Bingium (Bingen), lies at the confluence of the Nava (Nahe) and the Rhine. Ammianus records its fortification by Julian in 359 A.D. (XVIII. ii. 4).

[3] In the revolt of Civilis, the Treveri under Julius Tutor were crushed at Bingen by Sextilius Felix in 71 A.D. (Tac. *Hist.* iv. 70).

[4] Probably Densen, near Kirchberg.   [5] Berncastel.

[6] It was the custom in the later Empire to settle conquered barbarians in waste Roman territory: the Panegyric on

BOOK X

THE MOSELLE[1]

I HAD crossed over swift-flowing Nava's cloudy stream, and gazed with awe upon the ramparts lately thrown round ancient Vincum,[2] where Gaul once matched the Roman rout at Cannae, and where her slaughtered hordes lay scattered over the country-side untended and unwept.[3] Thence onward I began a lonely journey through pathless forest, nor did my eyes rest on any trace of human inhabitants. I passed Dumnissus,[4] sweltering amid its parched fields, and Tabernae,[5] watered by its unfailing spring, and the lands lately parcelled out to Sarmatian settlers.[6] And at length on the very verge of Belgic territory I descry Noiomagus, the famed camp of sainted Constantine.[7] Clearer the air which here invests the plains, and Phoebus, cloudless now, discloses glowing heaven with his untroubled light. No longer is the sky to seek, shut out by the green gloom of branches intertwined : but the free breath

Constantius Chlorus (ix. and xxi.) refers to such a settlement of Chamavi and Frisii ; and Maximian populated the waste lands of the Nervii and Treveri with Letts and Franks. This was *c.* 293-4 A.D. Ausonius clearly refers to a later settlement.

[7] Noiomagus or Noviomagus, the modern Neumagen, was probably occupied by Constantine in his war with the Franks and Alamanni, between 306 and 312 A.D.: *cp.* Eutropius, *Brev.* x. iii. 2.

sed liquidum iubar et rutilam visentibus aethram
libera perspicui non invidet aura diei.
in speciem quin me patriae cultumque nitentis
Burdigalae blando pepulerunt omnia visu,
culmina villarum pendentibus edita ripis   20
et virides Baccho colles et amoena fluenta
subter labentis tacito rumore Mosellae.

 Salve, amnis laudate agris, laudate colonis,
dignata imperio debent cui moenia Belgae :
amnis odorifero iuga vitea consite Baccho,   25
consite gramineas, amnis viridissime, ripas :
naviger, ut pelagus, devexas pronus in undas,
ut fluvius, vitreoque lacus imitate profundo
et rivos trepido potis aequiperare meatu,
et liquido gelidos fontes praecellere potu ;   30
omnia solus habes, quae fons, quae rivus et amnis
et lacus et bivio refluus manamine pontus.
tu placidis praelapsus aquis nec murmura venti
ulla, nec occulti pateris luctamina saxi :
non spirante [1] vado rapidos properare [2] meatus 35
cogeris, extantes medio non aequore terras
interceptus habes, iusti ne demat honorem
nominis, exclusum si dividat insula flumen.
tu duplices sortite vias, et cum amne secundo
defluis, ut celeres feriant vada concita remi,   40
et cum per ripas nusquam cessante remulco

---

[1] *G* : speranti, *Vat.*: sperante, *RBL* : superante, *Hummel-berg* (which is perhaps preferable).
[2] *G* : preparare, *V* : reparare, *RB*.

of transparent day withholds not sight of the sun's pure rays and of the aether, dazzling to the eyes. Nay more, the whole gracious prospect made me behold a picture of my own native land, the smiling and well-tended country of Bordeaux—the roofs of country-houses, perched high upon the overhanging river-banks, the hill-sides green with vines, and the pleasant stream of Moselle gliding below with subdued murmuring.

[23] Hail, river, blessed by the fields, blessed by the husbandmen, to whom the Belgae owe the imperial honour which graces their city:[1] river, whose hills are o'ergrown with Bacchus' fragrant vines, o'ergrown, river most verdant, thy banks with turf: ship-bearing as the sea, with sloping waters gliding as a river, and with thy crystal depths the peer of lakes, brooks thou canst match for hurrying flow, cool springs surpass for limpid draughts; one, thou hast all that belongs to springs, brooks, rivers, lakes, and tidal Ocean with his ebb and flow. Thou, with calm waters onward gliding, feel'st not any murmurs of the wind nor check from hidden rocks; nor by foaming shallows art thou forced to hurry on in swirling rapids, no eyots hast thou jutting in mid-stream to thwart thy course—lest the glory of thy due title be impaired, if any isle sunder and stem thy flow. For thee two modes of voyaging are appointed: this, when boats move down thy stream with current favouring and their oars thrash the churned waters at full speed; that, when along the banks, with tow-rope never slackening, the boatmen

---

[1] sc. Augusta Treverorum (Trèves, Trier), the capital of Belgica Prima and an imperial residence from the days of Constantine to those of Gratian.

intendunt collo malorum vincula nautae.
ipse tuos quotiens miraris in amne recursus.
legitimosque putas prope segnius ire meatus?
tu neque limigenis ripam praetexeris ulvis,   45
nec piger inmundo perfundis litora caeno:
sicca in primores pergunt vestigia lymphas.

    I nunc, et Phrygiis sola levia consere crustis
tendens marmoreum laqueata per atria campum.
ast ego despectis, quae census opesque dederunt, 50
naturae mirabor opus, non dira nepotum
laetaque iacturis ubi luxuriatur egestas.
hic solidae sternunt umentia litora harenae,
nec retinent memores vestigia pressa figuras.

    Spectaris vitreo per levia terga profundo,   55
secreti nihil amnis habens: utque almus aperto
panditur intuitu [1] liquidis obtutibus aer
nec placidi prohibent oculos per inania venti,
sic demersa procul durante per intima visu
cernimus, arcanique patet penetrale profundi,   60
cum vada lene meant liquidarum et lapsus aquarum
prodit caerulea dispersas luce figuras:
quod sulcata levi crispatur harena meatu,
inclinata tremunt viridi quod gramina fundo:
usque sub ingenuis agitatae fontibus herbae   65
vibrantes patiuntur aquas lucetque latetque
calculus et viridem distinguit glarea muscum.
tota Caledoniis talis patet ora Britannis,
cum virides algas et rubra corallia nudat
aestus et albentes concharum germina bacas,   70
delicias hominum, locupletibus atque sub undis

---

[1] *MSS.*: introitu, *Peiper.*

strain on their shoulders hawsers bound to the masts. Thyself how often dost thou marvel at the windings of thine own stream, and think its natural speed moves almost too slowly! Thou with no mud-grown sedge fringest thy banks, nor with foul ooze o'erspread'st thy marge; dry is the treading down to thy water's edge.

⁴⁸ Go now, and with Phrygian slabs lay out smooth floors spreading an expanse of marble through thy fretted halls! But I, scorning what wealth and riches have bestowed, will marvel at Nature's handiwork, and not at that wherein ruin wantons, recklessly prodigal and delighting in her waste. Here firm sands spread the moist shores, and the foot resting on them leaves no recording print behind.

⁵⁵ Thou through thy smooth surface showest all the treasures of thy crystal depths—a river keeping naught concealed: and as the calm air lies clear and open to our gaze, and the stilled winds do not forbid the sight to travel through the void, so, if our gaze penetrates thy gulfs, we behold things whelmed far below, and the recesses of thy secret depth lie open, whenas thy flood moves softly and thy waters limpid-gliding reveal in azure light shapes scattered here and there: how the furrowed sand is rippled by the light current, how the bowed water-grasses quiver in thy green bed: down beneath their native streams the tossing plants endure the water's buffeting, pebbles gleam and are hid, and gravel picks out patches of green moss. As the whole Caledonian shore spreads open to the Briton's gaze, when ebbing tides lay bare green seaweed and red coral and whitening pearls, the seed of shells, man's gauds, and under the enriched

adsimulant nostros imitata monilia cultus:
haud aliter placidae subter vada laeta Mosellae
detegit admixtos non concolor herba lapillos.

Intentos tamen usque oculos errore fatigant   75
interludentes, examina lubrica, pisces.
sed neque tot species obliquatosque natatus
quaeque per adversum succedunt agmina flumen,
nominaque et cunctos numerosae stirpis alumnos
edere fas aut ille sinit, cui cura secundae   80
sortis et aequorei cessit tutela tridentis.
tu mihi flumineis habitatrix Nais in oris
squamigeri gregis ede choros liquidoque sub alveo
dissere caeruleo fluitantes amne catervas.

Squameus herbosas capito inter lucet harenas,   85
viscere praetenero fartim congestus aristis
nec duraturus post bina trihoria mensis,
purpureisque salar stellatus tergora guttis
et nullo spinae nociturus acumine rhedo
effugiensque oculos celeri levis umbra natatu.   90
tuque per obliqui fauces vexate Saravi,
qua bis terna fremunt scopulosis ostia pilis,
cum defluxisti famae maioris in amnem,
liberior laxos exerces, barbe, natatus:
tu melior peiore aevo, tibi contigit omni   95
spirantum ex numero non inlaudata senectus.

---

[1] *sc.* Neptune (Poseidon), who received the waters as his share in the universe (*cp.* Hom. *Hymn to Demeter*, 86), as Zeus received the upper air and Aidoneus the lower world.

waves mimic necklaces counterfeit our fashions; even
so beneath the glad waters of still Moselle weeds of
different hue reveal the pebbles scattered amidst
them.

[75] Howbeit, though fixed upon the depths, the
eyes grow weary with straying after fishes who in
slippery shoals sport midway between. But their
many kinds, their slanting course in swimming,
and those companies which ascend up against the
stream, their names, and all the offspring of their
countless tribe, it is not lawful for me to declare, nor
does he permit to whom passed the charge of the
second element[1] and the safe-keeping of the watery
trident. Do thou for me, O Nymph, dweller in the
river's realm, declare the hosts of the scaly herd,
and from the depths of thy watery bed discourse of
those throngs which glide in the azure stream.[2]

[85] The scaly Chub gleams amid the weeds that
deck the sands, of flesh most tender, full of close-set
bones, and destined to keep fit for the table but
twice three hours; the Trout, too, whose back is
starred with purple spots, the Roach without pointed
bones to do mischief, and the swift Grayling darting
out of sight with his swift stroke. And thou, who
after buffeting amid the gorges of crooked Saravus
(the Sarre, or Saar) where its mouth frets at twice
three craggy piers,[3] when thou hast been carried
down into a stream of greater note, O Barbel, dost
more freely ply an easy stroke: improving with
declining life, to thee alone of the whole number of
living things belongs an old age not unpraised.

[2] The list which follows is imitated, but at far less length,
by Pope, *Windsor Forest*, 132 ff.

[3] *sc.* of the Roman bridge Consarbrück, near the confluence
of the Saar and the Moselle.

AUSONIUS

Nec te puniceo rutilantem viscere, salmo,
transierim, latae cuius vaga verbera caudae
gurgite de medio summas referuntur in undas,
occultus placido cum proditur aequore pulsus.   100
tu loricato squamosus pectore, frontem
lubricus et dubiae facturus fercula cenae,
tempora longarum fers incorrupte morarum,
praesignis maculis capitis, cui prodiga nutat
alvus opimatoque fluens abdomine venter.   105
quaeque per Illyricum, per stagna binominis Histri
spumarum indiciis caperis, mustela, natantum,
in nostrum subvecta fretum, ne laeta Mosellae
flumina tam celebri defrudarentur alumno.
quis te naturae pinxit color! atra superne   110
puncta notant tergum, qua lutea circuit iris;
lubrica caeruleus perducit tergora fucus;
corporis ad medium fartim pinguescis, at illinc
usque sub extremam squalet cutis arida caudam.

Nec te, delicias mensarum, perca, silebo,   115
amnigenos inter pisces dignande marinis,
solus puniceis facilis contendere mullis:
nam neque gustus iners solidoque in corpore partes
segmentis coeunt, sed dissociantur aristis.
hic etiam Latio risus praenomine, cultor   120
stagnorum, querulis vis infestissima ranis,
lucius, obscuras ulva caenoque lacunas
obsidet.   hic nullos mensarum lectus ad usus
fervet fumosis olido nidore popinis.

---

¹ *sc.* a dinner at which the guest does not know which
dish to prefer above another.   See Ter. *Phormio*, ii. 2.

THE MOSELLE

[97] Nor shall I pass thee by, O Salmon, with flesh of rosy red, the random strokes of whose broad tail from the mid-depths are reproduced upon the surface, when the still water's face betrays thy hidden course. Thou, with breastplate of scales, in the fore-part smooth, and destined to form a course at some "doubtful dinner,"[1] endurest untainted through seasons of long delay—thou distinguished by the markings of thy head, whose generous paunch sways and whose belly droops with rolls of fat. And thou, the Eel-pout, who o'er Illyricum, o'er the marshes of twice-named[2] Ister art betrayed and taken through tell-tale streaks of floating foam, hast been carried to our waters lest the glad streams of Moselle should be cheated of so famed a fosterling. With what colours has Nature painted thee! Above, dark spots pick out thy back, and rings of saffron surround them; azure hue continues the length of thy sleek back; up to the middle of thy length thou art full-fleshed and fat, but from there right on to thy tail's tip, thy skin is rough and dry.

[115] Neither shalt thou, O Perch, the dainty of our tables, be unsung—thou amongst fishes river-born worthy to be ranked with the sea-bred, who alone canst vie on equal terms with the rosy mullet; for not insipid is thy flavour, and in thy plump body the parts meet as segments, but are kept apart by the backbone. Here, too, doth he, jestingly known by a Latin proper name—that dweller in the marshes, most deadly enemy to plaintive frogs—Lucius (the Pike), beset pools dim with sedge and ooze: he, chosen for no service at banquets, is fried in cook-shops rank with the fumes of his greasy flavour.

[2] The Ister is also the Danube.

Quis non et virides, vulgi solacia, tincas   125
norit et alburnos, praedam puerilibus hamis,
stridentesque focis, obsonia plebis, alausas ?
teque inter species geminas neutrumque et utrumque,
qui nec dum salmo, nec iam salar ambiguusque
amborum medio, sario, intercepte sub aevo ?   130
tu quoque flumineas inter memorande cohortes,
gobio, non geminis maior sine pollice palmis,
praepinguis, teres, ovipara congestior alvo
propexique iubas imitatus, gobio, barbi.
    Nunc, pecus aequoreum, celebrabere, magne silure:
quem velut Actaeo perductum tergora olivo   136
amnicolam delphina reor : sic per freta magnum
laberis et longi vix corporis agmina solvis
aut brevibus deprensa vadis aut fluminis ulvis.
at cum tranquillos moliris in amne meatus,   140
te virides ripae, te caerula turba natantum,
te liquidae mirantur aquae : diffunditur alveo
aestus et extremi procurrunt margine fluctus.
talis Atlantiaco quondam ballena profundo,
cum vento motuve suo telluris ad oras   145
pellitur : exclusum exundat mare magnaque surgunt
aequora vicinique timent decrescere montes.
hic tamen, hic nostrae mitis ballena Mosellae
exitio procul est magnoque honor additus amni.
    Iam liquidas spectasse vias et lubrica pisces   150
agmina multiplicesque satis numerasse catervas.
inducant aliam spectacula vitea pompam
sollicitentque vagos Baccheia munera visus,

[125] Who shall not know of the green Tench also, the comfort of the commons, of Bleak, a prey for boyish hooks, of Shad, hissing on the hearth, food for the vulgar, and of thee, something between two species, who art neither and yet both, not yet salmon, no longer trout, and undefined betwixt these twain, art caught midway in thy life? Thou also must be mentioned amid the battalions of the stream, Gudgeon, no longer than the width of two palms without the thumbs, full-fat, rounded, and yet more bulky when thy belly teems with spawn—Gudgeon, who art bearded like the tufted barbel.

[135] Now, creature of the surface, shall thy praise be sung, O mighty Sheat-fish, whom, with back glistening as though with olive-oil of Attica,[1] I look on as a dolphin of the river—so mightily thou glidest through the waters and canst scarce extend thy trailing body to its full length, hampered by shallows or by river-weeds. But when thou urgest thy peaceful course in the stream, at thee the green banks marvel, at thee the azure throng of the finny tribe, at thee the limpid waters: in the channel a tide is rolled abroad on either hand, and the ends of the waves drive onward at the marge. So, when at times on the Atlantic deep a whale by wind or his own motion is driven to the verge of land, the sea displaced o'erflows, great waters rise, and neighbouring mountains fear to lose their height. Yet this—this gentle whale of our Moselle is far from havoc and brings glory to the mighty stream.

[150] Now 'tis enough to have viewed the watery paths and to have told o'er the fishes in their glistening hosts and legions manifold. Let show of vines lead on another pageant, and let Bacchus' gifts attract

qua sublimis apex longo super ardua tractu
et rupes et aprica iugi flexusque sinusque   155
vitibus adsurgunt naturalique theatro.
Gauranum sic alma iugum vindemia vestit
et Rhodopen proprioque nitent Pangaea Lyaeo;
sic viret Ismarius super aequora Thracia collis;
sic mea flaventem pingunt vineta Garumnam.   160
summis quippe iugis tendentis in ultima clivi
conseritur viridi fluvialis margo Lyaeo.
laeta operum plebes festinantesque coloni
vertice nunc summo properant, nunc deiuge dorso,
certantes stolidis clamoribus. inde viator   165
riparum subiecta terens, hinc navita labens,
probra canunt seris cultoribus: adstrepit ollis
et rupes et silva tremens et concavus amnis.

  Nec solos homines delectat scaena locorum:
hic ego et agrestes Satyros et glauca tuentes   170
Naidas extremis credam concurrere ripis,
capripedes agitat cum laeta protervia Panas
insultantque vadis trepidasque sub amne sorores
terrent, indocili pulsantes verbere fluctum.
saepe etiam mediis furata e collibus uvas   175
inter Oreiadas Panope fluvialis amicas
fugit lascivos paganica numina Faunos.
dicitur et, medio cum sol stetit igneus orbe,
ad commune fretum Satyros vitreasque sorores

---

[1] Now Monte Barbaro, in Campania.
[2] In Thrace: now Despoto Dagh.

our wandering gaze where lofty ridge, far-stretching
above scarped slopes, and spur, and sunny hill-side
with salient and reëntrant rise in a natural theatre
overgrown with vines. So does the gracious vintage
clothe the ridge of Gaurus[1] and Rhodope,[2] and so
Lyaeus decks the Pangaean hills,[3] his chosen haunt;
so Ismarus raises his green slopes above the Thracian
sea; so do my own vineyards cast their reflection on
the yellowing Garonne. For from the topmost ridge
to the foot of the slope the river-side is thickly
planted with green vines. The people, happy in
their toil, and the restless husbandmen are busy,
now on the hill-top, now on the slope, exchanging
shouts in boisterous rivalry. Here the wayfarer
tramping along the low-lying bank, and there the
bargeman floating by, troll their rude jests at the
loitering vine-dressers; and all the hills, and shiver-
ing woods, and channelled river, ring with their
cries.

[169] Nor does the scenery of this region please men
alone; I can believe that here the rustic Satyrs and
the grey-eyed Nymphs meet together on the border
of the stream, when the goat-footed Pans are seized
with merry ribaldry, and splashing in the shallows,
frighten the trembling sister-nymphs beneath the
stream, while they thresh the water with unskilful
strokes. Oft also, when she has stolen clusters
from the inland hills, Panope, the river lady, with a
troop of Oread friends, flees the wanton Fauns, gods
of the country-side. And it is said that when the
sun's fiery orb stops in the midst of his course,
the Satyrs and the sister-Nymphs of the crystal

---

[3] On the border-line between Thrace and Macedonia : now
Pilaf Tepeh.

consortes celebrare choros, cum praebuit horas   180
secretas hominum coetu flagrantior aestus.
tunc insultantes sua per freta ludere Nymphas
et Satyros mersare vadis rudibusque natandi
per medias exire manus, dum lubrica falsi
membra petunt liquidosque fovent pro corpore fluctus.
sed non haec spectata ulli nec cognita visu   186
fas mihi sit pro parte loqui : secreta tegatur
et commissa suis lateat reverentia rivis.

   Illa fruenda palam species, cum glaucus opaco
respondet colli fluvius, frondere videntur   190
fluminei latices et palmite consitus amnis.
quis color ille vadis, seras cum propulit umbras
Hesperus et viridi perfundit monte Mosellam !
tota natant crispis iuga motibus et tremit absens
pampinus et vitreis vindemia turget in undis.   195
adnumerat virides derisus navita vites,
navita caudiceo fluitans super aequora lembo
per medium, qua sese amni confundit imago
collis et umbrarum confinia conserit amnis.

   Haec quoque quam dulces celebrant spectacula
     pompas,   200
remipedes medio certant cum flumine lembi

---

[1] This passage is imitated by Pope in his description of
the Loddon :

   "Oft in her glass the musing shepherd spies
     The headlong mountains and the downward skies,

depths meet here beside the stream and ply the dance in partnership, what time the fiercer heat affords them hours set free from mortal company. Then, wantonly frolicking amid their native waters, the Nymphs duck the Satyrs in the waves, and slip away right through the hands of those unskilful swimmers, as, baffled, they seek to grasp their slippery limbs and, instead of bodies, embrace yielding waves. But of these things which no man has looked upon and no eye beheld, be it no sin for me to speak in part : let things secret be kept hid, and let Reverence dwell unspied upon, in the safe-keeping of her native streams.

[189] Yon is a sight that may be freely enjoyed : when the azure river mirrors the shady hill,[1] the waters of the stream seem to bear leaves and the flood to be all o'ergrown with shoots of vines. What a hue is on the waters when Hesperus has driven forward the lagging shadows and o'erspreads Moselle with the green of the reflected height ! Whole hills float on the shivering ripples : here quivers the far-off tendril of the vine, here in the glassy flood swells the full cluster. The deluded boatman tells o'er the green vines—the boatman whose skiff of bark floats on the watery floor out in mid-stream, where the pictured hill blends with the river and where the river joins with the edges of the shadows.

[200] And when oared skiffs join in mimic battle in mid-stream, how pleasing is the pageant which this

> The wat'ry landscape of the pendent woods,
> *And absent trees that tremble in the floods* ;
> In the clear, azure gleam the flocks are seen,
> And floating forests paint the waves with green."
> *Windsor Forest,* 211 ff.

et varios meunt flexus viridesque per oras
stringunt attonsis pubentia germina pratis!
puppibus et proris alacres gestire magistros
impubemque manum super amnica terga vagantem 205
dum spectat [viridis qua surgit ripa colonus,
non sentit [1]] transire diem, sua seria ludo
posthabet [2]; excludit veteres nova gratia curas.
quales Cumano despectat in aequore ludos
Liber, sulphurei cum per iuga consita Gauri
perque vaporiferi graditur vineta Vesevi,   210
cum Venus Actiacis Augusti laeta triumphis
ludere lascivos fera proelia iussit Amores,
qualia Niliacae classes Latiaeque triremes
subter Apollineae gesserunt Leucados arces;
aut Pompeiani Mylasena pericula belli   215
Euboicae referunt per Averna sonantia cumbae;
innocuos ratium pulsus pugnasque iocantes
naumachiae Siculo quales spectante Peloro
caeruleus viridi reparat sub imagine pontus:
non aliam speciem petulantibus addit ephebis   220
pubertasque amnis et picti rostra phaseli.
hos Hyperionio cum sol perfuderit aestu,
reddit nautales vitreo sub gurgite formas
et redigit pandas inversi corporis umbras.
utque agiles motus dextra laevaque frequentant   225

---

[1] Suppl. *Böcking*.
[2] *cp.* Virgil, *Ecl.* vii. 17 : posthabui . . . mea seria ludo.

---

[1] *i.e.* the Temple of Apollo at Actium, where the Egyptian
fleet of Antony and Cleopatra was defeated by Augustus
(B.C. 31).
[2] *i.e.* Cumaean, Cumae being a colony of Euboea.
[3] *Mylasena . . . pericula* should strictly mean a battle off
Mylasa (on the coast of Caria); but there is no doubt that
the reference is to the action off Mylae, where Agrippa

sight affords ! They circle in and out, and graze the
sprouting blades of the cropped turf along the green
banks. The husbandman, standing upon the rise of
the green bank, watches the light-hearted owners as
they leap about on stern or prow, the boyish crew
straggling over the river's wide expanse, and never
feels the day is slipping by, but puts their play before
his business, while present pleasure shuts out whilom
cares. As those games which Liber beholds on the
Cumaean tide, whenas he walks abroad over the
planted hills of reeking Gaurus, or passes through
the vineyards of smoke-plumed Vesuvius, when Venus,
glad at Augustus' victory of Actium, bade the pert
Loves enact in mimicry such fierce combats as the
navies of the Nile and Roman triremes waged below
Leucas and Apollo's hold ; [1] or as when Euboean [2]
barks repeat upon the waters of echoing Avernus the
hazards of the strife at Mylae in the Pompeian War ; [3]
or as the harmless onsets of boats and playful battles
of the *naumachia* which the dark sea repeats in his
green imagery while Sicilian Pelorus [4] looks down ;—
such the appearance which youth, river, skiffs with
painted prows, lend to these merry lads. But when
Hyperion pours down the sun's full heat, the crystal
flood reflects sailor-shapes and throws back crooked
pictures of their downward forms.[5] And as they ply
their nimble strokes with the right hand and the left,

defeated Dinochares, the admiral of Sextus Pompeius
(B.C. 36).

[4] Now Capo di Faro at the N.E. extremity of Sicily.

[5] *Pandas . . . umbras* are probably the distorted reflections
seen on a rippled surface, or possibly shadows foreshortened
owing to the height of the sun in the heavens. For *inversi
corporis, cp.* Pope's " The headlong mountains and the down-
ward skies " (*Windsor Forest*, 212).

et commutatis alternant pondera remis,
unda refert alios simulacra umentia nautas.
ipsa suo gaudet simulamine nautica pubes,
fallaces fluvio mirata redire figuras.
sic, ubi compositos ostentatura capillos   230
(candentem late speculi explorantis honorem
cum primum carae nutrix admovit alumnae)
laeta ignorato fruitur virguncula ludo
germanaeque putat formam spectare puellae :
oscula fulgenti dat non referenda metallo   235
aut fixas praetemptat acus aut frontis ad oram
vibratos captat digitis extendere crines :
talis ad umbrarum ludibria nautica pubes
ambiguis fruitur veri falsique figuris.

Iam vero accessus faciles qua ripa ministrat,   240
scrutatur toto populatrix turba profundo
heu male defensos penetrali flumine pisces.
hic medio procul amne trahens umentia lina
nodosis decepta plagis examina verrit ;
ast hic, tranquillo qua labitur agmine flumen,   245
ducit corticeis fluitantia retia signis ;
ille autem scopulis deiectas pronus in undas
inclinat lentae convexa cacumina virgae,
inductos escis iaciens letalibus hamos.
quos ignara doli postquam vaga turba natantum   250
rictibus invasit patulaeque per intima fauces
sera occultati senserunt vulnera ferri,
dum trepidant, subit indicium crispoque tremori
vibrantis saetae nutans consentit harundo,
nec mora et excussam stridenti verbere praedam   255
dexter in obliquum raptat puer ; excipit ictum

and throwing their weight in turn now upon this oar, now upon that, the wave reflects a watery semblance of sailors to match them. The boys themselves delight in their own counterfeits, wondering at the illusive forms which the river gives back. Thus, when hoping soon to display her braided tresses ('tis when the nurse has first placed near her dear charge the wide-gleaming glory of the searching mirror), delighted, the little maid enjoys the uncomprehended game, deeming she gazes on the shape of a real girl: she showers on the shining metal kisses not to be returned, or essays those firm-fixed hairpins, or puts her fingers to that brow, trying to draw out those curled locks; even so, at sight of the reflections which mock them, the lads afloat amuse themselves with shapes which waver between false and true.

240 Now, where the bank supplies easy approaches, a devastating throng ransacks all the depths for fish ill-sheltered — alack! — by the river's sanctuary. This man far out in mid-stream trails dripping nets and sweeps up shoals of fish, snared in the knotty folds; but this, where the river glides with peaceful flood, draws his seins, buoyed up with floats of cork; while yonder on the rocks one leans over the waters which flow beneath, and lets droop the curved tip of his pliant rod, casting hooks baited with deadly food. All unsuspecting, the wandering finny tribe rush upon them agape; and when — too late!—their opened gullets feel the concealed barbs pierce deep within, they struggle, and their struggles are betrayed above, when the wand bends in response to the tremulous vibrations of the quivering line. Straightway the boy skilfully whisks his prey from the water, swinging it sidelong with a whistling stroke: a hissing

spiritus, ut raptis quondam per inane flagellis
aura crepat motoque adsibilat aere ventus.
exultant udae super arida saxa rapinae
luciferique pavent letalia tela diei.   260
cuique sub amne suo mansit vigor, aere nostro
segnis anhelatis vitam consumit in auris.
iam piger invalido vibratur corpore plausus,
torpida supremos patitur iam cauda tremores
nec coeunt rictus, haustas sed hiatibus auras   265
reddit mortiferos expirans branchia flatus.
sic, ubi fabriles exercet spiritus ignes,
accipit alterno cohibetque foramine ventos
lanea fagineis adludens parma cavernis.
vidi egomet quosdam leti sub fine trementes   270
collegisse animas, mox in sublime citatos
cernua subiectum praeceps dare corpora in amnem,
desperatarum potientes rursus aquarum.
quos impos damni puer inconsultus ab alto
impetit et stolido captat prensare natatu.   275
sic Anthedonius Boeotia per freta Glaucus,
gramina gustatu postquam exitialia Circes
expertus carptas moribundis piscibus herbas
sumpsit, Carpathium subiit novus accola pontum.
ille hamis et rete potens, scrutator operti   280
Nereos, aequoream solitus converrere Tethyn,
inter captivas fluitavit praedo catervas.

    Talia despectant longo per caerula tractu
pendentes saxis instanti culmine villae,

follows on the blow, even as the breeze whines and
whistles when sometimes a scourge is whirled through
empty space and disturbs the air. The dripping
catch flounders on the parched rocks and quakes at
the deadly shafts of light-bringing day. Beneath
his native waters, his strength endured : enfeebled by
our atmosphere his life wastes away in the air he
gasps. Now his weakening body quivers with feeble
beats, now his nerveless tail endures its last throbs :
his gaping mouth no longer closes : his panting gills
give back the air they have drained and blow forth
the death-dealing breath of day. Even so, when the
blast fans a smithy-fire, the valve of wool which plays
in the hollow of the beechen bellows alternately
sucks in and confines the winds now by this hole,
now by that. I myself have seen fish, already quiver-
ing in the throes of death, summon up their last gasp
and, leaping high into the air, cast themselves with a
somersault into the river beneath, gaining once more
the waters which they never looked to find again.
Thereat, impatient at his loss, the lad impetuously
plunges in from on high, seeking—poor fool—to
catch them as he swims. So Glaucus of Anthedon,
the fisher of the Boeotian sea, having tasted Circe's
deadly herbs, when he had plucked those plants
cropped by his dying fish,[1] plunged into the Carpathian
sea, there to find a new home : that fisherman, so
skilful with his hooks and nets, who ransacked Nereus'
hidden depths and swept the surface which is Tethys'
realm—that spoiler tossed on the waves amid the
shoals he once took captive.

[283] Such sights unfold themselves along the azure
reaches of the river in sight of country seats which

[1] The story is told by Ovid, *Metam.* xiii. 917 ff.

quas medius dirimit sinuosis flexibus errans   285
amnis, et alternas comunt praetoria ripas.

    Quis modo Sestiacum pelagus, Nepheleidos Helles
aequor, Abydeni freta quis miretur ephebi?
quis Chalcedonio constratum ab litore pontum,
regis opus magni, mediis euripus ubi undis   290
Europaeque Asiaeque vetat concurrere terras?
non hic dira freti rabies, non saeva furentum
proelia caurorum; licet hic commercia linguae
iungere et alterno sermonem texere pulsu.
blanda salutiferas permiscent litora voces,   295
et voces et paene manus: resonantia utrimque
verba refert mediis concurrens fluctibus echo.

    Quis potis innumeros cultusque habitusque retexens
pandere tectonicas per singula praedia formas?
non hoc spernat opus Gortynius aliger, aedis   300
conditor Euboicae, casus quem fingere in auro
conantem Icarios patrii pepulere dolores:
non Philo Cecropius, non qui laudatus ab hoste
clara Syracosii traxit certamina belli.
forsan et insignes hominumque operumque labores 305

---

[1] *sc.* Xerxes: see Herodotus vii. 33 ff.

[2] Euripus, primarily the name of the narrow channel be-
tween Euboea and Bœotia, came to be used as a common
noun denoting any narrow water channel. According to
Cicero (*de Leg.* II. i. 2) aqueducts were so called; and Auso-
nius so uses the word in *Ordo Nobilium Urbium*, **xx.** 21.

[3] The reference is to Daedalus: *cp.* Virgil, *Aen.* **vi.** 12–33,
a passage closely imitated here.

perched on the toppling summits of the rocks, are
parted by the stream wandering on midways with
winding curves, while lordly halls grace either bank.

287 Who now can marvel at the waters on which
Sestos looks down—that sea named after Helle,
daughter of Nephela; who at the waves, once bridged
across from the Chalcedonian shore—a labour of the
Great King [1]—where the Channel [2] with intervening
waves forbids the lands of Europe and of Asia to
clash together? Here is not the dread fury of that
strait, not the wild turmoil of its north-western gales;
here two may link interchanging speech, and weave
discourse with alternating waves of sound. The
kindly shores intermingle cries of greeting—cries and
almost the grip of hands: words which resound from
either side Echo returns, speeding with them o'er
the intervening waves.

298 Who has the skill to unfold the countless
embellishments and forms, and to display the
architectural beauties of each demesne? Such work
the flying man of Gortyn would not scorn—he who
built that temple at Euboean Cumae and, essaying to
reproduce in gold the fate of Icarus, was thwarted by
a father's grief; [3] nor Philo of Athens; [4] nor yet he
who won admiration from his foe by the devices with
which he prolonged the famed struggles of besieged
Syracuse.[5] Perchance, too, even that company of
Seven Architects, whose praise is told in Marcus'

---

[4] Philo (c. 300 B.C.) designed the great arsenal at Athens
and the portico of the temple at Eleusis.

[5] sc. Archimedes, who by his mechanical devices enabled
Syracuse to hold out against its Roman besiegers. Marcellus,
the Roman general, was so struck by his genius that he
gave orders that Archimedes should be spared, when the city
was stormed in 212 B.C. cp. Pliny, N.H. vii. 37.

AUSONIUS

hic habuit decimo celebrata volumine Marcei
hebdomas, hic clari viguere Menecratis artes
atque Ephesi spectata manus vel in arce Minervae
Ictinus, magico cui noctua perlita fuco
adlicit omne genus volucres perimitque tuendo.   310
conditor hic forsan fuerit Ptolomaidos aulae
Dinochares, quadrata cui in fastigia cono
surgit et ipsa suas consumit pyramis umbras,
iussus ob incesti qui quondam foedus amoris
Arsinoen Pharii suspendit in aere templi.   315
spirat enim tecti testudine virus achates
adflatamque trahit ferrato crine puellam.

Hos ergo aut horum similes est credere dignum
Belgarum in terris scaenas posuisse domorum,
molitos celsas fluvii decoramina villas.   320
haec est natura sublimis in aggere saxi,

---

¹ Marcus Terentius Varro produced between *c.* 60–40 B.C.
a work in fifteen volumes (one introductory), known as
Imagines or *Hebdomades*. It contained portraits and brief
notices of nearly seven hundred famous personages, Romans
and foreigners. The title *Hebdomades* was due to the plan
of the actual work which consisted of fourteen volumes (or
two *hebdomades*), and each volume of seven groups of seven
personages each. Apparently one such group was devoted
to the seven greatest architects.

² No famous architect of this name is known. It is pro-
bable that Ausonius has unconsciously or deliberately sub-
stituted this name for the metrically impossible Metagenes,
who with his father Chersiphron, or Ctesiphon, built the
fourth-century temple of Artemis at Ephesus.

³ *sc.* Chersiphron (or Ctesiphon) : see preceding note.

⁴ Ictinus was the architect of the Parthenon. Nothing
further is known of the remarkable owl, which seems to have
been furnished with eyes so lifelike as to fascinate the birds.

tenth volume,[1] produced these marvellous works of
human hands; perchance here flourished the craft
of renowned Menecrates,[2] and that skill [3] which draws
all eyes at Ephesus, or the genius of Ictinus [4] displayed
in Minerva's citadel, where is that owl painted with
colours of such magic power as to lure to it fowls of
all kinds and to destroy them by its stare. Here also
may have been the designer of Ptolemy's palace,
Dinochares, builder of the pyramid which towers up,
foursided, to a point and itself devours its own shadow[5]
—he who, when bidden to commemorate Arsinoë,
the incestuous bride,[6] poised her image in mid-air
beneath the roof of her Pharian temple. For from
the vaulted roof a load-stone sheds its influence and
by its attraction draws the young queen towards it
by her iron-wrought hair.[7]

318 These, then, or such as these, we may well
believe to have raised these splendid dwellings in the
Belgic land, and to have piled these lofty mansions
to be the river's ornament. This one stands high
upon a mass of natural rock, this rests upon the

---

[5] Ammianus Marcellinus (XXII. xv. 29) describes a pyramid
as dwindling away like a flame (hence the name) to a point
(*in conum*), and explains that owing to the ratio of the height
to the base a pyramid "devours its shadows" (*umbras . . .
consumit*). When the sun is at a certain altitude above the
horizon, the shadow cast by the apex of a pyramid does, in
fact, fall within the area of its base.

[6] Arsinoë was sister and wife of Ptolemy II. Philadelphus.

[7] Dinochares planned the city of Alexandria (Pliny, *N.H.*
vii. 125): with him Ausonius has confused Timochares who
commenced, but did not complete, the Temple of Arsinoë
(*ib.* xxxiv. 148). Rufinus asserts that a figure of the Sun,
similarly poised, existed in the Serapeum at Alexandria at
the time of its destruction in 391 A.D. A similar figure of
Mercury is alleged to have been one of the wonders at Trèves,
and may have prompted this reference. No doubt such
figures were really suspended by a fine wire.

haec procurrentis fundata crepidine ripae,
haec refugit captumque sinu sibi vindicat amnem.
illa tenens collem, qui plurimus imminet amni,
usurpat faciles per culta, per aspera visus   325
utque suis fruitur dives speculatio terris.
quin etiam riguis humili pede condita pratis
compensat celsi bona naturalia montis
sublimique minans irrumpit in aethera tecto,
ostentans altam, Pharos ut Memphitica, turrim.   330
huic proprium clausos consaepto gurgite pisces
apricas scopulorum inter captare novales.
haec summis innixa iugis labentia subter
flumina despectu iam caligante tuetur.
atria quid memorem viridantibus adsita pratis?   335
innumerisque super nitentia tecta columnis?
quid quae fluminea substructa crepidine fumant
balnea, ferventi cum Mulciber haustus operto
volvit anhelatas tectoria per cava flammas,
inclusum glomerans aestu spirante vaporem?   340
vidi ego defessos multo sudore lavacri
fastidisse lacus et frigora piscinarum,
ut vivis fruerentur aquis, mox amne refotos
plaudenti gelidum flumen pepulisse natatu.

---

¹ i e. a weir is formed by blocking the spaces between the
rocks, into which fish are swept by the stream.
² The villa standing high up on the ridge which bounds
the valley looks down (despectu) upon the river, but at such
a distance that the view is slightly obscured (iam caligante)
with the haze natural to a river-valley.
³ Ausonius here refers to the system of hypocausts, with
connected flue-tiles let into the thickness of the walls, by
which Roman houses and baths were heated.

verge of the jutting bank, this stands back and claims
the river for its own, making it prisoner in an enfolding
bay. Yon occupies a hill whose bulk looms high
above the stream, claiming free prospect o'er tilth,
o'er waste, and the rich outlook enjoys the lands
about as though its own. Nay, and another, though
it rests its foot low down in the well-watered
meadows, makes up the natural advantage of a
mountain's height rearing its threatening steep until
the soaring roof breaks in upon the aether, display-
ing like Memphian Pharos, its lofty tower. This
has for its own the catching of fish imprisoned in
the fenced flood between the sunny, grass-grown
rocks ;[1] this, perched upon the ridge's topmost
crest, looks down with prospect just bedimmed in
haze [2] upon the stream which slides below. What
need to make mention of their courts set beside
verdant meadows, of their trim roofs resting upon
countless pillars ? What of their baths, contrived
low down on the verge of the bank, which smoke
when Vulcan, drawn by the glowing flue, pants
forth his flames and whirls them up through the
channelled walls,[3] rolling in masses the imprisoned
smoke before the scorching blast ! I myself have
seen some, exhausted by the intense heat of the baths,
scorn the pools and cold plunge-baths,[4] preferring to
enjoy running water, and, straightway refreshed by
the river, buffet the cool stream, threshing it with

[4] The reference in ll. 341–2 is to the three main divisions
in a Roman bathing establishment. The first (*tepidarium*)
was a room warmed by hot air to induce perspiration : in
the second (*caldarium*), a hot bath was taken. The swimmers
here mentioned refused the usual plunge into the basin of
cold water in the third division (*frigidarium*), preferring
running water.

quod si Cumanis huc adforet hospes ab oris,   345
crederet Euboicas simulacra exilia Baias
his donasse locis: tantus cultusque nitorque
adlicit et nullum parit oblectatio luxum.

  Sed mihi qui tandem finis tua glauca fluenta
dicere dignandumque mari memorare Mosellam, 350
innumeri quod te diversa per ostia late
incurrunt amnes? quamquam differre meatus
possent, sed celerant in te consumere nomen.
namque et Promeae Nemesaeque adiuta meatu
Sura tuas properat non degener ire sub undas,   355
Sura interceptis tibi gratificata fluentis,
nobilius permixta tuo sub nomine, quam si
ignoranda patri confunderet ostia Ponto.
te rapidus Celbis, te marmore clarus Erubris
festinant famulis quam primum adlambere lymphis:
nobilibus Celbis celebratus piscibus, ille   361
praecipiti torquens cerealia saxa rotatu
stridentesque trahens per levia marmora serras
audit perpetuos ripa ex utraque tumultus.
praetereo exilem Lesuram tenuemque Drahonum 365
nec fastiditos Salmonae usurpo fluores:
naviger undisona dudum me mole Saravus
tota veste vocat, longum qui distulit amnem,
fessa sub Augustis ut volveret ostia muris.

---

[1] *cp.* Statius, *Silv.* I. iii. 73: *vitreasque natatu Plaudit aquas.*   [2] *cp.* Statius, *Silv.* I. v. 60.
[3] The Sauer, into which fall the Prüm (Promea) and the Nims (Nemesa).
[4] The Kyll and the Ruwar.

their strokes.[1]   But if a stranger were to arrive here
from the shores of Cumae,[2] he would believe that
Euboean Baiae had bestowed on this region a minia-
ture copy of its own delights : so great is the charm
of its refinement and distinction, while its pleasures
breed no excess.

[349] But how can I ever end the theme of thy
azure tributaries, or tell all thy praises, O Moselle,
comparable with the sea for the countless streams
which throughout thy length flow into thee through
various mouths ?   Though they might prolong their
courses, yet they haste to lose their names in thee.
For, albeit swelled by the waters of Promea and
Nemesa, Sura,[3] no weakling stream, hurries to plunge
beneath thy waves—Sura, who delights thee with
the affluents she has cut off, and who enjoys ampler
renown when wholly merged in thee and bearing thy
name than if she blended with Father Ocean an
outfall unworthy fame.   Thee swift Celbis, thee
Erubris,[4] famed for marble, hasten full eagerly to
approach with their attendant waters : renowned is
Celbis for glorious fish, and that other, as he turns
his mill-stones in furious revolutions and drives the
shrieking saws through smooth blocks of marble,[5]
hears from either bank a ceaseless din.   I pass by
feeble Lesura and scanty Drahonus, nor turn to use
Salmona's despised rivulet :[6] long has Saravus,[7] bearing
ships upon the volume of his sounding waves, been
calling me with all his robe outspread :[8] far has he
prolonged his stream that he might roll his wearied

[5] cp. Pliny, N.H. xxxvi. 159.

[6] The Lieser, the Thron, and the Salm.   [7] The Saar.

[8] tota veste vocat is a loan (unfelicitously employed) from
Virgil, Aen. viii. 712 : Nilum Pandentemque sinus et tota
veste vocantem Caeruleum in gremium.

nec minor hoc, tacitum qui per sola pinguia labens 370
stringit frugiferas felix Alisontia ripas.
mille alii, prout quemque suus magis impetus urget,
esse tui cupiunt: tantus properantibus undis
ambitus aut mores.   quod si tibi, dia Mosella,
Smyrna suum vatem vel Mantua clara dedisset,   375
cederet Iliacis Simois memoratus in oris
nec praeferre suos auderet Thybris honores.
da veniam, da, Roma potens! pulsa, oro, facessat
invidia et Latiae Nemesis non cognita linguae:
[contigit haec melior, Thybris, tibi gloria, quod
        tu[1]]
                                                            379A
imperii sedem Romaeque tuere penates.[2]   380
    Salve, magne parens frugumque virumque, Mosella!
te clari proceres, te bello exercita pubes,
aemula te Latiae decorat facundia linguae.
quin etiam mores et laetum fronte serena
ingenium natura tuis concessit alumnis.   385
nec sola antiquos ostentat Roma Catones,
aut unus tantum iusti spectator et aequi
pollet Aristides veteresque inlustrat Athenas.
    Verum ego quid laxis nimium spatiatus habenis
victus amore tui praeconia detero? conde,   390
Musa, chelyn, pulsis extremo carmine netis.
tempus erit, cum me studiis ignobilis oti
mulcentem curas seniique aprica foventem
materiae commendet honos; cum facta viritim

---

[1] Suppl. *Translator.*
[2] *Translator*: Romaeque tuere parentes, *P*[3]: Romae tenuere
parentes, *Peiper* (with other MSS.).

---

[1] The reference cannot be to Trèves, which lies some six
miles from the mouth of the Saar: probably an imperial
residence situated at Saarbrücken is indicated.

outfall beneath imperial walls.[1]　No whit beneath
him is blest Alisontia [2] who laps fruit-laden banks as
he glides silently through rich corn-lands.　A
thousand others, according to the vehemence of each
which drives him on, long to become thine : such is
the ambition of these hurrying streams or such their
character.　But if to thee, O divine Moselle, Smyrna
or famed Mantua had given its own poet,[3] then would
Simoïs, renowned on Ilium's coasts, yield place, and
Tiber would not dare to set his glories above thine.
Pardon, O pardon me, mighty Rome !　Rebuffed—I
pray—let Envy withdraw, and Nemesis who knows
no Latin name !　To thee, O Tiber, belongs this
higher praise, that thou dost guard the seat of empire
and the homes of Rome.

[381] Hail, mighty mother both of fruits and men '
Thy illustrious nobles, thy youth trained to war, thy
eloquence which vies with the tongues of Rome—
these are thy glories, O Moselle !　And withal, Nature
has bestowed upon thy sons virtue and a blithe spirit
with unclouded brows.　Not Rome alone vaunts her
old-time Catos, nor does Aristides stand alone as the
one only critic of Justice and of Right.

[389] But why, coursing along too freely with loose
rein, do I, o'ercome with love, wear out thy praises ? [4]
Put by the lyre, my Muse, striking the last chords
which end thy song !　The time shall come when,
as I soothe my sorrows and cherish age that loves
sunny nooks with the pursuits of inglorious ease,[5]
the glory of my theme shall commend me, when to
their glory and renown I shall sing the achievements

---

[2] The Elz.　　　[3] sc. either Homer or Virgil.
[4] cp. Hor. *Carm.* I. vi. 12 : *laudes egregii Caesaris et tuas
Culpa deterere ingeni.*
[5] i.e. with non-epic poetry : cp. Virgil, *Georg.* iv. 564.

Belgarum patriosque canam decora inclita mores: 395
mollia subtili nebunt mihi carmina filo
Pierides tenuique aptas subtemine telas
percurrent: dabitur nostris quoque purpura fusis.
quis mihi tum non dictus erit? memorabo quietos
agricolas legumque catos fandique potentes,   400
praesidium sublime reis; quos curia summos
municipum vidit proceres propriumque senatum,
quos praetextati celebris facundia ludi
contulit ad veteris praeconia Quintiliani,
quique suas rexere urbes purumque tribunal   405
sanguine et innocuas inlustravere secures;
aut Italum populos aquilonigenasque Britannos
praefecturarum titulo tenuere secundo;
quique caput rerum Romam, populumque patresque,
tantum non primo rexit sub nomine, quamvis   410
par fuerit primis: festinet solvere tandem
errorem Fortuna suum libataque supplens
praemia iam veri fastigia reddat honoris
nobilibus repetenda nepotibus.   at modo coeptum
detexatur opus, dilata et laude virorum   415
dicamus laeto per rura virentia tractu
felicem fluvium Rhenique sacremus in undas.

   Caeruleos nunc, Rhene, sinus hyaloque virentem
pande peplum spatiumque novi metare fluenti

---

[1] The reference is not (as sometimes stated) to the *Professores* and *Parentalia*, since these deal with people of Aquitaine. No doubt Ausonius planned but did not execute a similar series commemorating the great and learned of Trèves.

[2] *i.e.* the *vicarii* of Italy and Britain who, as deputies of the praetorian prefects of Gaul and Italy, were prefects of the second class.

and native virtues of each hero of the Belgae:
the Muses of Pieria shall spin me smooth songs of
soft yarn and speed at looms fitted with fine-spun
woof: our spindles also shall not lack for purple. Of
whom then shall I not tell? I shall mention thy
peaceful husbandmen, thy skilful lawyers, and thy
mighty pleaders, high bulwark for men accused—
those in whom the Council of their townsmen has
seen its chief leaders and a Senate of its own, those
whose famed eloquence in the schools of youth has
raised them to the height of old Quintilian's re-
nown,[1] those who have ruled their own cities and
shed glory on tribunals unstained with blood and
axes guiltless of slaughter, or who as prefects of
second rank[2] have governed the peoples of Italy
and Britons, children of the North, and him who
ruled Rome, head of the world, both People and
Senate, bearing a title all but the highest, though
he was peer of the highest:[3] let Fortune haste at
length to unravel her mistake, give him full draught
of the prized cup already sipped, and give him back
this time the substance of that proud dignity—to
be reclaimed by his illustrious posterity! But let
the task lately begun be fully wrought, and, putting
off the praise of famous men, let me tell of the
happy river in its joyous course through the green
country-side, and hallow it in the waters of the
Rhine.

418 Now spread thine azure folds and glass-green
robe, O Rhine, and measure out a space for thy new

---

[3] The reference is to Probus, who in 370 A.D. held the
consulship with Gratian as his "senior" colleague (for the
differentiation cp. Praef. i. 38). Probus had therefore fallen
just short of the highest distinction, though, as associated
with Gratian, he was "peer of the highest."

fraternis cumulandus aquis. nec praemia in undis 420
sola, sed augustae veniens quod moenibus urbis
spectavit iunctos natique patrisque triumphos,
hostibus exactis Nicrum super et Lupodunum
et fontem Latiis ignotum annalibus Histri.
haec profligati venit modo laurea belli : 425
hinc alias aliasque feret.   vos pergite iuncti
et mare purpureum gemino propellite tractu.
neu vereare minor, pulcherrime Rhene, videri :
invidiae nihil hospes habet.   potiere perenni
nomine : tu fratrem famae securus adopta. 430
dives aquis, dives Nymphis, largitor utrique
alveus extendet geminis divortia ripis
communesque vias diversa per ostia pandet.
accedent vires, quas Francia quasque Chamaves
Germanique tremant : tunc verus habebere limes. 435
accedet tanto geminum tibi nomen ab amni,
cumque unus de fonte fluas, dicere bicornis.

Haec ego, Vivisca ducens ab origine gentem,
Belgarum hospitiis non per nova foedera notus,
Ausonius, nomen Latium, patriaque domoque 440

---

[1] sc. Trèves (Augusta Treverorum).
[2] Nicer is the Neckar, Lupodunum probably Ladenburg.
Ammianus speaks of the victory of Valentinian and Gratian
(the "father and son" of l. 422) in 368 as near Solicinum,
but does not mention L.   Probably the two references are
to the same victory.
[3] The Waal which diverges from the left bank of the
Rhine at Panaerden in Holland, and the Yssel which flows

stream : a brother's waters come to swell thee. Nor
is his treasure waters alone, but also that, coming
from the walls of the imperial city,[1] he has beheld
the united triumphs of father and son over foes
vanquished beyond Nicer and Lupodunum and Ister's
source,[2] unknown to Latin chronicles. This laureate
dispatch which tells of their o'erwhelming arms is
but now come to thee : hereafter others and yet
others shall he bring. Press on united both, and
with twin streams drive back the deep-blue sea.
Nor do thou fear to lose esteem, most beauteous
Rhine : a host has naught of jealousy. Thou shalt
enjoy endless fame : do thou, assured of renown, take
to thyself a brother. Rich in waters, rich in Nymphs,
thy channel, bounteous to both, shall stretch forth
two branching streams[3] from either bank and open
ways for you both through various outfalls. So shalt
thou gain strength to make Franks and Chamaves
and Germans quake : then shalt thou be held their
boundary indeed. So shalt thou gain a name be-
speaking double origin, and though from thy source
thou dost flow a single stream, thou shall be called
twy-horned.[4]

[438] Such is the theme I compass—I, who am sprung
of Viviscan[5] stock, yet by old ties of guestship no
stranger to the Belgae ; I, Ausonius, Roman in name
yet born and bred betwixt the frontiers of Gaul and

from the left bank of the (Old) Rhine further down and falls
into the Zuider Zee.

[4] Ausonius suggests that the horns with which personified
rivers are endowed were suggested by the confluence of two
forking streams to form the headwaters of the river proper.
The Rhine, he finds, lacks this characteristic, but the defect
is remedied lower down by the junction of the Moselle.

[5] *i.e.* a native of Bordeaux, the capital of the Bituriges
Vivisci : *cp.* Strabo, p. 190.

AUSONIUS

Gallorum extremos inter celsamque Pyrenen,
temperat ingenuos qua laeta Aquitanica mores,
audax exigua fide concino.   fas mihi sacrum
perstrinxisse amnem tenui libamine Musae.
nec laudem adfecto, veniam peto.   sunt tibi multi, 445
alme amnis, sacros qui sollicitare fluores
Aonidum totamque solent haurire Aganippen.
ast ego, quanta mei dederit se vena liquoris,
Burdigalam cum me in patriam nidumque senectae
Augustus, pater et nati, mea maxima cura,   450
fascibus Ausoniis decoratum et honore curuli
mittent emeritae post munera disciplinae,
latius Arctoi praeconia persequar amnis.
addam urbes, tacito quas subterlaberis alveo,
moeniaque antiquis te prospectantia muris;   455
addam praesidiis dubiarum condita rerum,
sed modo securis non castra, sed horrea Belgis;
addam felices ripa ex utraque colonos
teque inter medios hominumque boumque labores
stringentem ripas et pinguia culta secantem.   460
non tibi se Liger anteferet, non Axona praeceps,
Matrona non, Gallis Belgisque intersita finis,
Santonico refluus non ipse Carantonus aestu.
concedes gelido, Durani, de monte volutus
amnis, et auriferum postponet Gallia Tarnen   465

---

¹ *i.e.* between the Garonne and the Pyrenees: *cp.* Caesar,
de Bell. Gall. i.1. Pyrene is a poetical name for the Pyrenees:
cp. Herodotus ii. 33.
² *sc.* Valentinian I. and his sons Gratian and Valentinian II.
(the latter born 371 A.D.).

high Pyrene,[1] where blithe Aquitaine mellows the
native temper of her sons : great is my daring though
my lute is small.   Be it no sin for me to have touched
lightly on thy holy stream with the poor offering my
Muse affords.   'Tis not for praise I hanker : I sue
for pardon.   Many thou hast, O gentle stream, who
use to trouble the rills of the Aonian maids and drain
all Aganippe.   But as for me, so far as the flow of
my poetic vein shall serve—when the Emperor and
his sons [2] (my chiefest care) shall give me my discharge
from service as their tutor, and shall dispatch me,
invested with the emblems and dignity of the
Ausonian [3] consulship, home to Bordeaux, my native
land, the nest of my old age—I will pursue yet further
the praises of thy Northern stream.   I will tell also
of cities below which with voiceless channel thou
dost glide, of strongholds which look out on thee from
ancient walls ; I will tell also of fortresses raised
for defence in times of peril, now not fortresses but
granaries for the unmenaced Belgic folk ; I will tell
also of prosperous settlers upon either shore, and how
thy waters lap their banks midway between the toils
of men and oxen, parting the rich fields.   Not Liger
shall prefer himself before thee, not headlong Axona,
not Matrona, set as a border-line between Gauls and
Belgae, not Carantonus [4] himself whose stream is
driven back by the Santonic tide.   Thou too,
Duranius,[5] whose waters roll down from their chill
mountain-source, shalt yield, and Gaul shall rank

[3] The epithet is to be taken in the double sense of
"Italian," *i.e.* "Roman," and "of Ausonius."

[4] Liger is the Loire ; Axona, the Aisne ; Matrona, the
Marne ; Carantonus, the Charente.

[5] The Dordogne : the rivers next mentioned are the Tarn
and the Adour respectively.

insanumque ruens per saxa rotantia late
in mare purpureum, dominae tamen ante Mosellae
numine adorato, Tarbellicus ibit Aturrus.

   Corniger externas celebrande Mosella per oras,
nec solis celebrande locis, ubi fonte supremo   470
exeris auratum taurinae frontis honorem,
quave trahis placidos sinuosa per arva meatus,
vel qua Germanis sub portibus ostia solvis :
si quis honos tenui volet adspirare camenae,
perdere si quis in his dignabitur otia musis,   475
ibis in ora hominum laetoque fovebere cantu.
te fontes vivique lacus, te caerula noscent
flumina, te veteres pagorum gloria luci ;
te Druna, te sparsis incerta Druentia ripis
Alpinique colent fluvii duplicemque per urbem   480
qui meat et Dextrae Rhodanus dat nomina ripae ;
te stagnis ego caeruleis magnumque sonoris
amnibus, aequoreae te commendabo Garumnae.

---

   [1] This verse is partly imitated by Pope, *Windsor Forest*,
330, 332 :
     " Old Father Thames advanced his rev'rend head

     His shining horns diffused a golden gleam."

gold-bearing Tarnes in lower place; and, though he rushes madly 'mid wide-rolling rocks, yet shall Tarbellic Aturrus only pass into the dark sea when he has first done homage to the deity of sovereign Moselle.

[469] Horned Moselle, worthy to be renowned throughout foreign lands, and not to be renowned in those parts alone where at thy farthest source thou dost reveal the gilded glory of a bull-like brow;[1] or where amid embaying fields thou dost wind thy peaceful course; or where below German harbours thou dost clear thy outfall;—if any praise shall choose to breathe upon this feeble strain, if anyone shall deign to waste his leisure on my verse, thou shalt pass upon the lips of men, and be cherished with joyful song. Of thee springs and living lakes shall learn, of thee azure rivers, of thee ancient groves, the glory of our villages; to thee Druna, to thee Druentia,[2] wandering uncertainly between her shifting banks, shall do reverence with all the Alpine streams, and Rhodanus who, flowing through that two-fold city, gives a name to the Right Bank;[3] thee will I praise to the dark meres and deep-voiced tributaries, thee will I praise to sea-like Garonne.

[2] The Drôme and the Durance.
[3] The city is Arles, which was intersected by the Rhodanus (Rhone): cp. *Ordo Urbium Nobilium*, x. 1. An inscription from Narbonne (*C.I.L.* xii. 4398) shows that Ripa Dextra was a recognised place-name.

AUSONIUS

EPISTULA SYMMACHI AD AUSONIUM

Symmachus Ausonio

Petis a me litteras longiores : est hoc in nos veri
amoris indicium. sed ego, qui sim paupertini ingenii
mei conscius, Laconicae malo studere brevitati, quam
multiiugis paginis infantiae meae maciem publicare.
nec mirum, si eloquii nostri vena tenuata est, quam
dudum neque ullius poematis tui neque pedestrium
voluminum lectione iuvisti. unde igitur sermonis
mei largam poscis usuram, qui nihil litterati faenoris
credidisti? volitat tuus Mosella per manus sinusque
multorum divinis a te versibus consecratus : sed tan-
tum nostra ora praelabitur. cur me istius libelli,
quaeso, exortem esse voluisti? aut ἀμουσότερος tibi
videbar, qui iudicare non possem, aut certe malignus,
qui laudare nescirem. itaque vel ingenio meo pluri-
mum vel moribus derogasti. et tamen contra inter-
dictum tuum vix ad illius operis arcana perveni.
velim tacere, quid sentiam ; velim iusto de te silentio
vindicari ; sed admiratio scriptorum sensum frangit
iniuriae.

  Novi ego istum fluvium, cum aeternorum prin-
cipum iam pridem signa comitarer, parem multis,

THE MOSELLE

A LETTER OF SYMMACHUS TO AUSONIUS

Symmachus to Ausonius

THAT you ask me to send you a longer letter is a proof of the reality of your affection for me. But I am so fully aware of the poverty of my natural equipment that I think it better to cultivate a Spartan brevity than to expose my starved and stunted faculty of expression by adding page to page. And it is no wonder that the vein of my eloquence has run low; for it is a long time now since you allowed me the pleasure of reading any of your works in verse or prose. What right have you, then, to demand of me heavy usury in the matter of words, when you have advanced me no loan in the shape of literary work? Your *Moselle*—that poem which has immortalized a river in heavenly verse—flits from hand to hand and from bosom to bosom of many: I can only watch it gliding past. Pray tell me, why did you choose to deny me part or lot in that little book? You thought me either too uncultivated to be able to appreciate it, or at all events too grudging to praise it, and thereby have offered the greatest possible affront to my head or to my heart, as the case may be. However, despite your ban I have penetrated with difficulty to the sanctuary of that work. I should like to withhold my opinion, I should like to take a fair revenge on you by saying nothing; but my admiration for the work breaks down my sense of wrong.

I know that river from of old when I was on the staff of the immortal Emperors: 'tis a match for many though no match for the greatest. And

imparem maximis. hunc tu mihi inproviso clarorum versuum dignitate Aegyptio Nilo maiorem, frigidiorem Scythico Tanai clarioremque hoc nostro populari Tiberi reddidisti. nequaquam tibi crederem de Mosellae ortu ac meatu magna narranti, ni scirem, quod nec in poemate mentiaris. unde illa amnicorum piscium examina repperisti quam nominibus varia, tam coloribus, ut magnitudine distanti, sic sapore, quae tu pigmentis istius carminis supra naturae dona fucasti? atquin in tuis mensis saepe versatus cum pleraque alia, quae tunc in pretio erant, esui obiecta mirarer, numquam hoc genus piscium deprehendi. quando tibi hi pisces in libro nati sunt, qui in ferculis non fuerunt? iocari me putas atque agere nugas? ita deus me probabilem praestet, ut ego hoc tuum carmen libris Maronis adiungo.

Sed iam desinam mei oblitus doloris inhaerere laudibus tuis, ne hoc quoque ad gloriam tuam trahas, quod te miramur offensi. spargas licet volumina tua et me semper excipias: fruemur tamen tuo opere, sed aliorum benignitate. vale.

yet your noble and stately verse has upset my pre-
conceptions and made this stream for me greater
than the Nile of Egypt, cooler than the Don of
Scythia, and more famous than this Tiber we all
know so well.   I should certainly not believe all the
great things you say of the source of the Moselle and
its flow, did I not know that you never tell a lie—
even in poetry.   How did you discover all those
shoals of river-fish, whose names are no less varied
than their hues, whose size differs as widely as their
flavour—qualities which are painted in your poem in
colours more glowing than any Nature gave?   And
yet, though I have often found myself at your table
and there have marvelled at most other articles
of food which at the time were highly esteemed, I
have never found there fish such as you describe.
Tell me : when were these fish spawned which
appear in your book, but did not upon your board ?
You think I am jesting and merely trifling?   So
may Heaven make me honest, as I rank your poem
with the works of Virgil!

But it is time I ceased to dwell upon your praises,
forgetting my own vexation ; otherwise you may wrest
the fact that I admire your work despite my annoy-
ance into an additional tribute.   You may spread
abroad copies of your poems and always leave me
out ; but I will enjoy your work all the same, though
it be through the kindness of others.   Farewell.

LIBER XI

ORDO URBIUM NOBILIUM

I.—ROMA

PRIMA urbes inter, divum domus, aurea ROMA.

II., III.—CONSTANTINOPOLIS ET CARTHAGO

CONSTANTINOPOLI adsurgit CARTHAGO priori,
non toto cessura gradu, quia tertia dici
fastidit, non ausa locum sperare secundum,
qui fuit ambarum.   vetus hanc opulentia praefert,
hanc fortuna recens ; fuit haec, subit ista novisque 5
excellens meritis veterem praestringit honorem
et Constantino concedere cogit Elissam.
accusat Carthago deos iam plena pudoris,
nunc quoque si cedat, Romam vix passa priorem.

Conponat vestros fortuna antiqua tumores.   10
ite pares, tandem memores, quod numine divum
angustas mutastis opes et nomina : tu cum
Byzantina Lygos, tu Punica Byrsa fuisti.

---

[1] The original name of Byzantium (see Pliny, *N.H.* IV.
xi. 18).

BOOK XI

THE ORDER OF FAMOUS CITIES

I.—Rome

First among cities, the home of gods, is golden
Rome.

II., III.—Constantinople and Carthage

Carthage yields precedence in rank to Constan-
tinople, but will not stand a full step lower; for she
scorns to be counted third, yet dares not hope for
the second place, which both have held. One has
the advantage in her ancient wealth, the other in
her new-born prosperity: the one has seen her day,
the other is now rising and by the loftiness of new
achievements eclipses old-time renown, forcing Elissa
to give place to Constantine. Carthage reproaches
Heaven, now fully shamed if this time also she must
give place who scarcely brooked the pre-eminence
of Rome.
[10] Let your earlier conditions reconcile your
jealousies. Go forward equal, mindful at length
that 'twas through Heaven's power ye changed
your narrow fortunes and your names; thou, when
thou wast Byzantine Lygos[1]; and thou, Punic Byrsa.[2]

---

[2] The citadel of Carthage: Virgil, *Aen.* i. 367.

AUSONIUS

IV., V.—Antiochia et Alexandria

Tertia Phoebeae lauri domus Antiochia,
vellet Alexandri si quarta colonia poni:
ambarum locus unus. et has furor ambitionis
in certamen agit vitiorum: turbida vulgo
utraque et amentis populi male sana tumultu.   5
haec Nilo munita quod est penitusque repostis
insinuata locis, fecunda et tuta superbit,
illa, quod infidis opponitur aemula Persis.

    Et vos ite pares Macetumque adtollite nomen.
magnus Alexander te condidit; illa Seleucum   10
nuncupat, ingenuum cuius fuit ancora signum,
qualis inusta solet, generis nota certa; per omnem
nam subolis seriem nativa cucurrit imago.

VI.—Treveris

Armipotens dudum celebrari Gallia gestit
Trevericaeque urbis solium, quae proxima Rheno
pacis ut in mediae gremio secura quiescit,
imperii vires quod alit, quod vestit et armat.
lata per extentum procurrunt moenia collem: 5
largus tranquillo praelabitur amne Mosella,
longinqua omnigenae vectans conmercia terrae.

---

[1] Daphne, near Antioch, was famed for its laurel grove, in
which was a temple of Apollo.
[2] Before the birth of Seleucus Nicator—afterwards founder
of Antioch—his mother Laodice dreamed that she had be-
gotten a child of Apollo, who also gave her a ring with an

THE ORDER OF FAMOUS CITIES

IV., V.—Antioch and Alexandria

Third would be Antioch, the home of Phoebus' laurel,[1] if Alexander's settlement were willing to be placed fourth : both hold the same rank. These also doth frenzied ambition drive into rivalry of vices : each is disordered with her mob, and half-crazed with the riots of her frantic populace. This, fertile and secure, vaunts herself because she has the Nile for bulwark and is deep-embayed in her sheltered site ; that, because her rival power confronts the faithless Persians.

[9] Ye, too, go forward equal and uphold the Macedonian name. Great Alexander founded thee ; while she claims that Seleucus whose birthmark was an anchor,[2] whereof the branded likeness is wont to be the sure token of his race ; for through his whole succeeding line this natal sign has run.

VI.—Trèves

Long has Gaul, mighty in arms, yearned to be praised, and that royal [3] city of the Treveri, which, though full near the Rhine, reposes unalarmed as if in the bosom of deep profound peace, because she feeds, because she clothes and arms the forces of the Empire. Widely her walls stretch forward over a spreading hill ; beside her bounteous Moselle glides past with peaceful stream, carrying the far-brought merchandise of all races of the earth.

anchor engraved on the bezel. When born, her son was found to have a birth-mark, shaped like an anchor, upon his thigh. The same sign reappeared in his descendants, and marked their legitimacy : *cp.* Justin, xv. iv. 8.

[3] See note on *Mosella*, l. 24.

AUSONIUS

VII.—Mediolanum

Et Mediolani mira omnia, copia rerum,
innumerae cultaeque domus, facunda virorum
ingenia et mores laeti ; tum duplice muro
amplificata loci species populique voluptas
circus et inclusi moles cuneata theatri ;   5
templa Palatinaeque arces opulensque moneta
et regio Herculei celebris sub honore lavacri ;
cunctaque marmoreis ornata peristyla signis
moeniaque in valli formam circumdata limbo :
omnia quae magnis operum velut aemula formis   10
excellunt : nec iuncta premit vicinia Romae.

VIII.—Capua

Nec Capuam pol agri [1] cultuque penuque potentem,
deliciis, opibus famaque priore silebo,
fortuna variante vices, quae freta secundis
nescivit servare modum.   nunc subdita Romae
aemula, nunc fidei memor ; ante infida, senatum   5
sperneret, an coleret dubitans, sperare curules
Campanis ausa auspiciis unoque suorum
consule, ut imperium divisi adtolleret orbis.

[1] *Peiper* : pelago, *MSS.*

---

[1] The ramparts of the city are noticed below (l. 9). Hopfensack conjectures that this double wall enclosed an annexe to the city in which lay the "enclosed" Theatre. But *inclusum* may possibly mean that the Theatre was roofed-in, like the Odeum of Herodes Atticus at Athens.

THE ORDER OF FAMOUS CITIES

VII.—MILAN

AT Milan also are all things wonderful, abundant wealth, countless stately houses, men able, eloquent, and cheerfully disposed; besides, there is the grandeur of the site enlarged by a double wall,[1] the Circus, her people's joy, the massy enclosed Theatre with wedge-like blocks of seats, the temples, the imperial citadels, the wealthy Mint, and the quarter renowned under the title of the Baths of Herculeus;[2] her colonnades all adorned with marble statuary, her walls piled like an earthen rampart round the city's edge :—all these, as it were rivals in the vast masses of their workmanship, are passing grand; nor does the near neighbourhood of Rome abase them.

VIII.—CAPUA

NOR, certes, shall I leave unsung Capua, mighty in tillage of fields and in fruits, in luxury, in wealth, and in earlier renown, who, despite Fortune's changing haps, relied on her prosperity and knew not how to keep the mean.   Now she, once rival, is subject to Rome; now she keeps faith, once faithless— when, at a stand whether to flout or court the Senate, she dared to hope for magistrates chosen under Campanian auspices, and that with one consul from among her sons she might take up the empire

[2] Or possibly "of Hercules."   In either case the epithet indicates that the Baths were built by or under Maximian, surnamed Herculeus, who according to Aurelius Victor (*Caes.* xxxix. 45) adorned Milan with many fine buildings.   To the same Emperor also the *Palatinae arces*, or imperial residence, is to be ascribed.

quin etiam rerum dominam Latiique parentem
adpetiit bello, ducibus non freta togatis.   10
Hannibalis iurata armis deceptaque in hostis
servitium demens specie transivit erili.
mox—ut in occasum vitiis communibus acti
conruerunt Poeni luxu, Campania fasto,
(heu numquam stabilem sortita superbia sedem!)— 15
illa potens opibusque valens, Roma altera quondam,
comere quae paribus potuit fastigia conis,
octavum reiecta locum vix paene tuetur.

IX.—AQUILEIA

NON erat iste locus: merito tamen aucta recenti,
nona inter claras AQUILEIA cieberis urbes,
Itala ad Illyricos obiecta colonia montes,
moenibus et portu celeberrima.   sed magis illud
eminet, extremo quod te sub tempore legit,   5
solveret exacto cui sera piacula lustro
Maximus, armigeri quondam sub nomine lixa.
felix, quae tanti spectatrix laeta triumphi
punisti Ausonio Rutupinum Marte latronem.

---

[1] See Livy, XXIII. vi. 6. After the battle of Cannae, Capua agreed to aid Rome against Hannibal, on condition that one of the consuls (*curules*) should be a Capuan.

[2] Magnus Maximus, a Spaniard, is said by Pacatus (*Paneg. in Theod.* § 31) to have been a menial and hanger-on (*negle-*

over half the globe.[1] Nay, and she attacked the
mistress of the world, the mother of Latium, trust-
ing not in leaders who wore the *toga*. Sworn to
Hannibal's allegiance, she, the beguiled, the seem-
ing mistress, passed in her folly into slavery to a
foe.   Thereafter—when they were driven to their
fall by the failings of them both, and came to ruin,
the Carthaginians through luxury, the Campanians
through pride (ah, never does arrogance find a firm-
fixed throne!)—that city with her power and might
of wealth, a second Rome once, who could rear her
crest as high, is thrust backwards and scarce can
manage to keep the eighth place.

IX.—AQUILEIA

THIS was not thy place ; yet, raised by late deserts,
thou shalt be named ninth among famous cities, O
Aquileia, colony of Italy, facing toward the moun-
tains of Illyria and highly famed for walls and
harbour.   But herein is greater praise, that in these
last days Maximus,[2] the whilom sutler posing as a
captain, chose thee to receive his late expiation after
five full years were spent.   Happy thou who, as the
glad witness of so great a triumph, didst punish with
western arms the brigand of Rutupiae.[3]

gentissimus vernula . . . statuarius lixa : *cp.* l. 7) in the house-
hold of Theodosius.   When the legions stationed in Britain
revolted, he was put at their head, crossed into Gaul, and,
after routing the forces of Gratian near Paris, put Gratian to
death at Lyons (383 A.D.).   For five years (*cp.* l. 6) he was
master of Britain, Gaul and Spain, but was crushed by Theo-
dosius in 388, and met his end at Aquileia.
   [3] Equivalent to "British" (as in *Parent.* vii. 2, xviii. 8).

X.—Arelas

Pande, duplex Arelate, tuos blanda hospita portus,
Gallula Roma Arelas, quam Narbo Martius et quam
accolit Alpinis opulenta Vienna colonis,
praecipitis Rhodani sic intercisa fluentis,
ut mediam facias navali ponte plateam,   5
per quem Romani commercia suscipis orbis
nec cohibes, populosque alios et moenia ditas,
Gallia quis fruitur gremioque Aquitania lato.

XI.—Hispalis. XII.—Corduba. XIII.—Tarraco. XIV.—Bracara

Cara mihi post has memorabere, nomen Hiberum,
Hispalis,[1] aequoreus quam praeterlabitur amnis,
submittit cui tota suos Hispania fasces.
Corduba non, non arce potens tibi Tarraco certat
quaeque sinu pelagi iactat se Bracara dives.   5

XV.—Athenae

Nunc et terrigenis patribus memoremus Athenas,
Pallados et Consi quondam certaminis arcem,

[1] *V*: Emerita, *P*[1].

---

[1] Ancient Arelate lay partly on the east bank of the
Rhone, partly on an island in the stream.

[2] The epithet is either commemorative of Q. Martius Rex,
who with M. Porcius Cato was consul when Narbo was
founded (B.C. 118), or of the military origin of the colony.

[3] Vienne was the chief city of the Alpine Allobroges.

[4] Or, possibly, "thou makest *him* (Rhone) thy central

THE ORDER OF FAMOUS CITIES

X.—Arles

Open thy havens with a gracious welcome, two-fold [1]
Arelate—Arelas, the little Rome of Gaul, to whom
Martian [2] Narbonne, to whom Vienne, rich in Alpine
peasantry,[3] is neighbour—divided by the streams
of headlong Rhone in suchwise that thou mak'st a
bridge of boats thy central street,[4] whereby thou
gatherest the merchandize of the Roman world and
scatterest it, enriching other peoples and the towns
which Gaul and Aquitaine treasure in their wide
bosoms.

XI.—Seville. XII.—Cordova. XIII.—Tarragona. XIV.— Braga

After these thou shalt be told, beloved Hispalis,[5]
name Iberian, by whom glides a river [6] like the sea,
to whom all Spain subjects her magistrates.[7]   Not
Cordova, not Tarragona with its strong citadel con-
tends with you, nor wealthy Braga, lying proudly in
her bay beside the sea.

XV.—Athens

Now also let us tell of Athens with her earth-born
fathers,[8] the stronghold for which Pallas and Consus [9]

street, spanned (covered) as he is with ships, and along
him . . ''   [5] Seville.   [6] The Baetis (Guadalquivir).
[7] Probably because it was the residence of the *vicarius*,
the deputy of the praetorian prefect of Gaul.
[8] The earliest inhabitants of Athens were believed to be
autochthonous, sprung from the soil itself.
[9] Neptune (Poseidon).   Athens was to be called after
whichever of the two deities produced the more useful gift.
Poseidon produced the horse; but Athena won by creating
the olive-tree.

paciferae primum cui contigit arbor olivae,
Attica facundae cuius mera gloria linguae,
unde per Ioniae populos et nomen Achaeum   5
versa Graia manus centum se effudit in urbes.

XVI.—Catina.   XVII.—Syracusae

Quis Catinam sileat? quis quadruplices Syracusas?
hanc ambustorum fratrum pietate celebrem,
illam conplexam miracula fontis et amnis,
qua maris Ionii subter vada salsa meantes
consociant dulces placita sibi sede liquores,   5
incorruptarum miscentes oscula aquarum.

XVIII.—Tolosa

Non umquam altricem nostri reticebo Tolosam,
coctilibus muris quam circuit ambitus ingens
perque latus pulchro praelabitur amne Garumna:
innumeris cultam populis, confinia propter
ninguida Pyrenes et pinea Cebennarum,   5
inter Aquitanas gentes et nomen Hiberum.
quae modo quadruplices ex se cum effuderit urbes,
non ulla exhaustae sentit dispendia plebis,
quos genuit cunctos gremio conplexa colonos.[1]

----

¹ *MSS.*: colono, *Peiper.*

----

¹ *i e.* those who with Neleus and Androclus, the sons of
Codrus, took part in the great Ionian migration.
² Syracuse comprised four quarters—Ortygia, Achradina,
Tyche, and Neapolis: see Cic. *in Verr*. Act. II. iv. 52 f.
³ Amphinomus and Anapias, who carried their parents
out of the burning town when Etna was in eruption: see
Strabo, p. 269; *Aetna*, ll. 624 ff.

once contended—of her to whom the peace-bearing olive tree first belonged, whose is the unmixed glory of the fluent Attic tongue, from whom went abroad a Grecian band and throughout the peoples of Ionia and the Achaean race poured into a hundred cities.[1]

XVI.—Catana.   XVII.—Syracuse

Who would not tell of Catana?   Who not, of four-fold [2] Syracuse?—the one renowned for the devotion of the fire-scathed brethren,[3] the other enfolding the marvellous fount and river,[4] where, flowing beneath the salt waves of the Ionian Sea, they join in fellowship their sweet waters in the abode which pleases them—exchanging there the kisses of their waters untainted by the brine.

XVIII.—Toulouse

Never will I leave unmentioned Toulouse, my nursing-mother, who is girt about with a vast circuit of brick-built walls, along whose side the lovely stream of the Garonne glides past, home of uncounted people, lying hard by the barriers of the snowy Pyrenees and the pine-clad Cevennes between the tribes of Aquitaine and the Iberian folk.   Though lately she has poured forth from her womb four several cities, she feels no loss of her drained populace, enfolding in her bosom all whom she has brought forth, though emigrants.[5]

[4] Arethusa and Alpheus, believed to emerge, with their streams still fresh, on the island of Ortygia in Syracuse : see Strabo, p. 270, and *cp*. Virgil, *Ecl*. x. 4.

[5] *i.e.* Toulouse had thrown out four new suburbs, and thus, while founding new "cities," did not lose her "emigrants." In *Epist*. xxx. 83 Ausonius speaks of Toulouse as *quinqueplicem* in allusion to the same extension.

XIX.—Narbo

Nec tu, Martie Narbo, silebere, nomine cuius
fusa per inmensum quondam Provincia regnum
optinuit multos dominandi iure colonos.
insinuant qua se Grais Allobroges oris
excluduntque Italos Alpina cacumina fines,   5
qua Pyrenaicis nivibus dirimuntur Hiberi,
qua rapitur praeceps Rhodanus genitore Lemanno
interiusque premunt Aquitanica rura Cebennae,
usque in Teutosagos paganaque nomina Belcas,
totum Narbo fuit : tu Gallia prima togati   10
nominis adtollis Latio proconsule fasces.
   Quid memorem portusque tuos montesque la-
      cusque ?
quid populos vario discrimine vestis et oris ?
quodque tibi Pario quondam de marmore templum
tantae molis erat, quantam non sperneret olim   15
Tarquinius Catulusque iterum, postremus et ille,
aurea qui statuit Capitoli culmina, Caesar ?
te maris Eoi merces et Hiberica ditant
aequora, te classes Libyci Siculique profundi,
et quidquid vario per flumina, per freta cursu   20
advehitur : toto tibi navigat orbe cataplus.

---

[1] See note on x. 2.

[2] The Belcae (Volcae) were subdivided into the Volcae
Arecomii and the Volcae Teutosagi (in Caesar, *B.G.* vi. 20,
Ptol. ii. x. 8 called Tectosages) : the latter lived in the west
of Gallia Narbonnensis, with Toulouse as their chief town.

[3] In 121 B.C., after the defeat of the Allobroges and Arverni
by Gn. Domitius and Q. Fabius Maximus.

THE ORDER OF FAMOUS CITIES

XIX. —NARBONNE

NOR shalt thou be unsung, Martian [1] Narbonne, who gav'st thy name to that Province (Provence) which once spread over a vast realm and held sovereign sway over its numerous inhabitants. Where the Allobroges encroach upon the Graian borders and Alpine peaks shut out Italy, where the Iberians are parted from thee by Pyrenaean snows, where Rhone sweeps headlong from his sire Leman, and the Cevennes thrust deep into the plains of Aquitaine, right on to the Teutosagi and Belcae,[2] rustic folk, —all was Narbonne: thou in all Gaul wast first to display the insignia of the Roman race under an Italian proconsul.[3]

[12] What shall I say of thy harbours, mountains, lakes? What of thy peoples with their varied differences of garb and speech? Or of the temple of Parian marble, once thine, so vast in bulk that old Tarquin, the first builder,[4] would not scorn it, nor Catulus [5] the second, nor he who last raised the golden roofs of the Capitol, Caesar himself? [6] Thee the merchandise of the eastern sea and Spanish main enrich, thee the fleets of the Libyan and Sicilian deeps, and all freights which pass by many different routes o'er rivers and o'er seas: the whole world over no argosy is afloat but for thy sake.

[4] Either Tarquinius Priscus who began, or Superbus who completed, the building of the Capitol.

[5] Q. Lutatius Catulus finished the restoration of the Capitol, which had been burnt in the struggle between Sulla and Marius.

[6] Domitian, who restored the Capitol, which had again been destroyed under Vitellius, at a cost of over 12,000 talents.

AUSONIUS

XX.—Burdigala

Impia iamdudum condemno silentia, quod te,
o patria, insignem Baccho fluviisque virisque,
moribus ingeniisque hominum procerumque senatu,
non inter primas memorem, quasi conscius urbis
exiguae inmeritas dubitem contingere laudes.   5
non pudor hinc nobis; nec enim mihi barbara Rheni
ora nec arctoo domus est glacialis in Haemo:
Burdigala est natale solum; clementia caeli
mitis ubi et riguae larga indulgentia terrae,
ver longum brumaeque novo cum sole tepentes   10
aestifluique amnes, quorum iuga vitea subter
fervent aequoreos imitata fluenta meatus.
quadrua murorum species, sic turribus altis
ardua, ut aerias intrent fastigia nubes.
distinctas interne vias mirere, domorum   15
dispositum et latas nomen servare plateas,
tum respondentes directa in compita portas;
per mediumque urbis fontani fluminis alveum,
quem pater Oceanus refluo cum impleverit aestu,
adlabi totum spectabis classibus aequor.   20
  Quid memorem Pario contectum marmore fontem
Euripi fervere freto? quanta unda profundi!
quantus in amne tumor! quanto ruit agmine praeceps

---

[1] *contingere* (like our "contact" in certain senses) carries
an implication of defilement or degradation.

282

THE ORDER OF FAMOUS CITIES

XX.—Bordeaux

Long have I censured my unduteous silence in
that of thee, my country famed for thy wine, thy
rivers, thy famous men, the virtue and the wit of
thy inhabitants and for the Senate of thy nobles, I
did not tell among the foremost; as though, well
knowing thee a little town, I shrank from touching [1]
praises undeserved. For this no shame is mine;
for mine is neither a barbarous land upon the
banks of Rhine, nor icy home on frozen Haemus.
Bordeaux is my native soil, where are skies tem-
perate and mild, and well-watered land generously
lavish; where is long spring, and winters growing
warm with the new-born sun, and tidal rivers whose
flood foams beneath vine-clad hills, mimicking the
sea's ebb and flow. Her goodly walls four-square
raise lofty towers so high that their tops pierce the
soaring clouds. Within her, thou mayest marvel at
streets clearly laid out, at houses regularly plotted
out, at spacious boulevards which uphold their
name,[2] as also gates facing in direct line the cross-
ways opposite; and, where the channel of thy
spring-fed stream divides the town, soon as old
Ocean has filled it with his flowing tide, thou shalt
behold "a whole sea gliding onward with its
fleets." [3]

[21] What shall I say of that fountain, o'erlaid with
Parian marble, which foams in the strait of its
Euripus? [4] How deep the water! How swelling
the stream! How great the volume as it plunges

---

[2] *Platea*, the Greek πλατεῖα (ὁδός) "broad," is the modern
French *place*.   [3] = Virgil, *Aen.* x. 269.
[4] See note on *Mosella*, l. 290.

marginis extenti bis sena per ostia cursu,
innumeros populi non umquam exhaustus ad usus ! 25
hunc cuperes, rex Mede, tuis contingere castris,
flumina consumpto cum defecere meatu,
huius fontis aquas peregrinas ferre per urbes,
unum per cunctas solitus potare Choaspen.

Salve, fons ignote ortu, sacer, alme, perennis, 30
vitree, glauce, profunde, sonore, inlimis, opace.
salve, urbis genius, medico potabilis haustu,
Divona Celtarum lingua, fons addite divis.
non Aponus potu, vitrea non luce Nemausus
purior, aequoreo non plenior amne Timavus. 35

Hic labor extremus celebres collegerit urbes.
utque caput numeri ROMA inclita, sic capite isto
BURDIGALA ancipiti confirmet vertice sedem.
haec patria est : patrias sed Roma supervenit omnes.
diligo Burdigalam, Romam colo ; civis in hac sum, 40
consul in ambabus ; cunae hic, ibi sella curulis.

---

[1] See Herodotus, vii. 108 : *cp.* Juv. iv. 176, *Credimus altos
Defecisse amnes epotaque flumina Medo Prandente.*
[2] See Herodotus, i. 188.
[3] According to Vinetus, this implies that the stream was
conducted into the city by a subterranean piping, remains of
which he himself saw and describes ; but this is hardly sup-
ported by the description in ll. 20 ff. which shows that the
water was visible.
[4] Divona was also the name of Cahors on the Lot. Ihm

in its headlong course through the twice six sluices
in its long-drawn brink, and never fails to meet the
people's countless purposes? This would'st thou
long to reach with thy hosts, King of the Medes,
when streams were consumed and rivers failed;[1]
from this fount to carry waters through strange
cities, thou who through them all wast wont to drink
Choaspes alone![2]

[30] Hail, fountain of source unknown,[3] holy,
gracious, unfailing, crystal-clear, azure, deep, mur-
murous, shady, and unsullied! Hail, guardian deity
of our city, of whom we may drink health-giving
draughts, named by the Celts Divona,[4]—a fountain
added to the roll divine! Not Aponus in taste, not
Nemausus[5] in azure sheen is more clear, nor
Timavus'[6] sea-like flood more brimming-full.

[36] Let this last task conclude the muster of famous
cities. And as illustrious Rome leads at one end of
the rank, so at this end let Bordeaux establish her
place, leaving the precedence unsettled. This is
my own country; but Rome stands above all coun-
tries. I love Bordeaux, Rome I venerate; in this I
am a citizen, in both a consul; here was my cradle,
there my curule chair.

(Pauly-Wissowa, *Realencycl.*) gives its meaning as "God-
like, gleaming": George Long (*Dict. of Class. Geog.*) derives
it from the Celtic *di* or *div* (= God), and *on* or *von* (= water).
It is perhaps connected with *Deva* (the River Dee).

[5] Aponus (now Bagni d'Abano), near Patavium, was a
famous Roman watering place (see Claudian, *Idyll.* vi.):
Nemausus is Nîmes.

[6] Now the Timao, between Aquileia and Trieste: *cp.*
Virgil, *Aen.* i. 245 f.

LIBER XII

TECHNOPAEGNION

I.—Praefatio

Ausonius Pacato Proconsuli

Scio mihi aput alios pro laboris modulo laudem
non posse procedere. quam tamen si tu indulseris,
ut ait Afranius in Thaide—

Maiorem laudem quam laborem invenero.[1]

quae lecturus es monosyllaba sunt, quasi quaedam
puncta sermonum: in quibus nullus facundiae locus
est, sensuum nulla conceptio, propositio, redditio,
conclusio aliaque sophistica, quae in uno versu esse
non possunt: set cohaerent ita, ut circuli catenarum
separati. et simul ludicrum opusculum texui, ordiri
maiuscula solitus: set "in tenui labor, at non tenuis
gloria," [2] si probantur. tu facies, ut sint aliquid.
nam sine te monosyllaba erunt vel si quid minus. in

---

[1] frag. 2 (*ed.* Ribbeck).   [2] Virgil, *Georg.* iv. 6.

---

[1] From τέχνη and παίγνιον, a "game of skill."

BOOK XII

THE TECHNOPAEGNION[1]

I.—The Preface

Ausonius to Pacatus the Proconsul

I know that from others I cannot win approval commensurate with my modicum of pains. But if you will generously grant it, as Afranius[2] says in his *Thaïs*—

"Then shall I find the praise outweighs the pains."

These verses you are about to read deal with monosyllables which serve, if I may put it in that way, as so many full-stops. Consequently there is no opportunity for elaborate expression, no handling of ideas through concepts, premises, apodoses, and conclusions, or other scholastic tricks which cannot find room in single lines. They merely hold together like the individual links in a chain. And at the same time this is a trifling little work that I have woven, though used to spin something a little greater; but—"though slight the task, not slight the praise"—if my verse wins credit. You will endow them with a certain value. For without you they will be just monosyllables or, if possible, something still

---

[2] Lucius Afranius lived in the earlier part of the first century B.C. His *comediae togatae* were highly esteemed, despite their immorality. Only fragments are now extant.

quibus ego, quod ad usum pertinet, lusi, quod ad molestiam, laboravi. libello Technopaegnii nomen dedi, ne aut ludum laboranti, aut artem crederes defuisse ludenti.

II.—Ausonius Paulino Suo[1]

Misi ad te Technopaegnion, inertis otii mei inutile opusculum. versiculi sunt monosyllabis coepti et monosyllabis terminati. nec hic modo stetit scrupea difficultas, sed accessit ad miseriam conectendi, ut idem monosyllabon, quod esset finis extremi versus, principium fieret insequentis. dic ergo: o mora, o poena! rem vanam quippe curavi: exigua est, et fastiditur: inconexa est et implicatur: cum sit aliquid, vel nihili deprehenditur. laboravi tamen, ut haberet aut historicon quippiam, aut dialecticon. nam poeticam vel sophisticam levitatem necessitas observationis exclusit. ad summam, non est quod mireris: sed paucis litteris additis, est cuius miserearis neque aemulari velis. et si huc quoque descenderis, maiorem molestiam capias ingenii et facundiae detrimento, quam oblectationem imitationis affectu.

[1] This heading, which is omitted by the *Z* group of MSS., depends on the authority of the Lyons editors.

smaller. In composing them, if it is a question of utility, I have been at play: if of trouble, I have been hard at work. I have called this little book *Technopaegnion*, that you might not think it has been all work without play for me, or all play without skill.

II.—Ausonius to his Friend Paulinus

I AM sending you my *Technopaegnion*, the poor un-profitable outcome of inactive leisure. It consists in verses begun with monosyllables and ended with monosyllables. But the rock-strewn[1] difficulty of the task did not stop there, but went on further to the heart-breaking business of linking up, so that the monosyllable which was the ending of one verse might also become the beginning of the line follow-ing. You may well exclaim, then: "Heavens, what time and toil!" Of a surety I have spent my pains upon a useless task: it is small, yet it brings a sense of surfeit; it is disjointed, yet a hopeless tangle; though it is something, it is proved to be worth just nothing. Nevertheless, I have taken pains to give it something of learning and lore; for the rule I was bound to keep debarred the lighter graces of poetry and rhetoric. To sum up, you will find here nothing pretty, but (with the change of a few letters) something to pity and to resolve never to imitate. And if you should come down into these depths also, you will find the cramping of your ideas and powers of expression causes you greater discomfort than your effort at imitation affords you delight.

---

[1] Ausonius here has in mind a difficult mountain-path.

AUSONIUS

III.—Versus Monosyllabis et Coepti et Finiti
ita ut a Fine Versus ad Principium Re-
currant

Res hominum fragiles alit et regit et perimit Fors
Fors dubia aeternumque labans: quam blanda fovet
    Spes
Spes nullo finita aevo: cui terminus est Mors
Mors avida, inferna mergit caligine quam nox
nox obitura vicem, remeaverit aurea cum lux   5
lux dono concessa deum, cui praevius est Sol
Sol, cui nec furto in Veneris latet armipotens Mars
Mars nullo de patre satus, quem Thraessa colit gens
gens infrena virum, quibus in scelus omne ruit fas
fas hominem mactare sacris: ferus iste loci mos   10
mos ferus audacis populi, quem nulla tenet lex
lex naturali quam condidit inperio ius
ius genitum pietate hominum, ius certa dei mens
mens, quae caelesti sensu rigat emeritum cor
cor vegetum mundi instar habens, animae vigor et vis:
vis tamen hic nulla est: tantum est iocus et ni-
    hili res.   16

IV.—Praefatio Monosyllabarum Tantum in Fine Positarum

Ut in vetere proverbio est "sequitur vara vibiam,"
similium nugarum subtexo nequitiam. et hi versi-

---

[1] The monosyllables in this and the following pieces are
distinguished by italics.

THE TECHNOPAEGNION

III.—Verses Beginning and Ending with Monosyllables so contrived that the Word which Ends one Verse makes the Beginning of the Next [1]

Things that concern men are frail, prospered,
guided, and destroyed by *Chance—Chance* the unstable,
ever-changing goddess, who is flattered by fond *Hope*
—*Hope,* who knows no bounds of time; whose only
end is *Death—Death* the insatiate, who is steeped in
infernal gloom by *Night—Night,* who must yield place
on the return of golden *Light—Light* bestowed by
Heaven's gift, whose harbinger is the *Sun—the Sun,*
who even in their stolen loves beholds Venus and
warrior *Mars—Mars* unbegotten of a father, who is
worshipped by the Thracian *race—a race* of uncurbed
folk, with whom every crime is *right:—Right* bids
them offer men in sacrifice: such is their savage *wont*
—*wont* of a savage and a daring folk, all unrestrained
by *Law—Law,* which was founded by the natural
sway of *Right—Right* which is sprung from man's
natural affection, Right which is God's unerring *mind*
—*mind* which bedews with heavenly influence the
deserving *heart—the heart,* alive, formed like the
globe, the life's power and its *strength:—strength,*
however, there is none in this: 'tis but a jest and a
worthless *thing.*

IV.—Preface to Verses with Monosyllables only at the End

The old saw runs: "Misfortunes never come
singly;"[2] and so I append to the foregoing some
perverse trifles of the same sort. In this case,

---

[2] Literally "the trestle follows the plank," *i.e.* one evil is
followed by another to match.

culi monosyllabis terminantur, exordio tamen libero,
quamquam fine legitimo. set laboravi, ut quantum
eius possent aput aures indulgentissimas, absurda
concinerent, insulsa resiperent, hiulca congruerent;
denique haberent et amara dulcedinem et inepta
venerem et aspera lenitatem. quae quidem omnia,
quoniam insuavis materia devenustat, lectio benigna
conciliet. tu quoque mihi tua crede securior, quippe
meliora, ut, quod per adagionem coepimus, proverbio
finiamus et "mutuum muli scalpant."

V

AEMULA dis, naturae imitatrix, omniparens ars,
Pacato ut studeat ludus meus, esto operi dux.
arta, inamoena licet nec congrua carminibus lex,
iudice sub tanto fandi tamen accipiet ius.
quippe et ridiculis data gloria, ni prohibet fors.   5

VI.—DE MEMBRIS

INDICAT in pueris septennia prima novus dens,
pubentes annos robustior anticipat vox.
invicta et ventis et solibus est hominum frons.
ecdurum nervi cum viscere consociant os.
palpitat inrequies, vegetum, teres, acre, calens cor, 5

---

[1] Or "Harsh, unlovely, and with verse ill-agreeing though
be the *law*, yet with so great a judge, my work to plead
shall win the *right*."

however, the lines end in monosyllables, while their beginnings are free though the ending is bound by rule. But I have taken pains—so far as is possible, given the utmost lenience on my hearers' part—to harmonize what is harsh, to give a flavour to the insipid, to couple up the disconnected; in short, to lend sweetness to the bitter, grace to the awkward, smoothness to the rough. And since the dreariness of the subject-matter robs all these allurements of their charm, the reader's kindness must make them agreeable. Do you also entrust your work to me; and that with the less misgiving, since it is better than mine, that so—for as I have begun with a saw, so I must end with an adage—"mules may ease each other's itch."

V

THOU rival of the gods, Nature's mimic, universal mother, *Art*, that Pacatus may approve my trifles, be to my work a *guide*! Harsh, unlovely, and for verse ill-suited though be my *rule*, yet before such a judge of eloquence it shall receive *right*.[1] For even fooling may win praise, save when forbid by *Chance*.

VI.—ON THE PARTS OF THE BODY

A BOY's entry on his seventh year is marked by a second growth of *teeth*: the approach of ripening years is foretold by a more manly *voice*. Unconquered both by wind and sun is the human *face*.[2] The sinews link the flesh in partnership with the hard *bone*. Restless, full of life, round, eager, warm throbs the *heart*, wherefrom the feelings have their strength:

[2] *i.e.* the face needs no covering to protect it from the weather.

unde vigent sensus, dominatrix quos vegetat mens,
atque in verba refert modulata lege loquax os.
quam validum est, hominis quota portio, caeruleum
 fel !
quam tenue et molem quantam fert corpoream crus!
pondere sub quanto nostrum moderatur iter pes ! 10

VII.—DE INCONEXIS

SAEPE in coniugiis fit noxia, si nimia est, dos.[1]
sexus uterque potens, set praevalet inperio mas.
qui recte faciet, non qui dominatur, erit[2] rex.
vexat amicitias et foedera dissociat lis.
incipe, quidquid agas : pro toto est prima operis pars.[3] 5
insinuat caelo disque inserit emeritos laus.
et disciplinis conferta est et vitiis urbs.
urbibus in tutis munitior urbibus est arx.
auro magnus honos, auri pretium tamen est aes.
longa dies operosa viro, sed temperies nox, 10
qua caret Aethiopum plaga, pervigil, inrequies gens,
semper ubi aeterna vertigine clara manet lux.

VIII.—DE DIS

SUNT et caelicolum monosyllaba. prima deum Fas,
quae Themis est Grais; post hanc Rea, quae Latiis Ops;

---

[1] cp. Juvenal, vi. 460.
[2] cp. Horace, *Epist.* I. i. 59 : " Rex eris," aiunt, "Si recte facies."
[3] cp. *id.* I. ii. 40 f.: Dimidium facti qui coepit habet : sapere aude ; Incipe !

they are enlivened by their mistress, *Mind,* and translated into words by law articulate through the chattering *mouth.* How potent, yet how small a part of man is the dark *bile!* How great a mass of body rests on that slender prop, the *leg!* Beneath how great a load moves that which controls our way, the *foot!*

VII.—On Things which have no Connexion

In wedlock mischief often follows if too great is the wife's *dot.* Each sex has its powers, but in authority paramount is the *male.* He who acts rightly, not he who holds sway, will be a *king.* Friendships are troubled, treaties dissolved by *strife.* Whatever you are about, begin it: good as the whole is a task's first *half.*[1] Their way to Heaven and their place among the gods the worthy win through *praise.* Crowded with virtues and with vices is the *town.* In guarded cities yet more strongly guarded is the *keep.* Gold is in high esteem; and yet gold has its price in *bronze.* Long day is full of toil for men; but relief comes with the *night,* which never falls on the realm of the Ethiopians—a sleepless, restless *tribe*; for there, moving in unbroken circle through the sky, shines ever the bright *light.*

VIII.—On the Gods

The inhabitants of Heaven also have their monosyllables. First of the gods is *Right,* who is Themis to the Greeks; next Rhea, whom the Romans know

[1] A saying ἀρχὴ δέ τοι ἥμισυ παντός is attributed to Hesiod by Lucian, *Hermot.* 3: see Rzach, *Hes.* (1913), *fragm. fals.* 5. This is probably due to confusion with Hesiod, *W. and D.* 40: ὅσῳ πλέον ἥμισυ παντός.

tum Iovis et Consi germanus, Tartareus Dis,
et soror et coniunx fratris, regina deum,[1] Vis,
et qui quadriiugo curru pater invehitur Sol,   5
quique truces belli motus ciet armipotens Mars,
quem numquam pietas, numquam bona sollicitat Pax.
nec cultor nemorum reticebere, Maenalide Pan,
nec genius domuum, Larunda progenitus Lar,
fluminibusque Italis praepollens, sulphureus Nar,[2] 10
quaeque pias divum periuria, nocticolor Styx,
velivolique maris constrator, leuconotos Libs,
et numquam in dubiis hominem bona destituens Spes.

IX.—DE CIBIS

NEC nostros reticebo cibos, quos priscus habet mos,
inritamentum quibus additur aequoreum sal.
communis pecorique olim cibus atque homini glans,
ante equidem campis quam spicea suppeteret frux.
mox ador atque adoris de polline pultificum far,   5
instruxit mensas quo quondam Romulidum plebs.
hinc cibus, hinc potus, cum dilueretur aqua puls.
est inter fruges morsu piper aequiperans git,
et Pelusiaco de semine plana, teres lens,
et duplici defensa putamine quinquegenus nux,   10

---

[1] cp Virgil, *Aen.* i. 46 f.: Ast ego, quae divum incedo
regina Iovisque Et soror et coniunx . . .
[2] *cp. id.* vii. 517.

---

[1] Larunda or Lara was the daughter of the river-god Almo.
Her tongue was cut out by Jupiter for betraying his amour

as *Ops*; then, brother of Jove and Consus, Tartarean
Dis, her brother's sister and his wife, the queen of
the gods, *Might*, and he who rides in a four-horse
chariot, the old *Sun*, and he who wakens war's fierce
tumult—the warrior *Mars*, by love of kindred never
roused nor by kind *Peace*. Thou also shalt be named,
thou haunter of the woods, Maenalian *Pan*; and thou,
the genius of our homes, born of Larunda,[1] *Lar*; and
thou, eminent above the streams of Italy, sulphureous
Nar;[2] and thou who dost punish the gods for perjury,[3]
night-dark *Styx*; the calmer also of the sea whereon
sails flit, white-backed *Libs*;[4] and thou, who never
leav'st poor man in trouble, kindly *Hope*.

IX.—On Articles of Food

I will tell also of our articles of food, as fixed by
ancient *use*, to which for relish we add sea-born *salt*.
Of old food for beast and man alike was furnished
by the *oak*,[5] ere that in fields there was store of
wheaten *ears*. Next came spelt, and from spelt
pottage-making *meal*, that 'mid the sons of Romulus
furnishes the tables of the common *folk*. Thereafter,
food and drink both (when mixed with water), *pulse*.
Another fruit, no less hot than pepper, is the cori-
ander-*pip*, and, grown from Pelusian seed, the smooth,
round lentil-*bean*,[6] and five kinds, shielded by double

---

with Juturna : hence she was worshipped at Rome under the
name of Tacita or Muta. To Mercury she bare the Lares.

[2] The Nera, a tributary of the Tiber.

[3] *cp.* Hesiod, *Theog.* 775 ff.

[4] = Λίψ, the " Libyan " or S.W. wind.

[5] See Hesiod, *W. and D.* 233.

[6] *cp.* Virgil, *Georg.* i. 228.

quodque cibo et potu placitum, labor acer apum,
    mel :
naturae liquor iste novae, cui summa natat faex.

X.—De Historiis

Solamen tibi, Phoebe, novum dedit Oebalius flos.
flore alio reus est Narcissi morte sacer fons.
caedis Adoneae mala gloria fulmineus sus.
periurum Lapitham Iunonia ludificat nubs
ludit et Aeaciden Parnasia Delphicolae sors.　　5
Thraeicium Libycum freta Cimmeriumque secat bos.
non sine Hamadryadis fato cadit arborea trabs.
quo generata Venus, Saturnia desecuit falx.
sicca inter rupes Scythicas stetit alitibus crux,
unde Prometheo de corpore sanguineus ros　　10
adspargit cautes et dira aconita creat cos.
Ibycus ut periit, index fuit altivolans grus.
Aeacidae ad tumulum mactata est Andromachae glos.
carcere in Argivo Philopoemena lenta adiit mors.
tertia opima dedit spoliatus Aremoricus Lars.[1]　　15

　　　　　　[1] *cp.* Virgil, *Aen.* vi. 859.

---

[1] *i.e.* bivalved shells like those of the walnut.

[2] Honey was the chief ingredient of *mulsum* (mead).

[3] Honey being an extremely dense liquid, all foreign matter
floats on its surface : *cp.* Macrobius, *Sat.* vii. 8.

[4] The hyacinth, named after Hyacinthus, son of Oebalus.

[5] Ixion.

[6] Pyrrhus, inquiring of the oracle whether he would
conquer the Romans, received the ambiguous reply, " Aio te,
Aeacida, Romanos vincere posse" (I say that you the Romans
can defeat).　　[7] *sc.* Io.

shells,[1] of *nuts*. Besides, what is agreeable for food
and drink,[2] the bees' industrious toil, honey of the
comb: that fluid has strange properties; for on its
surface float the *dregs*.[3]

X.—On Points of Learning

Phoebus, to thee new consolation came through
the Oebalian *bloom*.[4] Another bloom sprang through
the fault of that which is accursed for Narcissus'
death—a *fount*. For slain Adonis ill-renowned is the
bright-tusked *boar*. The forsworn Lapith[5] is beguiled
by Juno's shape—a *cloud*, and she who dwells at
Parnassian Delphi beguiles the son of Aeacus with
her *voice*.[6] Across Thracian, Libyan, and Cimmerian
waves cleaves her way the *cow*.[7] Except the Hama-
dryad perishes ne'er falls the tree's *trunk*.[8] That
from which Venus was begotten Saturn cut off with
his *hook*.[9] Amid Scythian crags, a mark for birds,
stood that parched *cross*, whence from Prometheus'
body dripped a bloody *dew*, besprinkling the rocks,
till deadly aconite sprang from the *flint*. When
Ibycus was slain, the tale was told by the high-flying
crane.[10] At the tomb of the son of Aeacus was sacri-
ficed Andromache's *coz*.[11] In Grecian prison Philo-
poemen met a lingering *death*.[12] The third "spolia

[8] See the Homeric *Hymn to Aphrodite*, 272.
[9] See Hesiod, *Theogony*, 173 ff.
[10] Ibycus of Rhegium (*flor. c.* 560 B.C.), the lyric poet, was
murdered by robbers; the cranes, who witnessed the crime,
caused the murderers to betray themselves in the theatre at
Corinth.
[11] Properly "sister-in-law."
[12] Philopoemen, leader of the Achaean League, was captured
by the Messenians and forced to drink poison while in prison
at Messene.

sera venenato potu abstulit Hannibalem nex.

res Asiae quantas leto dedit inmeritas fraus![1]

ultrix flagravit de rupibus Euboicis fax.

stat Iovis ad cyathum, generat quem Dardanius Tros.

praepetibus pennis super aera vectus[2] homo Cres. 20

intulit incestam tibi vim, Philomela, ferus Thrax.

barbarus est Lydus, pellax Geta, femineus Phryx,[3]

fallaces Ligures, nullo situs in pretio Car.

vellera depectit nemoralia vestifluus Ser.[4]

nota in portentis Thebana tricorporibus Sphinx.   25

nota Caledoniis nuribus[5] muliebre secus Strix,

XI.—De Vere Primo

Annus ab exortu cum floriparum reserat ver,

cuncta vigent: nemus omne viret, nitet auricomum rus

et fusura umbras radicitus exigitur stirps.

[1] *cp.* Virgil, *Aen.* iii. 1 f.   [2] *cp.* Catullus, *Attis*, 1.
[3] *cp.* Plautus, *Bacchides*, 121 ; Terence, *Phormio*, 672 ;
Virgil, *Aen.* xii. 99.   [4] *cp.* Virgil, *Georg.* ii. 121.
[5] *V* : nota et parvorum cunis, *CZ.*

---

[1] Lars was an Etruscan title (as in Lars Porsena). The
reference is to Viridomarus, king of the Insubres, slain by
M. Claudius Marcellus, the Roman consul, in 222 B.C.
[2] In 183 B.C.
[3] *i.e.* the beacon lit by Nauplius, father of Palamedes (who
was stoned to death by the Greeks before Troy), on the pro-
montory of Caphareus. This caused the wreck of the home-
ward-bound fleet of the Greeks.

opima'' were yielded by a Gaulish *lord*.[1] Through
poisoned draught Hannibal was carried off by a
late *death*.[2] How great the realm of Asia, brought
to undeserved doom by *wrong*! From the crags
of Euboea blazed forth the avenging *flame*.[3] Beside
Jove's cup stands the son of Dardanian *Tros*.[4] On
soaring wings above the air was borne the man of
Crete.[5] To thee, Philomela, incestuous violence was
offered by the brutal king of *Thrace*.[6] Lydians are
savages, Getae treacherous, effeminate the children
of Phrygia's *land*, Ligurians are cheats, worthless is
counted the Carian *breed*. Carding the woodland-
fleeces see the loose-robed *Chink*![7] Famous among
monsters of triple form is the Theban *Sphinx*. Well
known to Caledonian mothers is that bird, woman in
kind, the screech-*owl*.[8]

XI.—On the Beginning of Spring

When the year at its uprising unlocks flower-
bearing *Spring*, all things flourish: green is every
grove, gay the gold-tressed *field*, and, soon to spread
shade, up from its root shoots the *sprout*. No longer

---

[4] Ganymedes.   [5] Daedalus.   [6] Tereus.

[7] Modern slang for Chinese. The "fleeces" are probably
silk, or possibly cotton.

[8] The screech-owl was believed to suck the blood of young
children : see Ovid, *Fasti*, vi. 135 ff. It seems to have been
regarded as the embodiment through magic (*cp.* Ovid, *op. cit.*
141 : *seu carmine fiunt*) of *strigae* (hags, witches: see Petronius,
Sat. 63); and in Apuleius, *Metam.* iii. 21, the witch Pam-
phile actually transforms herself into an owl. *Muliebre secus*
may be understood either in the light of these passages, or
with reference to the female characteristics noticed by
Statius, *Theb.* i. 597 ff. No other reference to the ill-repute
of the Caledonian owls appears to be extant.

non denso ad terram lapsu glomerata fluit nix.
florum spirat odor, Libani ceu montis honor tus.   5
[iam pelago volitat mercator vestifluus Ser [1]]

XII.—Per Interrogationem et Responsionem

Quis subit in poenam capitali iudicio?   vas.
quid si lis fuerit nummaria, quis dabitur?   praes.
quis mirmilloni contenditur?   aequimanus Thraex.
inter virtutes quod nomen Mercurio?   fur.
turibula et paterae, quae tertia vasa deum?   lanx.   5
cincta mari quaenam tellus creat Hippocratem?   Co.
grex magis an regnum Minoida sollicitat?   grex.
quid praeter nubem Phaeacibus inpositum?   mons.[2]
dic cessante cibo somno quis opimior est?   glis.[3]
tergora dic clipeis accommoda quae faciat?   glus.   10
sponte ablativi casus quis rectus erit?   spons.
quadrupes oscinibus quis iungitur auspiciis?   mus.[4]
quid fluitat pelago, quod non natat in fluvio?   pix.[5]
bissenas partes quis continet aequipares?   as.
tertia defuerit si portio, quid reliquum?   bes.   15

XIII.—De Litteris Monosyllabis Graecis ac Latinis

Dux elementorum studiis viget in Latiis A
et suprema notis adscribitur Argolicis Ω.

[1] *CZ*: omitted by *V*.   The line seems to be compounded
of elements taken from x. 24 and xii. 13.
[2] *cp.* Homer, *v* 177.   [3] *cp. Ephemeris*, i. 5 f.
[4] *cp.* Pliny, *N.H.* viii. 221.   [5] *id.* ii. 103.

in thick shower streams to earth the billowing *snow*.
The smell of flowers fills the air like that pride of
Mount Libanus, the *spice* (incense). Now o'er the
sea flits the loose-robed merchant *Chink*.

XII.—BY QUESTION AND ANSWER

ON whom does the penalty devolve in a capital
charge? On him who gives *bail*. But if the case be
one of money, what assurance will be given? A
bond. Who is matched with the "mirmillo"? The
ambidextrous gladiator of *Thrace*. Amongst good folk
what is Mercury called? A *thief*. Besides the censer
and the bowl, what third vessel is the gods'? The
dish. What island girdled by the sea produced Hip-
pocrates? *Cos*. Did Minos' wife care more for herds
or realms? For *herds*. What besides a cloud was
hung over the Phaeacians? A *hill*.[1] Say, what grows
more fat on sleep though it ceases to eat? The *shrew*.
Tell me, what makes hides fit for shields? *Glue*.
"Sponte" is ablative; what will be its nominative?
"*Spons*." What four-footed thing shares with birds
in the auspices?[2] The *mouse*. What floats on the
sea which sinks in a river? *Pitch*. What contains
twice six equal parts? The (Roman) *pound*. If four
ounces are subtracted, what is left? Two-*thirds*.

XIII.—ON MONOSYLLABIC LETTERS GREEK AND LATIN

LEADER of letters in the Roman alphabet proud
stands *A*, and last in the list of Argive characters is

---

[1] See Homer, *ν* 177.
[2] See Pliny, *N.H.* viii. 57.

Hτα quod Aeolidum, quodque ε[1] valet, hoc Latiare E.

praesto quod E Latium semper breve Dorica vox Є.

hoc tereti argutoque sono negat Attica gens O.   5

Ω quod, et O, Graecum conpensat Romula vox O.

littera sum, Iotae similis vox plena, iubens I.

Cecropiis ignota notis, ferale sonans V.

Pythagorae bivium, ramis pateo ambiguis Y.[2]

vocibus in Grais numquam ultima conspicior M.   10

Zeta iacens, si surgat, erit nota, quae legitur N.

Maeandrum flexusque vagos imitata vagor Ƶ.

dividuum Betae monosyllabon Italicum B.

non formam, at vocem Deltae gero Romuleum D.

hostilis quae forma iugi est, hanc efficiet Π.   15

Ausonium si Pe scribas, ero Cecropium P,

et Rho quod Graeco, mutabitur in Latium P.

malus ut antemnam fert vertice, sic ego sum T.

spiritus hic, flatu tenuissima vivificans, H.

haec tribus in Latio tantum addita nominibus, K ; 20

praevaluit post quam, Gammae vice functa prius, C,

---

[1] *Turnebus* : *V* omits : *Peiper* inserts ει.
[2] *cp.* Persius, iii. 56 f.: et tibi quae Samios diduxit littera ramos Surgentem dextro monstravit limite callem.

---

[1] *i.e.* in the word *oὐ*. From this line and from *Epist.* xxix. 36–7 it appears that Ausonius regarded *oὐ* as a distinct letter rather than as a diphthong.
[2] *sc.* as the imperative of *ire*.
[3] *V* (resembling *W* in sound) sounded ill-omened (*cp.* Pliny,

entered Ω. That value which the "Eta" of the
Aeolian race and that which ε have, that has Latin
E. The sound of short Latin E I always render—the
Dorian letter Є. The smooth, clear sound wherewith
the Attic race denies, is O.[1] To the Greek Ω and O,
equivalent is the Roman letter O. I am a letter
like Iota and a complete word of command,[2] I. A
stranger to the Cecropian alphabet is ominous-sound-
ing V.[3] I stretch forth arms alternative—the Two
Ways of Pythagoras[4]—and I am Y. I am a letter
never seen at the end of a Greek word, M.[5] If Zeta
lying on its side gets up, it will be the character
which is read N. Copying Maeander and its strag-
gling curves, here straggles Ƶ. Half Beta's length
has the Italian monosyllabic B. Though not her
form, I have Delta's sound, and I am Roman D.
The shape of the "hostile yoke"[6] will be given you
by Π. I am Ausonian P: write me, and I shall be
Cecropian P, and what is Rho for the Greek will be
changed into Latin P. Like a mast carrying a yard
at its top, so am I, T. This aspirate is a breathing
which gives life to the smallest words, H. In Latin
this letter is used in three words alone,[7] K; after
which became general the letter which once served

N.H. x. 12, 34), as in Virgil, Aen. iv. 460 f. : hinc exaudiri
voces et verba vocantis visa viri.

[4] See note on *Prof.* xi. 5.   [5] *cp.* Quintilian, XII. x. 31.

[6] The yoke, under which a conquered army had to pass,
was formed of two spears fixed upright with a third lashed
horizontally to connect their tops : see Livy iii. 28.

[7] Kalendae, K (for Caeso, the proper name), Kaput :
Kalumnia is sometimes added.

atque alium pro se titulum replicata dedit G.

ansis cincta duabus erit cum Iota, leges ⌒.[1]

in Latio numerus denarius, Argolicum X.

haec gruis effigies Palamedica porrigitur φ.　　25

Coppa fui quondam Boeotia, nunc Latium Q.

furca tricornigera specie paene ultima sum Ψ.

XIV.—Grammaticomastix

Et logodaedalia? stride modo, qui nimium trux

frivola condemnas: nequam quoque cum pretio est

　　mers!

Ennius ut memorat, repleat te laetificum gau.[2]

livida mens hominum concretum felle coquat pus.

dic, quid significent Catalepta Maronis? in his al　　5

Celtarum posuit; sequitur non lucidius tau:[3]　　6

estne peregrini vox nominis an Latii sil?　　8

et quod germano mixtum male letiferum min?　　9

---

[1] *Peiper*: *V* has Θ, which is not a monosyllable.

[2] *V*: et quod nonnumquam praesumit laetificum gau, *CZ* (placing this after l. 19).

[3] *V*: scire velim Catalepta (Catalecta, *C*) legens quid significet tau, *CZ* (omitting l. 6).

---

[1] To be understood in a double sense: the letter C, in becoming G, reverted to its early value as the equivalent of *gamma*, and its new form is differentiated in writing by a "twist." For the relation between γ, C and G, see Lindsay, *Hist. Lat. Grammar*, ch. i. § 5.

[2] *San* (or *sanpi*), an obsolete letter used only as a numeral sign = 900.

[3] According to Pliny, Palamedes invented the letters θ,

for Gamma, *C*, and with a twist back[1] gave a new name for itself, *G*. When Iota is flanked by a pair of handles, you will read ⌒.[2] In Latin for the number ten stands Argolic X. This is the picture of Palamedes' long-necked crane,[3] ϕ. Once I was Boeotian Coppa, now I am Latin *Q*. Shaped like a three-pronged fork, I am last letter but one, Υ.

XIV.—A Scourge for Grammarians

And what results from preciosity? Now raise a howl thou who, too *sour*, condemnest trifling: there is a price even for shoddy *wares*! As Ennius[4] says, "may you be filled with joy-causing *pleas*'." Let men's envious hearts distil gall-curdled *pus*. Pray what does Virgil's "Catalepta" mean? There he has put in Celtic *al*, and follows it up with a word no whit more clear, *tau*.[5] Does this sound like a foreign or a Latin word—*sil*?[6] Or that which is so deadly when confused with its next cousin—*min*?[7]

ξ, ϕ, and χ: Philostratus credits him with υ, ϕ and χ, υ representing the formation adopted by a number of cranes in flight, and ϕ a single crane asleep with its head under its wing, and standing on one leg.

[4] *Annales*, frag. lii. (*ed.* Müller): *gau = gaudium.*

[5] *Catalepton*, ii. 4 f.: Scaliger conjectures that *al, tau,* and *min* were abbreviations of *allium, taurus, minium,* current in the Latin spoken in Celtic regions. *Al,* however, is not found in the *Catalepton.*

[6] *Sil* (see Pliny, *N.H.* xxxiii. 12) was a pigment found in gold and silver mines.

[7] Red-lead, also called cinnabaris: it was therefore sometimes confused with the drug cinnabar in prescriptions—with unhappy results: see Pliny, *N.H.* xxxiii. 7.

imperium, litem, venerem cur una notat res?   7

lintribus in geminis constratus ponto sit an pons? 10

Bucolico saepes dixit Maro, cur Cicero saeps?

vox solita et cunctis notissima, si memores, lac

cur condemnatur, ratio magis ut faciat lact?

an, Libyae ferale malum, sit Romula vox seps?

si bonus est insons contrarius et reus, est sons?   15

dives opum cur nomen habet Iove de stygio dis?

unde Rudinus ait "divum domus altisonum cael"?[1]

et cuius de more, quod addidit, "endo suam do"?[2]

aut, de fronde loquens, cur dicit "populea fros"?[3]

   Sed quo progredior?   quae finis, quis modus et
     calx?   20

indulge, Pacate bonus, doctus, facilis vir;

totum opus hoc sparsum, crinis velut Antiphilae : pax.[4]

---

[1] Ennius, *Annales* (*ed.* Müller), frag. li.
[2] *id.* frag. l.   [3] *id.* frag. xxxiv.
[4] Terence, *Heaut.* 289 f.: capillus passus prolixe et circum caput Reiectus neclegenter ; pax.

---

[1] The French *affaire* seems nearly parallel : for *res*=imperium, litem, Venerem, *cp.* (1) x. 17 (above) ; (2) Hor. *Sat.* I. ix. 41 ; (3) Terence, *Eun.* 119.
[2] Properly a pontoon-bridge.   [3] *Ecl.* i. 54.
[4] Martianus Capella, iii. § 307 : quidam cum *lac* dicunt, adiiciunt *t*, propterea quod facit *lactis*.

State, law-proceedings, love, why are they all de-
noted by one word, *res*?[1] That which is laid on
boats ranged side by side, is it a brig'[2] or *bridge*?
In one of his Bucolics[3] Virgil wrote "hedge," why
did Cicero write "*hedg'*"? A common word and
one well-known to all, if you mention it, is *lac*
(milk); why then is it condemned that pedantry
may prefer the form *lact*?[4] Has it a Latin name,
that deadly pest of Libya, the *seps*?[5] If a good
man is sinless and, notwithstanding, guilty,[6] is he a
man of *sin*? Why is a rich man called after Stygian
Jove, *dis* (wealthy)? How comes the bard of Rudiae[7]
to say "the deep-echoing home of gods, *Heav'*"?
And what precedent has he for the phrase "into his
own *hou'*"? Or in speaking of a leaf, why does he
say "a poplar *le'f*"?

[20] But how far am I going? What end is there,
what limit, or what *goal*? Pardon me, Pacatus, good,
learned, kindly *Sir*. Here is the whole work spread
out—like Antiphila's hair: *peace!*

---

[5] A snake whose bite caused putrefaction. The name is
probably derived from the Greek σήπειν, "to rot": *cp.* Lucan,
Phars. ix. 723; ossaque dissolvens cum corpore tabificus
seps.

[6] It is impossible to reproduce the play on the alternative
meanings of *reus*, which may denote (1) a party in a legal
action, (2) a defendant, (3) a guilty person.

[7] *sc.* Ennius, born at Rudiae in Calabria, B.C. 239. The
words *cael* and *do* shortened by apocope (*cp.* the Homeric
δῶ and κρῖ) are for *coelum* and *domus*.

LIBER XIII

LUDUS SEPTEM SAPIENTUM

I.—Ausonius Consul Drepanio Proconsuli Sal.

Ignoscenda istaec an cognoscenda rearis,
    adtento, Drepani, perlege iudicio.
aequanimus fiam te iudice, sive legenda,
    sive tegenda putes carmina, quae dedimus.
nam primum est meruisse tuum, Pacate, favorem :   5
    proxima defensi cura pudoris erit.
possum ego censuram lectoris ferre severi
    et possum modica laude placere mihi :
novit equus plausae sonitum cervicis amare,
    novit et intrepidus verbera lenta pati.   10
Maeonio qualem cultum quaesivit Homero
    censor Aristarchus normaque Zenodoti !
pone obelos igitur primorum stigmata vatum :
    palmas, non culpas esse putabo meas ;
et correcta magis quam condemnata vocabo,   15
    adponet docti quae mihi lima viri.
interea arbitrii subiturus pondera tanti
    optabo, ut placeam ; si minus, ut lateam.

---

[1] Aristarchus of Samothrace, a disciple of Aristophanes of
Byzantium at Alexandria, flourished B C. 156. He is specially
famous for his recension of the Homeric Poems, in which he
used various critical signs, such as the *obelos* (" spit "), to
mark spurious verses.

310

BOOK XIII

THE MASQUE OF THE SEVEN SAGES

I.—Ausonius the Consul to Drepanius the Proconsul sends Greeting

READ through these lines, Drepanius, heedfully judging whether you think they should be pardoned or perused. With you as judge I shall be content, whether you think the verse I send worth conning or concealing. For my first aim, Pacatus, is to earn your countenance : to defend my modesty shall be my second thought. I can bear a stern reader's criticism, and I can satisfy myself with a modest meed of praise : a horse learns to love the sound of a patted neck, learns also to endure the pliant lash unterrified. What finish did critic Aristarchus[1] and Zenodotus[2] with his rules demand in Maeonian Homer ! Set down your brackets,[3] then—brands which distinguish the chiefest bards : I will consider them marks of fame, not blame ; and will call those passages corrected rather than condemned which the polish of a scholar's taste shall mark against me. Meanwhile, ere I face a verdict of such weight, I'll hope to impress you ; or else myself suppress.

[2] Zenodotus of Ephesus (flor. *c.* 208 B.C.) was the first head of the Alexandrian Library. His recension of the Homeric Poems was based largely on his study of their language.

[3] See note 1 (above).

AUSONIUS

II.—Prologus

Septem sapientes, nomen quibus istud dedit
superior aetas nec secuta sustulit,   20
hodie in orchestram palliati prodeunt.
quid erubescis tu, togate Romule,
scaenam quod introibunt tam clari viri?
nobis pudendum hoc, non et Atticis quoque:
quibus theatrum curiae praebet vicem.   25
nostris negotis sua loca sortito data:
campus comitiis, ut conscriptis curia,
forum atque rostra separat ius [1] civium.
una est Athenis atque in omni Graecia
ad consulendum publici sedes loci,   30
quam in urbe nostra sero luxus condidit.
aedilis olim scaenam tabulatam dabat
subito excitatam nulla mole saxea.
Murena sic et Gallius: nota eloquar.
postquam potentes nec verentes sumptuum   35
nomen perenne crediderunt, si semel
constructa moles saxeo fundamine
in omne tempus conderet ludis locum:

[1] *Scaliger*: separatis, *VP*.

---

[1] Ausonius has in mind a passage from Cornelius Nepos
(*Praef.* 5): magnis in laudibus *tota fere fuit Graecia* (*cp.* l. 29)
victorem Olympiae citari, *in scaenam vero prodire* ac populo
esse spectaculo *nemini in eisdem gentibus fuit turpitudini.*

[2] *i.e.* for different uses, the forum for legal business, the
rostra for public speaking.

[3] The statement is loose, since Athens (for example) had
its βουλευτήριον. But Ausonius is thinking of the use to
which the theatre was put in an emergency, as in 338 B.C.,
when, in the alarm which followed the capture of Elatea by
Philip, the Athenian people συνέδραμεν εἰς τὸ θέατρον (Diod.
Sic. XVI. lxxxiv. 3). The Roman envoys to Tarentum were
brought into the Theatre (in theatrum *ut est consuetudo*

THE MASQUE OF THE SEVEN SAGES

II.—PROLOGUE

THE Seven Sages, as an earlier age called them—
nor has a later withdrawn the title—to-day step
forth upon our stage, wearing Grecian cloaks. Why
do you blush so hotly, toga-clad Roman, because
such famous men are to appear upon the stage ?
With us this is a disgrace, but is not so also with men
of Greece,[1] whose theatre serves them in place of a
Senate House. Our proceedings have their own al-
lotted places: the Campus for elections, as the Curia
for the Senate, while the privilege of the citizens
sets apart the forum and the rostra.[2] At Athens
and everywhere in Greece the only public place for
debate [3] is that which luxury established in our city
at a late date.[4] The aedile in old times used to
provide a wooden theatre, hastily run up, and not a
massive pile of stone. That is what Murena and
Gallius [5] did—I will mention established facts. When
men, grown powerful and reckless of expense, be-
lieved their names would endure for ever if they
once raised a massy structure on stone foundations
to be a place for shows to all time, this immense

Graeciae introducti—Valerius Maximus, I. ii. 5). And the
enraged Ephesians of St. Paul's day "rushed with one accord
into the Theatre " (*Acts*, xix. 29).

[4] As late as B.C. 154 an attempt to raise a permanent
theatre was thwarted by the senate. The first permanent
stone theatre was built by Pompey (B.C. 55): that of Cor-
nelius Balbus (l. 40) was erected in B.C. 13, and in the same
year that of Octavian was dedicated in memory of his nephew
Marcellus.

[5] See Cic. *pro Muraena*, 19 ; Pliny, *N.H.* xxxiii. 53. L.
Gallius is mentioned as having given a gladiatorial show when
aedile, professedly in honour of his father: see Asconius
Pedianus, *Comm. in Cic. c. C. Antonius et L. Catilina.*

cuneata crevit haec theatri inmanitas :
Pompeius hanc et Balbus et Caesar dedit   40
Octavianus concertantes sumptibus.
sed quid ego istaec ? non hac de causa huc prodii,
ut expedirem, quis theatra, quis forum,
quis condidisset privas partes moenium :
set ut verendos disque laudatos viros   45
praegrederer aperiremque, quid vellent sibi.
    Pronuntiare suas solent sententias,
quas quisque iam prudentium anteverterit.
scitis profecto, quae sint ; set si memoria
rebus vetustis claudit, veniet ludius   50
edissertator harum, quas teneo minus.

III.—LUDIUS

DELPHIS Solonem scripse fama est Atticum
γνῶθι σεαυτόν, quod Latinum est : nosce te.
multi hoc Laconis esse Chilonis putant.
Spartane Chilon, sit tuum necne, ambigunt,   55
quod iuxta fertur, ὅρα τέλος μακροῦ βίου,
finem intueri longae vitae qui iubes.
multi hoc Solonem dixe Croeso existimant.
et Pittacum dixisse fama est Lesbium
γίγνωσκε καιρόν : tempus ut noris, iubet.   60
set καιρὸς iste tempestivum tempus est.
Bias Prieneus dixit οἱ πλεῖστοι κακοί,
quod est Latinum, plures hominum sunt mali ;
set inperitos scito, quos dixit malos.

---

¹ Literally "divided into wedges"—*i.e.* the wedge-shaped
segments into which the auditorium was divided by the
radiating gangways.
² See note 4, p. 313 : Ausonius loosely represents the three
as having all worked to produce a single theatre.

theatre with its radiating gangways¹ came into
being : this theatre Pompey and Balbus and Octa-
vianus Caesar² gave us, vying with each other in
their outlay. But what have I to do with all this?
I am not come forward on this stage to explain who
built theatres, or forums, or separate bits of our
walls, but to prepare the way for men worthy of
reverence and approved by the gods, and to reveal
what their purpose is.

⁴⁷ Their usage is to deliver their own sayings,
each that which he in his wisdom first hit upon.
You know, of course, what these are ; but if Memory
limps among ancient matters, Chorus³ will come
fully to explain these sayings on which I have too
slight a grip.

III.—Chorus

'Tis said that Attic Solon wrote at Delphi Γνῶθι
σεαυτόν, which in our tongue is " Know thyself."
Many think this to be by Chilon the Laconian.
Spartan Chilon, 'tis disputed whether the saw which
comes next is yours or no, ὅρα τέλος μακροῦ βίου—
wherein you bid us mark the ending of a long life.
Many consider that Solon said this to Croesus. And
'tis reported that Lesbian Pittacus⁴ said Γίγνωσκε
καιρόν : he bids you know the time. But this καιρός
means the timely time. Bias of Priene said οἱ πλεῖστοι
κακοί, which is translated " most men are bad " ; but
know that they are uncultured whom he called "bad."

---

³ sc. in the Elizabethan sense. In Henry V., for example,
" Chorus " serves the same purpose as " Ludius " here.
⁴ The dictator of Mitylene, who supported the commons
against the aristocratic party to which Alcaeus belonged :
he died 569 B.C.

μελέτη τὸ πᾶν, Periandri id est Corinthii, 65
meditationem posse totum qui putat.
ἄριστον μέτρον esse dicit Lindius
Cleobulus : hoc est, optimus cunctis modus.
Thales set ἐγγύα, πάρα δ' ἄτα protulit,
spondere qui nos, noxa quia praes est, vetat. 70
hoc nos monere faeneratis non placet.
    Dixi : recedam.   legifer venit Solon.

IV.—SOLON

DE more Graeco prodeo in scaenam Solon,
septem sapientum fama cui palmam dedit.
set famae [1] non est iudicii severitas ; 75
neque enim esse primum me, verum unum existimo,
aequalitas quod ordinem nescit pati.
recte olim ineptum Delphicus suasit deus
quaerentem, quisnam primus sapientum foret,
ut in orbe tereti nominum sertum inderet, 80
ne primus esset, ne vel imus quispiam.
eorum e medio prodeo gyro Solon,
ut, quod dixisse Croeso regi existimor,
id omnis hominum secta sibi dictum putet.
Graece coactum est ὅρα τέλος μακροῦ βίου, 85
quod longius fit, si Latine dixeris :
spectare vitae iubeo cunctos terminum.
proinde miseros aut beatos dicere
evita, quod sunt semper ancipiti in statu.
id adeo sic est.   si queam, paucis loquar. 90

[1] fama, *MSS.* (and *Peiper*).

---

[1] Son of Cypselus and tyrant of Corinth, 625–585 B.C.
[2] Flourished 580 B.C. He and his daughter Cleobulina were also famous for their riddles.

THE MASQUE OF THE SEVEN SAGES

Μελέτη τὸ πᾶν, 'tis the saw of Periander the Corinthian,[1] who considers that careful thought can achieve the whole. Ἄριστον μέτρον, says Cleobulus of Lindos:[2] that is, "moderation is always best." But Thales produced ἐγγύα, πάρα δ' ἄτα[3] and forbids us to stand surety, because to be a bondsman is ruin. Money-lenders do not like us to give this advice.

[72] I have said my say: I will retire. Lawgiver Solon enters.

IV.—SOLON

AFTER the Greek fashion I appear upon the stage, Solon, to whom among the Seven Sages the general voice has given the palm. But the general voice has not the strictness of the judgment-seat; for I regard myself not as the first, but one of them, because equality cannot brook gradation. When a fool once asked who was the first among the Sages, well did the Delphic god advise him to fasten a slip bearing their names about a round ball, that no one should be first or last. From that circle's midst I, Solon, come forward, in order that that word, which it is thought I spake to Croesus, all the human race may regard as spoken to itself. In Greek 'tis tersely put ὅρα τέλος μακροῦ βίου, but becomes somewhat longer if rendered in your tongue: I bid all men watch life's end. Therefore avoid calling men wretched or happy, because they are always in an uncertain state. The case stands thus. If I can, I will speak briefly.[4]

[3] "Give surety, but ruin is at hand": cp. *Proverbs* vi. 1 ff.
[4] This explains the cramped style of the following narrative.

Rex an tyrannus Lydiae, Croesus, fuit
his in beatis, dives insanum in modum,
lateribus aureis templa qui divis dabat.
is me evocavit.   venio dicto oboediens,
meliore ut uti rege possint Lydii.   95
rogat, beatum prodam, si quem noverim.
Tellena dico civem non ignobilem :
pro patria pugnans iste vitam obiecerat.
despexit, alium quaerit.   inveni Aglaum :
fines agelli proprii is numquam excesserat.   100
at ille ridens : " Quo dein me ponis loco,
beatus orbe toto qui solus vocor ? "
" Spectandum " dico " terminum vitae prius :
tum iudicandum, si manet felicitas."
dictum moleste Croesus accepit : ego   105
relinquo regem.   bellum ille in Persas parat.
profectus, victus, vinctus, regi deditus.
stat ille, captans funeris iam instar sui,
qua flamma totum se per ambitum dabat
volvens in altum fumidos aestu globos.   110
ac paene sero Croesus ingenti sono,
" O vere vates," inquit, " O Solon, Solon ! "
clamore magno ter Solonem nuncupat.
qua voce Cyrus motus, extingui iubet
gyrum per omnem et destrui ardentem pyram : 115
et commodum profusus imber nubibus
repressit ignem.   Croesus ad regem illico
per militarem ducitur lectam manum :
interrogatur, quem Solonem diceret
et quam ciendi causam haberet nominis ?   120
seriem per omnem cuncta regi edisserit.
miseratur ille vimque fortunae videns
laudat Solonem : Croesum inde in amicis habet

[91] The king or despot of Lydia, Croesus, was one of these "happy" men, extravagantly rich, one who used to give the gods temples built of golden bricks.[1] He summoned me abroad. I come, obeying his command that so the Lydians may be able to enjoy a better king. He asks: let me name a happy man, if I know one. I speak of Telles,[2] no mean citizen: he had offered up his life fighting for his country. He scorned this man—asks for another. I found one, Aglaus:[3] he had never gone outside the bounds of his little farm. But he asks, laughing: "In what place, then, do you put me, who alone am called happy by the whole world?" "We must behold," I answer, "the end of life first: then we can judge —if prosperity abides." Croesus took the saying badly: I leave the king. He plans war against the Persians. He marched, was beaten, bound, handed over to their king. He stands, trying to imagine his own end, while fire was spreading all round about and rolling aloft on its blast clouds of smoke. Almost too late, Croesus with a deep cry says: "O true seer! O Solon, Solon!" With a great clamour he calls on Solon thrice. Moved by this utterance Cyrus bids the encircling fire be put out and the blazing pyre pulled down; and happily a shower, poured from the clouds, quenched the flames. Croesus is straightway led to the king by a picked band of soldiers: he is asked whom he meant by Solon, and what reason he had for calling his name aloud? From first to last he relates all to the king. Cyrus feels pity, and seeing Fortune's power, praises Solon:

[1] See Herodotus, i. 50. Croesus sent 170 "bricks" of gold to Delphi.
[2] In Herodotus, i. 30, he is called Tellos.
[3] See Valerius Maximus, VII. i. 2.

vinctumque pedicis aureis secum iubet,
reliquum quod esset vitae, totum degere.   125
ego duorum regum testimonio
laudatus et probatus ambobus fui.
quodque uni dictum est. quisque sibi dictum putet.
   Ego iam peregi, qua de causa huc prodii.
venit ecce Chilon.   vos valete et plaudite.   130

V.—Chilon

Lumbi sedendo, oculi spectando dolent,
manendo Solonem, quoad ad se se recipiat.[1]
hui, quam pauca, di, locuntur Attici !
unam trecentis versibus sententiam
tandem peregit meque respectans abit.   135
   Spartanus ego sum Chilon, qui nunc prodeo.
brevitate nota, qua Lacones utimur,
commendo nostrum γνῶθι σεαυτόν, nosce te,
quod in columna iam tenetur Delphica.
labor molestus iste fructi est optimi,   140
quid ferre possis, quidve non, dinoscere ;
noctu diuque, quae geras, quae gesseris,
ad usque puncti tenuis instar quaerere.[2]
officia cuncta, pudor, honor, constantia
in hoc, et ulla spreta nobis gloria.   145
   Dixi : valete memores.   plausum non moror.

---

[1] A parody of Plautus, *Men.* 882 : lumbi sedendo, oculi
spectando dolent Manendo medicum dum se ex opere re-
cipiat : *cp.* also Terence, *Phorm.* 462 : ibo ad portum quoad
se recipiat.
[2] *cp. Ecl.* iii. 3, 7–8, 15–16.

---

[1] Probably an ironical allusion to l. 87.
[2] Literally "to betake himself back to himself"; *i.e.* to
remember what he is about and to retire.

thereafter he counts Croesus among his friends, and bids him be bound with golden chains and spend with him all the rest of his life. Two kings bare witness in my praise, and both proved me right. And what was said to one, that let each consider spoken to himself.

129 Now I have finished that for which I came forward here. Look! Chilon is coming. Fare ye well and applaud.

V.—CHILON

" My loins ache with sitting, my eyes with watching,[1] while I waited" for Solon "to come to himself."[2] Good Lord! What "brief speaking"[3] these Athenians use! When at last he has finished off a single saw in heaven knows how many lines, he goes off looking back at me regretfully.

136 I who now come on am Spartan Chilon. With that well-known curtness which we Laconians use I recommend my γνῶθι σεαυτόν, "know thyself," which is still preserved on a column at Delphi.[4] That irksome toil produces most excellent fruit—to distinguish what you can endure and what you cannot; by night and day to examine what you are doing, what you have done, down to the smallest atom.[5] All virtues—self-respect, honour, fortitude—lie in this, as well as any noble trait I have passed by.

146 I have done: farewell, be thoughtful. I do not wait for applause.

[3] A sarcastic reference to Solon's promise in l. 90.
[4] Pausanias (x. xxiv. 1) mentions a tradition that the Seven Sages dedicated to Apollo at Delphi the maxims γνῶθι σεαυτόν and μηδὲν ἄγαν.
[5] Literally "down to the likeness of a tiny point": cp. Eclogues, iii. 3.

VI.—CLEOBULUS

CLEOBULUS ego sum, parvae civis insulae,
magnae sed auctor, qua cluo, sententiae:
ἄριστον μέτρον quem dixisse existimant.
interpretare tu, qui orchestrae proximus   150
gradibus propinquis in quatuordecim sedes:
ἄριστον μέτρον an sit optimus modus,
dic! adnuisti? gratiam habeo.   persequar
per ordinem.   iam dixit ex isto loco
Afer poeta vester "ut ne quid nimis,"[1]   155
et noster quidam μηδὲν ἄγαν.[2]   huc pertinet
uterque sensus, Italus seu Dorius.
fandi, tacendi, somni, vigilii is modus,
beneficiorum, gratiarum, iniuriae,
studii, laborum: vita in omni quidquid est,   160
istum requirit optimae pausae modum.
  Dixi: recedam.   sit modus.   venit Thales.

VII.—THALES

MILESIUS sum Thales, aquam qui principem
rebus creandis[3] dixi, ut vates Pindarus,[4]
[cuique olim iussu Apollinis tripodem aureum[5]]
dedere piscatores extractum mari;   165
namque hi iubente Delio me legerant,
quod ille munus hoc sapienti miserat.

---

[1] Terence, *Andria* 61.   [2] Eur. *Hippol.* 264 f.
[3] *cp.* Diog. Laërt. I. i. 6: ἀρχὴν δὲ τῶν πάντων ὕδωρ
ὑπεστήσατο.
[4] *Olymp.* i. 1.   [5] Suppl. *Scaliger.*

---

[1] Literally "the fourteen seats"; *i.e.* the first fourteen
rows of seats in the theatre behind those reserved for magis-

THE MASQUE OF THE SEVEN SAGES

VI.—Cleobulus

I am Cleobulus, native of a small island, but author
of a great saying which makes me famous—he whom
they believe to have said ἄριστον μέτρον. Translate
please, you who sit next the orchestra in the
stalls close by:[1] is not ἄριστον μέτρον "modera-
tion is best"? Come, tell me! You nodded? Thank
you. I will go on to the next point. Your African
poet[2] has already said from this stage "do nothing
overmuch," and one of my own countrymen[3] says
μηδὲν ἄγαν. Both maxims, Latin and Greek, bear on
our purpose. 'Tis moderation in speech, in silence,
in slumber, in watching, in benefits, in gratitude, in
wrongs, in study, in toil. Whatever our whole life
can show demands this moderation, which is timely
cessation.

[162] I have said my say: I will go off. Let us be
moderate! Thales is coming.

VII.—Thales

Milesian Thales I, who declared that water was
the prime element in nature, as did the poet Pindar,
and to whom at Apollo's command fishermen once
gave the golden tripod dredged up from the sea;[4]
for they had chosen me at the behest of the Delian
god, because he had sent this gift to the Wise One.

trates, which in B.C. 67 were appropriated to the equites.
See Suet. *Julius*, xxxix.
[2] Terence, who was said to have been born at Carthage.
[3] Euripides. (See note on Text.)
[4] For this anecdote see Valerius Maximus, iv. 1, ext. 7:
Diog. Laërt. (I. i. 7) makes Solon dedicate the tripod to
Apollo.

ego recusans non recepi et reddidi
ferendum ad alios, quos priores crederem.
dein per omnes septem sapientes viros   170
missum ac remissum rursus ad me deferunt.
ego receptum consecravi Apollini ;
nam si sapientem deligi Phoebus iubet,
non hominem quemquam, set deum credi decet.
  Is igitur ego sum. causa set in scaenam fuit 175
mihi prodeundi, quae duobus ante me,
adsertor ut sententiae fierem meae.
ea displicebit, non tamen prudentibus,
quos docuit usus et peritos reddidit.
en ἐγγύα, πάρα δ' ἄτα, graece dicimus :   180
Latinum est, sponde, noxa set praesto tibi.
per mille possem currere exempla, ut probem
praedes vadesque paenitudinis reos.
sed nolo quemquam nominatim dicere :
sibi quisque vestrum dicat et secum putet,   185
spondere quantis damno fuerit et malo.
gratum hoc officium maneat ambobus tamen.
  Pars plaudite ergo, pars offensi explodite.

VIII.—Bias

Bias Prieneus [quod [1]] dixi οἱ πλεῖστοι κακοι,
Latine dictum suspicor : plures mali.   190
dixisse nollem ; veritas odium parit.[2]
malos sed imperitos dixi et barbaros,
qui ius et aequum et sacros mores neglegunt.
nam populus iste, quo theatrum cingitur,
totus bonorum est. hostium tellus habet,   195

---

[1] Suppl. *Peiper.*
[2] Terence, *Andr.* 68 : obsequium amicos, veritas odium parit.

I declined and did not accept it, returning it to be
taken to others such as I deemed more eminent.
Then, when to each of the Seven Sages it had been
sent and sent back, they brought it again to me. I
accepted and dedicated it to Apollo; for if Phoebus
bids the Wise One be chosen, 'tis fitting to believe
that not any man but a god is wise.

175 That man, then, am I. But the reason for
my appearing on the stage, as with the two who
have preceded me, is to become the champion of
my own maxim. It will offend some, but not those
canny ones who have learned from experience and
have been made worldly-wise. Well, ἐγγύα, πάρα
δ' ἄτα, we say in Greek: in your language, " Be
a surety, but Ruin stands near you.[1] " I could run
over a thousand instances to prove that those who
give bond or bail appear at the bar of regret. But
I do not care to mention anyone by name: let
each of you mention such to himself and reflect how
many have suffered loss and harm by standing surety.
Yet may both parties still find pleasure in this service!

188 Clap, then, some of you; the rest, affronted,
hiss me off the stage.

VIII.—BIAS

I AM Bias of Priene, and my saying οἱ πλεῖστοι κακοί
I fancy you would render " most men are bad." I
could wish I had never said it; " truth breeds hatred."
But by the " bad " I meant uncultured men and
savages, who disregard right and equity and hallowed
customs. For this throng filling the circle of the
theatre is of good men all. It is your enemies'

---

[1] cp. Proverbs, xi. 15: " He that is surety . . . shall
smart for it."

325

dixisse quos me creditis, plures malos.
sed nemo quisquam tam malus iudex fuat,
quin iam bonorum partibus se copulet,
sive ille vere bonus est, seu dici studet.
iam fugit illud nomen invisum mali.   200
    Abeo.   valete et plaudite, plures boni.[1]

IX.—Pittacus

Mytilena ego ortus Pittacus sum Lesbius,
γίνωσκε καιρὸν qui docui sententiam.
set iste καιρός, tempus ut noris, monet
et esse καιρόν, tempestivum quod vocant.   205
Romana sic et est vox : veni in tempore.[2]
vester quoque iste comicus Terentius
rerum omnium esse primum tempus autumat,
ad Antiphilam quom venerat servus Dromo[3]
nullo inpeditam, temporis servans vicem.   210
reputate cuncti, quotiens offensam incidat,
spectata cui non fuerit opportunitas.
    Tempus monet, ne sim molestus.   plaudite.

X.—Periander

Ephyra creatus huc Periander prodeo,
μελέτη τὸ πᾶν qui dixi et dictum iam probo,   215
meditationis esse, quod recte geras.
is quippe solus rei gerendae est efficax,
meditatur omne qui prius negotium.

---

[1] cp. Plautus, *Capt.* Prologue, 67 : abeo. valete, iudices
iustissimi.
[2] Terence, *Andr.* 758.

country that contains those of whom you think I
spoke, "the many bad." But no one would be so
bad a judge as not to attach himself to the side of
the good, whether he is really good or anxious to be
so called. So now that hated epithet "the bad"
takes flight.

201 I must move off. Farewell and applaud, you
who "most are good."

IX.—Pittacus

Born at Mitylene, I am Lesbian Pittacus who
taught the saying γίγνωσκε καιρόν. But this καιρός
advises you to know the time, and that καιρός is
what is called the timely time. Your own word too
has the same sense, as : " I am come in time." Your
comic poet also, Terence, speaks of time as the most
important of all things, when the slave Dromo was
come to Antiphila choosing the right time, when she
was disengaged. Reflect, all of you, how often a
man gets into trouble who has not watched for the
right opportunity.

213 Time warns me not to be wearisome. Give me
your applause.

X.—Periander

A son of Ephyra, I come forward on this stage,
Periander, who said μελέτη τὸ πᾶν, and now I make
good my saying that to do aught rightly needs careful
thought. For he alone succeeds in any business who
first ponders the whole matter. Whether things go

---

3 See Terence, *Heaut.* 364: in tempore ad eum veni, quod
rerum omniumst primum.

327

adversa rerum vel secunda praedicat
meditanda cunctis comicus Terentius.[1]   220
locare sedes, bellum gerere aut ponere,
magnas modicasque res, etiam parvas quoque
agere volentem semper meditari decet.
nam segniores omnes in coeptis novis,
meditatio si rei gerendae defuit.   225
nil est, quod ampliorem curam postulet,
quam cogitare, quid gerendum sit.   dehinc
incogitantes fors, non consilium regit.
    Sed ego me ad partes iam recipio.   plaudite,
meditando et vestram rem curetis publicam.   230

---

[1] *Phormio*, 241 f.: quom secundae res sunt maxume, tum
maxume Meditar secum oportet quo pacto advorsam aerum-
nam ferant.

well or ill—so Terence the comedian declares—every one should take careful thought. When you want to let a house, to carry on war or to end it, to transact affairs of great, less, or least importance, you always ought to think carefully. For in new enterprises everyone makes slow progress if careful thought is wanting to his action. There is nothing which can demand greater attention than to think what ought to be done. Therefore 'tis chance, not design, which governs the unreflecting.

229 But now I must rejoin my fellow-characters. Applaud, and take thought while you manage your state affairs.

LIBER XIV

AUSONII DE XII CAESARIBUS
PER
SUETONIUM TRANQUILLUM SCRIPTIS

[*MONOSTICHA*]

I.—Ausonius Hesperio Filio S. D.

Caesareos proceres, in quorum regna secundis
consulibus dudum Romana potentia cessit,
accipe bis senos.   sua quemque monosticha signant,
quorum per plenam seriem Suetonius olim
nomina, res gestas vitamque obitumque peregit.   5

II.—Monosticha de Ordine Imperatorum

Primus regalem patefecit *Iulius* aulam
Caesar et *Augusto* nomen transcripsit et arcem.
privignus post hunc regnat *Nero Claudius*, a quo
Caesar, cognomen caligae cui castra dederunt.
Claudius hinc potitur regno.   post quem *Nero* saevus,   5
ultimus Aeneadum.   post hunc tres, nec tribus annis :

---

¹ *i.e.* Gaius Caesar, nicknamed Caligula : see Suet. *Cal.* ix.;
Tac. *Ann.* i. xli. 69.

BOOK XIV

AUSONIUS ON THE TWELVE CAESARS
WHOSE LIVES WERE
WRITTEN BY SUETONIUS TRANQUILLUS

IN SINGLE VERSES

I.—AUSONIUS TO HIS SON HESPERIUS SENDS GREETING

HERE take the twice six Caesars into whose sove-
reignty the sway of Rome passed long ago, leaving
the consuls second in authority. A single verse here
records each of those emperors of whom through
all their array Suetonius once detailed the names,
the deeds, the lives and deaths.

II.—SINGLE VERSES ON THE SUCCESSION OF
THE EMPERORS

Julius Caesar first opened a royal court and to
Augustus bequeathed his name and stronghold. After
him his stepson, *Nero Claudius* (Tiberius) reigned,
and next *Caesar* whom the troops nicknamed after
the soldier's boot.[1] Then *Claudius* gained the throne.
Cruel *Nero* followed him, last of the sons of Aeneas.[2]
Then three emperors in scarce three years: aged

---

[2] Nero was the last of the Julian Dynasty which claimed
descent from Aeneas.

Galba senex, frustra socio confisus inerti;
mollis *Otho*, infami per luxum degener aevo
nec regno dignus nec morte *Vitellius* ut vir.
his decimus fatoque accitus *Vespasianus*   10
et *Titus* imperii felix brevitate.   secutus
frater, quem calvum dixit sua Roma Neronem.[1]

III.—De Aetate Imperii Eorum Monosticha

Iulius, ut perhibent, divus trieteride regnat.
Augustus post lustra decem sex prorogat annos,
et ter septenis geminos *Nero Claudius* addit.
tertia finit hiems grassantia tempora *Gai*.
Claudius hebdomadam duplicem trahit et *Nero* dirus 5
tantundem, summae consul sed defuit unus.
Galba senex, *Otho* lascive, famose *Vitelli*,
tertia vos Latio regnantes nesciit aestas,[2]
  *   *   *   *   *
implet fatalem decadam sibi *Vespasianus*.   10
ter dominante *Tito* cingit nova laurea Ianum:
quindecies, saevis potitur dum[3] frater habenis.

IV.—De Obitu Singulorum Monosticha

Iulius interiit *Caesar* grassante senatu.
addidit *Augustum* divis matura senectus.
sera senex Capreis exul *Nero* fata peregit.
expetiit poenas de *Caesare* Chaerea mollis.

---

[1] *cp.* Juv. *Sat.* iv. 38 : calvo serviret Roma Neroni.
[2] *cp.* Virgil, *Aen.* i.: tertia dum Latio regnantem viderit
aestas.   [3] *MSS.*: tum, *Peiper.*

Galba, vainly reliant on his slothful partner; effeminate *Otho,* degraded by a life made notorious by vice; *Vitellius,* as unworthy of the throne as unmanly in his death. Fate summoned *Vespasian* to make the tenth, and *Titus,* blessed in his brief reign. His brother[1] following was called "the bald Nero" by his subject Rome.

III.—Single Verses on the Length of their Reigns

Julius the Divine, 'tis said, reigned three years. *Augustus* after ten lustres prolonged his rule for six years, and to thrice seven years *Nero Claudius* (Tiberius) added two. The third winter ended the bloody days of *Gaius.* *Claudius* dragged out a double span of seven years, and frightful *Nero's* total was as great, save that one consulship was lacking. Old *Galba,* profligate *Otho,* ill-famed *Vitellius,* a third summer knew not your rule in Latium . . . *Vespasian* lived out the full decade of his destiny. Thrice under *Titus'* sway was Janus wreathed with fresh laurels, fifteen times while his brother held the reins of cruelty.

IV.—Single Verses on the Death of Each of Them

Julius Caesar perished under the daggers of the Senate. Ripe old age added *Augustus* to the number of the gods. In his retreat at Capri old *Nero* (Tiberius) ended his life at last. Effeminate Chaerea wreaked vengeance on (Gaius) *Caesar.* *Claudius* met

---

[1] *sc.* Domitian : on his baldness, see Suet. *Dom.* xviii.

AUSONIUS

Claudius ambiguo conclusit fata veneno.　　　　　5
matricida *Nero* proprii vim pertulit ensis.
Galba senex periit saevo prostratus *Othone*.
mox *Otho* famosus, clara set morte potitus.
prodiga succedunt perimendi sceptra *Vitelli*.
laudatum imperium, mors lenis *Vespasiano*.　　　10
at *Titus*, orbis amor, rapitur florentibus annis.
sera gravem perimunt, sed iusta piacula fratrem.

TETRASTICHA[1]

Nunc et praedictos et regni sorte sequentes
　　expediam, series quos tenet imperii.
incipiam ab divo percurramque ordine cunctos,
　　novi Romanae quos memor historiae.

I.—Iulius Caesar

Imperium, binis fuerat sollemne quod olim　　　　5
　　consulibus, Caesar Iulius optinuit.
set breve ius regni, sola trieteride gestum :
　　perculit armatae factio saeva togae.

II.—Octavius Augustus

Ultor successorque dehinc Octavius, idem
　　Caesar et Augusti nomine nobilior.　　　　　10

[1] This series is found only in *V* and allied MSS. representing the second edition.

---

[1] Suetonius regards his death as certainly due to poison, but states that it was not known where or by whom it was administered. The popular belief was that he died through eating mushrooms : *cp.* Juv. *Sat.* v. 146 f. : ancipites fungi . . . quales Claudius edit. *Ambiguo* therefore alludes to the doubtful quality of the mushrooms.

his end through poison in doubtful circumstances.[1]
Nero, his mother's slayer, felt the point of his own
sword. Old *Galba* died, o'erthrown by ruthless Otho.
Soon ill-famed *Otho* perished, but won a glorious end.
Then came the wasteful reign of *Vitellius*, doomed to
be massacred. *Vespasian's* rule was praised, his death
was easy. But *Titus*, the world's darling, was snatched
away in the flower of life. Late but righteous venge-
ance destroyed his tyrannous brother.

QUATRAINS

Now I will tell both of those already mentioned
and of those who, following them upon the throne,
fill up the list of Empire.[2] I will begin with the
divine [3] and run in sequence over all those princes
whom I know, mindful of Roman history.

I.—JULIUS CAESAR

THAT command which once had been the yearly
privilege of consuls twain, Julius Caesar grasped.
But brief was his kingly sway, wielded for but three
years: ruthless conspiracy of citizens in arms struck
it down.

II.—OCTAVIUS AUGUSTUS

NEXT came Octavius, a successor and avenger, he
too called Caesar, and under the title of Augustus

---

[2] This promise was never fulfilled, or the latter part of the
work has been lost, Heliogabalus being the last Emperor
commemorated.

[3] *i.e.* from "divus Julius": *cp. Caesares* (Monosticha),
iii. 1. But doubtless Ausonius is also thinking of the conven-
tional invocation prefixed to poetic efforts : *cp.* Virgil, *Ecl.*
iii. 60 : **ab Iove principium.**

longaeva et numquam dubiis violata potestas
   in terris positum prodidit esse deum.

III.—Tiberius Nero

Praenomen Tiberi nanctus Nero prima iuventae
   tempora laudato gessit in imperio.
frustra dehinc solo Caprearum clausus in antro,   15
   quae prodit vitiis, credit operta locis.

IV.—-Caesar Caligula

Post hunc castrensi caligae cognomine [1] Caesar
   successit saevo saevior ingenio,
caedibus incestisque dehinc maculosus et omni
   crimine pollutum qui superavit avum.   20

V.—Claudius Caesar

Claudius inrisae privato in tempore vitae,
   in regno specimen prodidit ingenii.
libertina tamen nuptarum et crimina passus
   non faciendo nocens, set patiendo fuit.

VI.—Nero

Aeneadum generis qui sextus et ultimus heres,   25
   polluit et clausit Iulia sacra Nero.
nomina quot pietas, tot habet quoque crimina vitae.
   disce ex Tranquillo : set meminisse piget.

---

[1] Suet. *Calig.* ix.: Caligulae cognomen castrensi ioco traxit
quia manipulario habitu inter milites educabatur.

more illustrious still. His sway, long-lived and by danger never outraged, revealed him as a god placed upon earth.

III.—Tiberius Nero

Nero, who also bore the first-name Tiberius, in the early season of his youth ruled with applause. Vainly thenceforth secluded in his cave on Capri, he fancies place can conceal what vice betrays.

IV.—Caesar Caligula

After him, nicknamed after the soldier's boot, Caesar succeeded—more cruel than that master of cruelty, with murders and incest thenceforth stained, and one who went farther than his grandfather besmirched with every vice.

V.—Claudius Caesar

Claudius, flouted in his private life, as emperor showed a pattern of ability. Even though he suffered his freedmen's and his wife's enormities, his guilt lay not in performance but in sufferance.

VI.—Nero

Sixth and last heir of Aeneas' race, Nero defiled and ended the rites of the Julian family. For every name that natural kinship bears, his life also shows a sin. Read them in Tranquillus: but to recall them disgusts.

AUSONIUS

VII.—Galba

Spe frustrate senex, privatus sceptra mereri
  visus et [1] imperio proditus inferior,[2]   30
fama tibi melior iuveni ; set iustior ordo est
  conplacuisse dehinc, displicuisse prius.

VIII.—Otho

Aemula polluto gesturus sceptra Neroni
  obruitur celeri raptus Otho exitio.
fine tamen laudandus erit, qui morte decora   35
  hoc solum fecit nobile, quod periit.

IX.—Vitellius

Vita ferox, mors foeda tibi, nec digne, Vitelli,
  qui fieres Caesar : sic sibi fata placent.
umbra tamen brevis imperii ; quia praemia regni
  saepe indignus adit, non nisi dignus habet.   40

X.—Vespasianus

Quaerendi adtentus, moderato commodus usu,[3]
  auget nec reprimit Vespasianus opes,
olim qui dubiam privato in tempore famam,
  rarum aliis, princeps transtulit in melius.[4]

---

[1] *V* : es, *Peiper.*
[2] *cp.* Tac *Hist.* i. 49 : maior privato visus dum privatus
fuit, et omnium consensu capax imperii nisi imperasset.
[3] *cp.* Suet. *Vesp.* xvi.: male partis optime usus est.
[4] *cp.* Suet. *Titus* i. : . . . quod difficillimum est in imperio,

VII.—GALBA

OLD man, deceptive in thy promise, who, uncrowned, seemed worthy to wield the sceptre, and by empire wast revealed incompetent, higher was thy repute in youth; yet 'tis a fitter order to satisfy men later, to dissatisfy them earlier.

VIII.—OTHO

LIKE to wield a sceptre vying with unclean Nero, Otho is cut off and o'erwhelmed by swift destruction. Yet for his end shall he be deserving praise, who by an honourable death did this one noble deed—he died.[1]

IX.—VITELLIUS

BRUTAL your life and base your death, nor were you worthy, Vitellius, to become Caesar; 'tis but the Fates' whim. Howbeit, 'twas a passing shadow of empire; for the unworthy often approach the prize of sovereignty: none but the worthy hold them.

X.—VESPASIAN

SET upon gathering, in reasonable spending generous, Vespasian increased his wealth, not straitened it; once in his uncrowned days bearing a blemished name,[2] as prince—rare act!—he changed it for the better.

[1] *cp. Macbeth*, I. iv. 7 f.
[2] According to Suetonius (*Vesp.* iv.), Vespasian was guilty of levying blackmail.

---

quando privatus .. ne odio quidem nedum vituperatione caruit.

XI.—Titus

Felix imperio, felix brevitate regendi,   45
    expers civilis sanguinis, orbis amor.[1]
unum dixisti moriens te crimen habere;[2]
    set nulli de te, nec tibi credidimus.

XII.—Domitianus

Hactenus edideras dominos, gens Flavia, iustos.
    cur duo quae dederant, tertius eripuit?   50
vix tanti est habuisse illos, quia dona bonorum
    sunt brevia; aeternum, quae nocuere, dolent.

DE CAESARIBUS POST TRANQUILLUM TETRASTICHA

XIII.—Nerva

Proximus extincto moderatur sceptra tyranno
    Nerva senex, princeps nomine, mente parens.
nulla viro suboles; imitatur adoptio prolem,   55
    quam legisse iuvat, quam genuisse velit.

---

[1] *cp.* Suet. *Titus* i.: Titus . . . amor ac deliciae generis humani.
[2] *cp. id.* x.: neque enim extare ullum suum factum paenitendum dumtaxat uno.

---

[1] See Suet. *Titus*, ix., who reports that Titus "declared that henceforth he would be neither the principal nor

XI.—Titus

HAPPY in thy sway, happy in the shortness of thy reign, guiltless of thy country's blood,[1] the world's darling, thou! Dying, thou saidst one only fault[2] was thine; but we believe none speaking thus of thee—not even thee thyself.

XII.—Domitian

So far thou hadst brought forth righteous princes, House of the Flavians. Why did the third snatch that away which the two had given? Scarce is it worth the price to have possessed those, for good men's gifts are passing; injuries once done rankle for ever.[3]

QUATRAINS ON THE CAESARS AFTER THE AGE OF TRANQUILLUS

XIII.—Nerva

THE tyrant destroyed, old Nerva next wields the sceptre—a prince in name, in heart a father. Childless is he; adoption gives him offspring's substitute —one whose choice delights him, whose birth he fain would own.

accessory in the death of any man, vowing that he would perish himself rather than destroy anyone."

[2] According to Suet. *Titus*, x., "Titus did not himself reveal its nature, nor can anyone easily conjecture it."

[3] *cp. Julius Caesar*, III. ii. 81 f. :

> " The evil that men do lives after them :
> The good is oft interred with their bones."

AUSONIUS

XIV.—Traianus

Adgreditur regimen viridi Traianus in aevo,
 belli laude prior, cetera patris habens.
hic quoque prole carens sociat sibi sorte legendi,
 quem fateare bonum, diffiteare parem.   60

XV.—Hadrianus

Aelius hinc subiit mediis praesignis in actis:
 principia et finem fama notat gravior.
orbus et hic: cui iunctus erit documenta daturus,[1]
 adsciti quantum praemineant genitis.

XVI.—Antoninus Pius

Antoninus abhinc regimen capit ille vocatu   65
 consultisque Pius, nomen habens meriti.
filius huic fato nullus; set lege suorum
 a patria sumpsit, qui regeret patriam.

XVII.—M. Antoninus

Post Marco tutela datur, qui scita Platonis
 flexit ad imperium patre Pio melior.   70
successore suo moriens, set principe pravo,
 hoc solo patriae, quod genuit, nocuit.

 ¹ *V*: sociansque virum . . . daturum, *Z.*

---

¹ The reference is to the execution of Nigrinus and four
other *consulares* early in Hadrian's principate, and of Severi-
anus and others suspected as likely to succeed him during
his last years: see Spartianus, *Hadr.* vii., xxii.
² Capitolinus, *Ant.* ii., says he was accorded this title by
the Senate because in its presence he supported his aged

THE TWELVE CAESARS

XIV.—Trajan

Trajan comes to the throne in life's prime, for
war's renown more eminent, for all else like his
father. He also, lacking offspring, takes for his
partner by hazard of choice such an one as we
allow worthy, but disallow as equal.

XV.—Hadrian

Then Aelius succeeded, highly distinguished for
the deeds of his mid-reign: repute more sinister
marks its beginning and its end.[1] He, too, is child-
less: with him shall be linked one to give proof
how far adopted sons can excel the natural-born.

XVI.—Antoninus Pius

Thereafter that Antoninus receives the sway,
who by general voice and by decree was called Pius,[2]
bearing a title which proclaims his worth. Fate
gives him no son; but after the custom of his house
he took from his country one to rule his country.

XVII.—M. Antoninus

Next, charge of the state is given to Marcus, who,
nobler than his father Pius, applied Plato's maxims[3]
to the task of empire. Dying with a natural heir
but an abandoned prince, the only wrong he did his
country was to have had a son.

father-in-law; but many alternative reasons are suggested by
the same writer.

[3] *cp.* Capitolinus, *M. Antoninus*, xxvii. 7: sententia
Platonis semper in ore illius fuit florere civitates si aut
philosophi imperarent aut imperantes philosopharentur; see
Plato, *Republic*, 473 D.

XVIII.—Commodus

Commodus insequitur, pugnis maculosus harenae,
  Thraecidico princeps bella movens gladio.
eliso tandem persolvens gutture poenas,   75
  criminibus fassus matris adulterium.

XIX.—Helvius Pertinax

Helvi, iudicio et consulto lecte senati,
  princeps decretis prodite, non studiis.
quod doluit male fida cohors, errore probato,
  curia quod castris cesserat imperio.   80

XX.—Didius Iulianus

Di bene, quod sceptri Didius non gaudet opimis
  et cito periuro praemia adempta seni.
tuque, Severe pater, titulum ne horresce novantis:
  non rapit imperium vis tua, sed recipit.

XXI.—Severus Pertinax

Impiger egelido movet arma Severus ab Histro,   85
  ut parricidae regna adimat Didio.
Punica origo illi; set qui virtute probaret
  non obstare locum, cum valet ingenium.

---

[1] Commodus did not fight in the arena as a *Thraex*, but as
a Thracian Amazon. For this reason he was nicknamed
Amazonius: see Lampridius, *Commodus*, xii. 9 ff.

[2] He was strangled by the athlete Narcissus at the instance
of one of his mistresses.

[3] *sc.* Faustina the Younger. Commodus was believed to
be the offspring of a gladiator: see Capitolinus, *M. Ant.* xix.

XVIII.—Commodus

Commodus follows next, disgraced by his battles in
the arena, a prince who made war with the Thracian
sword.[1] Strangled,[2] he paid full penalty at last,
when by his crimes he had revealed his mother's
unfaithfulness.[3]

XIX.—Helvius Pertinax

Helvius, chosen by the Senate's verdict and de-
cree,[4] a prince proclaimed by statute, not by favour,
thou! This angered the treacherous bodyguard,
once their delusion was made plain, for the Senate
had yielded place to the army in authority.[5]

XX.—Didius Julianus

Thank heaven that Didius has no joy of the fruits
of sovereignty, and that its prizes soon were snatched
from that false[6] old man! And thou, father Severus,
dread not the title of usurper: your arms do not
seize the empire, but receive it.

XXI.—Severus Pertinax

Unwearying, Severus marches from chill Ister to
wrest the sovereignty from Didius the parricide.
Punic[7] by birth was he, yet such as to prove by
manliness that place is no bar when native power
is strong.

[4] *cp.* Capitolinus, *Pertinax*, vi.: suscipere se etiam im-
perium a senatu dixit.

[5] Pertinax was murdered by the Praetorian guards, who
set up Didius Julianus in his place.

[6] Didius, by accepting the empire, showed himself lacking
in loyalty to his predecessor Pertinax.

[7] According to Spartianus (*Severus*, x.), Severus was a
native of Leptis (N. Africa).

AUSONIUS

XXII.—Bassianus Antoninus sive Caracalla

Dissimilis virtute patri et multo magis illi,
    cuius adoptivo nomine te perhibes,   90
fratris morte nocens, punitus fine cruento,
    inrisu populi tu Caracalla magis.

XXIII.—Opilius Macrinus

Principis hinc custos sumptum pro Caesare ferrum
    vertit in auctorem caede Macrinus iners.
mox cum prole ruit.   gravibus pulsare querellis   95
    cesset perfidiam : quae patitur, meruit.

XXIV.—Antoninus Heliogabalus

Tune etiam Augustae sedis penetralia foedas,
    Antoninorum nomina falsa gerens,
[quo nunquam neque turpe magis neque foedius ullum
    monstrum Romano sedit in imperio ? [1]]   100

    [1] Ll. 99–100 are recorded by *Dousa*.

---

[1] Severus.
[2] Antoninus Pius (Caracalla also assumed the title Pius).
[3] Geta Caesar, put to death 212 A.D.

THE TWELVE CAESARS

XXII.—Bassianus Antoninus or Caracalla

Unlike thy father[1] in manliness, and still less like
him[2] by whose usurped name thou dost style thyself
—thou, guilty of thy brother's death[3] and punished
with a bloody end, to thy jeering people art rather
Caracalla.[4]

XXIII.—Opilius Macrinus

Next Macrinus, the prince's guard, turns the sword
he wore for Caesar's sake against him who gave it
—even in murder sluggish.[5]   Soon with his son[6] is
he o'erthrown.   Let him cease to assail treachery
with sore complaints : what he suffers he deserved.

XXIV.—Antoninus Heliogabalus

Dost thou also defile the sanctuary of the Augustan
palace, falsely bearing the name of the Antonines[7]—
thou, than whom no fouler or more filthy monster
ever filled the imperial throne of Rome ?

[4] From the hooded Gaulish overall affected by Caracalla :
see Spartianus, *Carac.* ix.
[5] Probably because Macrinus did not commit the murder
himself, but through Martial, Caracalla's groom.
[6] Antoninus Diadumenus.
[7] *cp.* Lampridius, *Heliogab.* ii.: . . . quamvis sanctum illud
Antoninorum nomen polluerit.

LIBER XV

[LIBRI DE FASTIS] CONCLUSIO

I.—Ausonius Hesperio Filio Sal [1]

(Consulari Libro subiciendi quem ego ex cunctis Con-
sulibus unum coegi. Gregorio ex Praef.[2])

Ignota aeternae ne sint tibi tempora Romae,
   regibus et patrum ducta sub imperiis,
digessi fastos et nomina praepetis aevi,
   sparsa iacent Latiam si qua per historiam.
sit tuus hic fructus, vigilatas accipe noctes: 5
   obsequitur studio nostra lucerna tuo.
tu quoque venturos per longum consere Ianos,
   ut mea digessit pagina praeteritos.
exemplum iam patris habes, ut protinus [3] et te
   adgreget [4] Ausoniis purpura consulibus.   10

---

[1] Conclusio . . . sal. This heading is found only in *V*.
[2] So *M* (in place of the title read in *V*). *Peiper* transfers
this heading to iv.
[3] *V*: exemplo confide meo: sic protinus, *Z*
[4] *V*: applicet, *Z*.

BOOK XV

CONCLUSION OF THE BOOK OF ANNALS

I.—Ausonius to his Son Hesperius, Greeting

(*To be appended to my Book of the Consuls, where I have compressed into a single volume the names of all the Consuls. To Gregorius, formerly Prefect.*)[1]

That not unknown to you may be the ages which eternal Rome has passed under the sway of Princes and of Senate, I have compiled these Annals, gathering the names which Time in his swift career has left scattered along the path of Latin history. Be yours this fruit, take the produce of my night-watches: my midnight oil burns in the service of your delight. Do you, too, through a long life link together New Years yet to come, as my page has set in order those gone by. Even now the example of your father bids you also win forthwith the purple robe and join the company of Ausonian[2] Consuls.

[1] The existence of these alternative titles shows that Ausonius " dedicated " this book twice over, and the fact that each occurs in one of the two main groups of MSS. has an important bearing on the textual tradition of Ausonius. See *Introduction*.

[2] The epithet, of course, bears a double meaning.

AUSONIUS

II.—Supputatio ab Urbe Condita in Consulatum Nostrum [1]

Annis undecies centum coniunge quaternos,
undecies unumque super trieterida necte.
haec erit aeternae series ab origine Romae.

III.—In Fine Eiusdem Libri Additi [2]

Hactenus adscripsi fastos.   si sors volet, ultra
    adiciam : si non, qui legis, adicies.
scire cupis, qui sim? titulum, qui quartus ab imo est,
    quaere : leges nomen consulis Ausonii.

IV.—De Eodem [3]

Urbis ab aeternae deductam rege Quirino
    annorum seriem cum, Procule, accipies,
mille annos centumque et bis fluxisse novenos
    consulis Ausonii nomen ad usque leges.
fors erit, ut, lustrum cum se cumulaverit istis,   5
    confectam Proculus signet Olympiadam.

---

[1] This piece is omitted in the *Z* group of MSS.
[2] This piece is omitted by *V*.
[3] *M*: de eodem fastorum libro, *G*. This poem also is
omitted in *V*.

---

[1] *i.e.* 1118 years (*cp.* iv. 3-4); but since Ausonius was
consul in 379 A.D., this gives the date of the foundation of
Rome as 739 instead of 753 B.C., the traditional date.

CONCLUSION OF THE BOOK OF ANNALS

II.—A CALCULATION OF THE YEARS FROM THE FOUNDATION OF THE CITY DOWN TO MY CONSULATE

To eleven times a hundred years join four, then add eleven times one and three beside.[1] This will be the tale of years passed since the beginning of eternal Rome.

III.—LINES WRITTEN AT THE END OF THE SAME BOOK

UP to this point have I written my annals. If Fortune will, I will carry them yet further; if not, you who read will add to them. Would you know who I am? Look up the entry which is fourth from the last:[2] you will read the name of Ausonius the Consul.

IV.—ON THE SAME

WHEN you receive this sequence of the years of our eternal city traced down from the time of King Quirinus, you will read that a thousand years, a hundred and twice nine have ebbed away ere you come on the name of Ausonius the Consul. Perchance when five years have been added to that tale, Proculus[3] shall seal the complete Olympiad.

---

[2] These lines were therefore written in 382 A.D., while I. and II. were composed in 379 A.D. It is noteworthy that this poem addresses neither Hesperius nor Proculus, but the general reader (cp. l. 2, *qui legis* ; l. 3, *scire cupis qui sim ?*).

[3] Proculus Gregorius was *praefectus praetorio* of the Gauls 382–3, and this book was therefore re-dedicated to him in 383. Ausonius evidently anticipated that he would be consul in 384, but the arrangement was upset by the revolt of Maximus (383) and death of Gratian.

LIBER XVI

GRIPHUS TERNARII NUMERI

Ausonius Symmacho

Latebat inter nugas meas libellus ignobilis; utinamque latuisset neque indicio suo tamquam sorex periret. hunc ego cum velut gallinaceus Euclionis situ chartei pulveris eruissem, excussum relegi atque ut avidus faenerator inprobum nummum malui occupare quam condere. dein cogitans mecum, non illud Catullianum,[1]

> cui dono lepidum novum libellum,

set ἀμουσότερον et verius:

> cui dono inlepidum, rudem libellum,

non diu quaesivi. tu enim occurristi, quem ego, si mihi potestas sit ex omnibus deligendi, unum semper elegerim. misi itaque ad te haec frivola gerris Siculis vaniora, ut, cum agis nihil, haec legas et, ne nihil

----

[1] Catullus, i. 1.

----

[1] According to Hesychius, *griphus* (γρῖφος) was a form of riddle popular at wine-parties.

[2] *cp.* Ter. *Eun.* 1024 : egomet meo indicio miser quasi sorex hodie perii.

BOOK XVI

A RIDDLE[1] OF THE NUMBER THREE

AUSONIUS TO SYMMACHUS

HIDING away amongst my trash was a wretched
little book; and I would to Heaven it had kept
hidden and were not coming to grief by betraying
itself as the shrew-mouse did.[2]   When, like Euclio's
cock,[3] I had disinterred this from a litter of crumbling
paper and had shaken out the dust, I read it again,
and, as a grasping usurer, preferred to put a bad
coin out to interest rather than keep it by me. Then,
while reflecting, not in those words of Catullus,

"To whom do I give my pretty, new book?",

but less poetically and more truthfully,

"To whom do I give my ugly, rough book?",

I did not seek for long.   For you confronted me—
the man whom I, had I the power to pick from all
mankind, would ever have picked out alone.   And
so I send you this frivolous piece, more worthless
than Sicilian "junk,"[4] that, when you are doing
nothing, you may read it, and may find something to

---

[3] Plaut. *Aul.* 465 ff.   (The cock began to scratch up the
miser's pot of gold.)

[4] *Gerrae* were osier baskets: for the origin of the expression as a term of contempt, see Festus, *de Verb. Signif.* p. 83
(ed. Lindsay).

agas, defendas. igitur iste nugator libellus iam diu
secreta quidem, sed vulgi lectione laceratus perveniet
tandem in manus tuas. quem tu aut ut Aesculapius
redintegrabis ad vitam, aut ut Plato iuvante Vulcano
liberabis infamia, si pervenire non debet ad famam.

Fuit autem ineptiolae huius ista materia. in expe-
ditione, quod tempus, ut scis, licentiae militaris est,
super mensam meam facta est invitatio, non illa de
Rubrii convivio, ut Graeco more biberetur,[1] set illa
de Flacci ecloga,[2] in qua propter "mediam noctem"
et "novam lunam" et "Murenae auguratum" "ter-
nos ter cyathos attonitus petit vates." hunc locum
de ternario numero illico nostra illa poetica scabies
coepit exculpere: cuius morbi quoniam facile conta-
gium est, utinam ad te quoque prurigo commigret et
fuco tuae emendationis adiecto inpingas sphongiam,
quae inperfectum opus equi male spumantis absolvat.
ac ne me nescias gloriosum, coeptos inter pranden-

---

[1] See Cic. *in Verr.* II. i. 26: Rubrius istius comites invitat
. . . mature veniunt, discumbitur . . . fit sermo inter eos et
invitatio, ut Graeco more biberetur.
[2] Horace, *Od.* III. xix. 9 ff.: da lunae propere novae, Da
noctis mediae, da, puer, auguris Murenae . . . Ternos ter
cyathos attonitus petet Vates.

---

[1] Aesculapius restored to life Hippolytus after he had
been torn to pieces.
[2] Plato, after hearing Socrates, burned his tragedies : see
Diog Laërt. iii. 8, and *cp.* Apuleius, *de Mag.* x.
[3] *sc.* with fire.
[4] This was in the Alamannic campaign of 368-9 A.D.

do in defending it. Well, this trumpery booklet, long since mangled by its surreptitious but wide circulation, will at last come into your hands. You will either, like Aesculapius,[1] restore it to life, or, like Plato,[2] with aid of Vulcan,[3] will deliver it from disrepute, if it has no right to attain to repute.

The occasion of this bit of foolery was as follows. When I was on active service[4]—a season which, as you know, is one of military freedom—at my mess a challenge was issued to drink, not in Greek fashion[5] as at the banquet of Rubrius, but after the manner described by Flaccus in that piece of his where by reason of "midnight" and the "new moon" and "Muraena's augurship" "the bard inspired calls for thrice three cups." At this subject of the triple number that poetic itch of mine at once began scratching away: and since this disease is easily communicable, may the plaguy passion pass over to you also, and that, with some of your improving colour added, you may dash the sponge which shall give the finishing touch to the incomplete work of my badly-foaming Pegasus.[6] And that you may know me for a boaster—I began these bits of verses

---

[5] Asconius comments on Cicero, *in Verr.* II. i. 26 : "Now the Greek fashion is, as the Greeks express it, ' to drink together cup for cup,' when they make offering of unmixed wine from their cups, first saluting the gods and then naming their own friends ; for as often as they call by name upon the gods and those dear to them, so often do they drink unmixed wine."

[6] The third-century painter Nealces, dissatisfied with his rendering of a foaming horse, began to apply a sponge to delete his work, but found that the first touch had produced the effect he had vainly laboured to attain : see Pliny, *N.H.* xxxv. 10, § 104 (ed. Mayhoff). Almost the same story is related of the painter Protogenes : *ib.* §§ 102 f.

dum versiculos ante cenae tempus absolvi, hoc est,
dum bibo et paulo ante quam biberem. Sit ergo
examen pro materia et tempore. set tu quoque hoc
ipsum paulo hilarior et dilutior lege; namque iniu-
rium est de poeta male sobrio lectorem abstemium
iudicare.

Neque me fallit fore aliquem, qui hunc iocum nos-
trum acutis naribus et caperrata fronte condemnet
negetque me omnia, quae ad ternarium et novenarium
numeros pertinent, attigisse. quem ego verum di-
cere fatebor, iuste, negabo. quippe si bonus est,
quae omisi, non oblita mihi, sed praeterita existimet.
dehinc qualiscumque est, cogitet secum, quam multa
de his non repperisset, si ipse quaesisset. sciat etiam
me neque omnibus erutis usum et quibusdam oblatis
abusum. quam multa enim de ternario sciens nec-
lego! tempora et personas, genera et gradus, novem
naturalia metra cum trimetris, totam grammaticam
et musicam librosque medicinae, ter maximum Her-
men et amatorem primum philosophiae Varronisque
numeros et quidquid profanum vulgus ignorat. Post-
remo, quod facile est, cum ipse multa invenerit, com-

---

[1] Iambic, trochaic, dactylic, anapaestic, choriambic, anti-
apastic, the two Ionic metres, and the Paeonic.

[2] *sc.* Hermes Trismegistus. The title is Egyptian in
origin, and is applied to Thoth, the scribe-god. To him
were attributed forty "Hermetic" books. In the third

during tiffin and finished them before messtime,
that is to say, while drinking and a little before
drinking (again). Your criticism, therefore, must
allow for the subject and the season. Nay, do you
too read this same book when a trifle "gay" and
"wutty"; for it is unfair for a teetotal critic to
pass judgment on a poet half-seas over.

I do not forget either that there will be someone
who with keen scent and furrowed brow will damn
this jest of mine, and say that I have not touched
on all the aspects which the numbers three and nine
present. I will admit that he speaks truth, but deny
its fairness. For if he is a good sort, let him con-
sider that what I have left out has not been forgotten
by me, but passed over. Next, whatever he is like,
let him reflect how many of these instances he would
not have found if he himself had been searching.
Let him know also that I have not always employed
recondite instances, and have sometimes employed
the obvious excessively. For how many examples of
the number Three do I deliberately ignore! Tenses
and persons, genders and degrees of comparison, the
nine natural metres[1] together with the trimeters,
the whole field of grammar and music and the books
of medicine, thrice-greatest Hermes,[2] Philosophy's
first lover,[3] the numbers of Varro,[4] and all that the
uninitiate herd wots not of. Finally—and 'tis an easy
test—let him find out himself as many as he can and

and following centuries a mass of syncretistic literature was
fathered on him.

[3] Pythagoras, who first called himself φιλόσοφος instead of
σοφός.

[4] The reference is to a lost work by Varro entitled *De
Principiis Numerorum*.

paret se atque me, occupatum cum otioso, pransum
cum abstemio, iocum et ludum meum, diligentiam et
calumniam suam.   alius enim alio plura invenire
potest : nemo omnia.

Quod si alicui et obscurus videbor, aput eum me
sic tuebere : primum eiusmodi epyllia, nisi vel obscura
sint, nihil futura ; deinde numerorum naturam non
esse scirpum, ut sine nodo sint : postremo si etiam
tibi obscurus fuero, cui nihil neque non lectum est
neque non intellectum, tum vero ego beatus, quod
adfectavi, adsequar, me ut requiras, me ut desideres,
de me cogites.[1]   vale.

GRIPHUS TERNARII NUMERI

TER bibe vel totiens ternos : sic mystica lex est,
vel tria potanti vel ter tria multiplicanti,
inparibus novies ternis contexere coebum.[2]

Iuris idem tribus est, quod ter tribus : omnia in istis ;
forma hominis coepti plenique exactio partus   5
quique novem novies fati tenet ultima finis.
tris Ope progeniti fratres, tris ordine partae,

---

[1] *cp.* Ter. *Eun.*: dies noctisque me ames, me desideres,
Me somnies, me expectes, de me cogites.
[2] *cp.* Mart. Capella, ii. § 105 : numeri (ternarii) triplicatio
prima ex imparibus κύβον gignit.

---

[1] *lit.* " little poems."
[2] " To look for a knot in a bulrush " was proverbial for
looking for non-existent difficulties ; *cp.* Plaut. *Men.* 247.
[3] *i.e.* do not stop at three or nine, but complete the cube
by drinking twenty-seven cups.

then compare himself and me, a hurried worker with a leisured, one who has lunched well with one soberheaded, my playful *jeu d'esprit* with his studied artifices. For one can find more instances than another : none can find all.

But if anyone shall also think my meaning dark, you will defend me against him in this way : first, that such *tours de force* [1] will go for nothing unless they *are* dark ; secondly, that numbers are not like bulrushes, without knots ; [2] lastly, if you also find my meaning dark—you who have left nothing unconned, nothing unconquered—then indeed I shall be happy in attaining what I have sought after, to make you want me, long for me, think of me. Farewell !

A RIDDLE OF THE NUMBER THREE

THRICE drink or else as many times three cups : thus stands the mystic law—whether three draughts thou drinkest or three thrice multipliest, with nine times three uneven form the cube ! [3]

[4] The same virtue is in three as in thrice three : all things are in terms of these ; the first forming of the human shape, the due completion of the act of birth,[4] and the limit which marks man's extreme span, years nine times nine.[5] Three were the brethren born of Ops [6] (Rhea), three the sisters whom she

---

[4] The embryo first assumes human shape three months, and birth nine months, after conception : see above, *Eclogues*, viii. 15 ff., 39 f.

[5] See Censorinus, *de Die Natali*, who quotes Plato's view that the full period of man's life is represented by a square number, 9×9 years.

[6] See Hesiod, *Theog.* 453 ff.

Vesta, Ceres et Iuno, secus muliebre, sorores.
inde trisulca Iovis sunt fulmina, Cerberus inde,
inde tridens triplexque Helenae cum fratribus ovum.
ter nova Nestoreos implevit purpura fusos   11
et totiens trino cornix vivacior aevo.
quam novies terni glomerantem saecula tractus
vincunt aeripedes ter terno Nestore cervi,
tris quorum aetates superat Phoebeius oscen,   15
quem novies senior Gangeticus anteit ales,
ales cinnameo radiatus tempora nido.

    Tergemina est Hecate, tria virginis ora Dianae;
tris Charites, tria Fata, triplex vox, trina elementa.
tris in Trinacria Siredones; omnia terna: 20
tris volucres, tris semideae, tris semipuellae,
ter tribus ad palmam iussae certare camenis,
ore manu flatu buxo fide voce canentes.
tris sophiae partes, tria Punica bella, trimenstres
annorum caelique vices noctisque per umbram   25
tergemini vigiles.   ter clara instantis Eoi
signa canit serus deprenso Marte satelles.

---

   [1] For this and the following ll. *cp. Eclogue* v.
   [2] *i.e.* if the crow lived twenty-seven (human) lifetimes,
yet stags who live thirty-six lifetimes would surpass her by
nine.
   [3] The raven which brought news to Phoebus of the loves
of Ischys and Coronis, and by him was changed from white
to black: see Hesiod, *Cat. of Women* (Loeb Class. Lib.),
frag. 89 and note 3.
   [4] *sc.* the Phoenix: *cp.* Pliny, *N.H.* xii. 85.

bare in turn, Vesta, Ceres, and Juno, a female company. So triple-barbed are Jove's thunderbolts, so is it with Cerberus, so with the trident, and the triple egg whence Helen and her brethren came. Thrice was the distaff of Nestor's destiny replenished with purple yarn, and as many times doth the crow outlive that triple span.[1] And could she roll into one nine times the periods of three ages, yet by thrice Nestor's triple span do brazen-footed stags surpass her,[2] whereof three lifetimes doth the sacred bird of Phoebus[3] overpass, to be nine times outstripped by that fowl of Ganges, radiate of head within his nest of cinnamon.[4]

[1S] Triple in form is Hecate, three faces has virgin Diana; three the Graces, three the Fates, three tones hath the voice,[5] three are the elements.[6] Three Sirens were in three-cornered Sicily, triple in all respects: three birds, three demi-goddesses, three semi-maids,[7] with thrice three Muses[8] bidden to strive for the palm, employing lips, hands, and breath, making melody with pipes, strings, and voice. Three the branches of Philosophy,[9] three the Punic Wars, three months go to each change in the year and clime, threefold the watches which share Night's gloom. Thrice doth that tardy sentinel,[10] who let Mars be caught, sound the clear call of approaching

---

[5] Treble, tenor, and bass.   [6] Air, fire, and water.

[7] The Sirens were pictured as half-human and half-bird: the divine element in them was due to their birth from Phorcys.   [8] For this see Pausanias, IX. xxxiv. 2.

[9] Natural, Moral, and Rational: see Quintilian, XII. ii. 10.

[10] Alectryon, stationed by Ares to give warning of the approach of Helios (on the occasion celebrated by Demodocus), slept at his post and allowed Helios to descry the lovers. In punishment, he was changed into a cock: see Lucian, *Somnium*, 3.

et qui conceptus triplicatae vespere noctis
iussa quater ternis adfixit opima tropaeis.

 Et lyrici vates numero sunt Mnemosynarum, 30
tris solas quondam tenuit quas dextera Phoebi:
set Citheron totiens ternas ex aere sacravit
relligione patrum, qui sex sprevisse timebant.
trina Tarentino celebrata trinoctia ludo,
qualia bis genito Thebis trieterica Baccho. 35
tris primas Thraecum pugnas tribus ordine bellis
Iuniadae patrio inferias misere sepulcro.
illa etiam thalamos per trina aenigmata quaerens,
qui bipes et quadrupes foret et tripes, omnia solus,
terruit Aoniam volucris, leo, virgo triformis 40
sphinx, volucris pennis, pedibus fera, fronte puella.

 Trina in Tarpeio fulgent consortia templo.
humana efficiunt habitacula tergenus artes:
parietibus qui saxa locat, qui culmine tigna,
et qui supremo comit tectoria cultu. 45
hinc Bromii quadrantal et hinc Sicana medimna:
hoc tribus, hoc geminis tribus explicat usus agendi.

---

 [1] Hercules.
 [2] See Plautus, *Amphitryo*, 113, 271 ff.; Lucian, *Dial. of the Gods*, x.
 [3] The Nine Muses were *daughters* of Mnemosyne.
 [4] The reference is to an early statue of Apollo by Tectaeus and Angelion at Delos : see Plut. *de Mus.* xiv. It is figured on certain Athenian coins, for which see P. Gardner, *Types of Greek Coins*, Pl. XV. 29.
 [5] See Pausanias, ix. xxix. 2.

A RIDDLE OF THE NUMBER THREE

Dawn. And he[1] who was conceived in the darkness of a tripled night[2] hung up the spoils enjoined on thrice four trophies.

[30] Also the lyric poets are of one number with the Mnemosynae,[3] three of whom only Phoebus once held in his right hand:[4] but Cithaeron dedicated three times three in bronze[5]—such was our fathers' piety, who feared to slight the six. Thrice a year were games held at Tarentum[6] lasting three nights, like the three-yearly festival at Thebes for twice-born Bacchus. The three first combats of gladiators matched in three pairs—these were the offering made by the sons of Junius at their father's sepulchre.[7] She too, who asked her triple riddle of the suitors of the queen[8]—what one being was two-legged, four-legged, and three-legged, and yet the same—the Sphinx who affrighted Aonia, was of triple shape, part bird, part lioness, part maid—in wings a bird, in paws a beast, in face a girl.

[42] Three are the allied gods who shine in the temple on the Tarpeian rock. Threefold the crafts which shape man's dwelling-place: one man lays stones in the walls, a second beams in the roof, a third adds the last covering of tiles. Three is a factor of the quadrantal[9] of Bromius, as also of the Sicilian medimnus: this into three, that into twice three parts[10]

---

[6] In honour of Persephone and Dis. This Tarentum was a spot near the Campus Martius, and not the Campanian city.

[7] Gladiatorial combats were first held in 265 B.C. by Marcius and Decius Brutus at the obsequies of their father: see Valerius Max. II. iv. 7 (and cp. *Éclogues*, xxiii. 33 and note).

[8] Jocasta, whose hand was to reward the man who solved the riddle of the Sphinx. [9] *sc.* the *amphora*.

[10] The *quadrantal* or *amphora* contained three, the *medimnus* six *modii*.

in physicis tria prima, deus, mundus, data forma:
tergenus omnigenum, genitor, genetrix, generatum.

    Per trinas species trigonorum regula currit,   50
aequilatus vel crure pari vel in omnibus inpar.
tris coit in partes numerus perfectus,[1] ut idem
congrege ter terno per ter tria dissoluatur.
tris primus par, impar habet mediumque : sed ipse,
ut tris, sic quinque et septem quoque, dividit unus; 55
et numero in toto positus sub acumine centri
distinguit solidos coebo pergente [2] trientes,
aequipares dirimens partes ex inpare terno :
et paribus triplex medium, cum quattuor et sex
bisque quaternorum secernitur omphalos idem.   60

    Ius triplex, tabulae quod ter sanxere quaternae :
sacrum, privatum et populi commune quod usquam
    est.

---

[1] For this and ll. 54 ff. *cp.* Mart. Capella, vii. § 733 : trias
vero princeps imparium numerus perfectusque censendus.
Nam prior initium, medium finemque sortitur, et centrum
medietatis ad initium finemque interstitiorum aequalitate
congruit. Also Macrobius, *Comm. in Somn. Scip.* I. vi. 23 :
primo ergo ternario contigit numero ut inter duo summa
medium quo vinciretur acciperet.   [2] pereunte, *Z.*

---

[1] *i.e.* the Efficient, the Material, and the Formal Cause.
[2] The play on the root *gen-* cannot be reproduced without
taking certain liberties alike with Latin and English.
[3] The perfect number is *three* (*cp.* Mart. Capella, quoted
in note on text, l. 52), which when multiplied by three is
perfectly divisible by 3 × 3. It is the first to possess a medial
unit with a first and second unit (*par*, *impar*, l. 54) on either
side of it (or perhaps, to contain an even number, 2, and an

is broken up in common use. In natural science are three prime causes, God, matter, and the shape given:[1] three-formed is all formation, the former, the formatrix, and the formed.[2]

[50] Over three kinds ranges the figure of the triangle, equilateral, isosceles, and scalene. Three parts combined make up the perfect number,[3] in such wise that if a group thrice three be formed, by three times three the same may be resolved. Three is the first number which has an odd, an even, and a medial unit: but, as the unit itself divides[4] three, so does it five and seven; and when 'tis placed under[5] the central point of the full number, it parts in two a series of thirds forming a continuous cube,[6] by separating even and equal groups from the uneven threes: and even numbers thrice find a centre, when the same midmost point of four, six, and twice four, is bracketed.

[61] Triple the code which Tables[7] four times three ordained: the canon, the private, and the common

odd number, 3, with a unit differentiating them; since 2 + 1 = 3). Nine (3 × 3) contains *three* uneven numbers (3, 5, 7) possessing such a medial unit (ılı, ılıı, ıılıı) and, if the medial is placed "under" the centre (*i.e.* left out of count), itself is transformed from an odd group of three (*i.e.* of three threes: *impare terno*, l. 58) into two equal (*aequipares*, l. 58) of four each: the medial unit then marks the centre of the thirds (*trientes*, l. 57) which make up the cube 8 (*sc.* 2 × 2 × 2: *cp.* Mart. Capella, vii. § 740). Yet again, if the medial unit is treated as a mark *only*, it shows the centre of *three* even numbers also which are contained in nine, viz. 4, 6, 8 (ıılıı, ıılııı, ıılııı).

[4] *i.e.* divides it into two equal groups.
[5] *i.e.* when it is withdrawn from the sum and is treated as a mere mark.
[6] Literally, "the thirds solid (*sc.* united) in a continuous cube." [7] *sc.* the Twelve Tables.

interdictorum trinum genus : unde repulsus
vi fuero aut utrubi fuerit quorumve bonorum.
triplex libertas capitisque minutio triplex.   65
trinum dicendi genus est : sublime, modestum
et tenui filo.   triplex quoque forma medendi,
cui logos aut methodos cuique experientia nomen.
et medicina triplex : servare, cavere, mederi.
tris oratorum cultus ; regnata Colosso   70
quem Rhodos, Actaeae quem dilexistis Athenae
et quem de scaenis tetrica ad subsellia traxit
prosa Asiae, in causis numeros imitata chororum.

    Orpheos hinc tripodes, quia sunt tria, terra, aqua,
      flamma.

triplex sideribus positus, distantia, forma.   75
et modus et genetrix modulorum musica triplex,
mixta libris, secreta astris, vulgata theatris.
Martia Roma triplex : equitatu, plebe, senatu.
hoc numero tribus et sacro de monte tribuni.

---

[1] The three legal interdicts, known by the incipits of their
formulae as *Unde vi, De utrubi,* and *Quorum bonorum,* were
for recovering, retaining, and acquiring possession of pro-
perty respectively : see *Digest,* xliii. 16 ; *id.* 32 ; *id.* 2.

[2] See Cicero, *Top.* ii. § 10.   The three methods by which
a slave could obtain freedom were (1) by purchase, (2) by
manumission, (3) by will.

[3] *i.e.* in respect of personal liberty, civic rights, or family.

[4] *cp.* Quintilian, XII. x. 58 ff. (who calls the third mode
subtile or ἰσχνόν : *cp.* Milton, *Sonnet* xi. 2, " woven close ").

[5] For this division *cp.* Jerome, *Dial. contra Pelagianos,* xxi.
(A school of physicians who held that diseases might be
cured by specific treatment through diet and exercise were
known as " Methodists.")

law which is current everywhere. The legal inter-
dict has three formulae, the *whence by force* I have
been put out, the *wherever he has been*, and the *which
goods*.[1] In three ways freedom is acquired,[2] in three
ways civil rights may be attainted.[3] Three are the
modes of eloquence, the exalted, the restrained, and
the close-wove.[4] Medicine also has three branches,
called theory, practice, and empiric.[5] And Medicine
in aim is triple, to maintain health, prevent disease,
and heal. Three are the styles of oratory:[6] the
first from Rhodes, dominated by its Colossus, the
second beloved by thee, Attic Athens, and thirdly
that which the prose of Asia dragged from the stage
to the crabbed benches of the law, imitating in our
courts the lilt of choric songs.

[74] This number explains Orpheus' *Tripod*,[7] because
there are three elements, earth, water, fire. Triple
the classification of the stars, according to their
station, distance, and their magnitude. The modes [8]
also are threefold, and so is Music, mother of
measures—that woven into books,[9] that possessed in
secret by the stars, and that purveyed in our theatres.
Mars' city, Rome, hath three orders, Knights, Com-
mons, Senators. From this number the *tribe* [10] takes
its name, as do the *tribunes* of the Sacred Mount.[11]

[6] For these three styles see Quintilian, XII. x. 18.
[7] Either the title of a work attributed to Orpheus, or
some symbolical figure in which the three elements were
conceived of as the legs of a tripod supporting the universe.
[8] The Dorian, Phrygian, and Lydian.
[9] *i.e.* rhythm.
[10] *Tribus*, denoting originally a third part of the Roman
people, is derived, according to Corssen, from *tri* + a root
$b(h)u = φυ$- (as in φυλή).
[11] The tribunate was established 494 B.C., after the secession
of the plebs to the Sacred Mount.

tres equitum turmae, tria nomina nobiliorum.　　　80

nomina sunt chordis tria, sunt tria nomina mensi.

Geryones triplices, triplex conpago Chimaerae:

Scylla triplex, commissa tribus: cane, virgine, pisce.

Gorgones Harpalycaeque et Erinyes agmine terno,

et tris fatidicae, nomen commune, Sibyllae,　　　85

quarum tergemini fatalia carmina libri,

quos ter quinorum servat cultura virorum.

　　Ter bibe.　tris numerus super omnia, tris deus unus.

hic quoque ne ludus numero transcurrat inerti,

ter decies ternos habeat deciesque novenos.　　　90

---

[1] *sc.* the *praenomen*, or personal name, the *nomen*, determining the *gens* of the individual, and the *cognomen*: *e.g.* Marcus Junius Brutus.

[2] The bass (*gravis*, ὑπάτη), the tenor (*media*, μέση), and the treble (*acuta*, νητή).

A RIDDLE OF THE NUMBER THREE

Three are the squadrons of the Knights, three the names borne by the nobility.[1] The chords have three names,[2] and three names each month[3] owns. Geryones was three in one, triple the compound of Chimaera: Scylla was triple, a mixture of three forms, part dog, part woman, and part fish. The Gorgons, Harpies, and Erinyes lived in bands of three, and three the soothsaying Sibyls,[4] bearers of a common name, whose fateful verses, couched in volumes three, are preserved in the keeping of the thrice five men.[5]

[88] Thrice drink! The number three is above all, Three Persons and one God! And that this conceit may not run its course without significance of number, let it have verses thrice ten times three, or nine times ten!

[3] *i.e.* each month contains the three days, Calends, Nones, and Ides.

[4] Presumably the Sibyls of Delphi, Cumae, and Erythrae; but many other Sibyls were known.

[5] The Sibylline books were first in the charge of Duumviri, then of Decemviri, and (from the first century B.C.) of Quindecimviri.

LIBER XVII

CENTO NUPTIALIS

Ausonius Paulo S.

Perlege hoc etiam, si operae est, frivolum et
nullius pretii opusculum, quod nec labor excudit
nec cura limavit, sine ingenii acumine et morae
maturitate.

Centonem vocant, qui primi hac concinnatione
luserunt. solae memoriae negotium sparsa colligere
et integrare lacerata, quod ridere magis quam laudare
possis. pro quo, si per sigillaria in auctione veniret,
neque Afranius naucum daret, neque ciccum suum
Plautus offerret. piget enim Vergiliani carminis dig-
nitatem tam ioculari dehonestasse materia. sed quid
facerem? iussum erat: quodque est potentissimum
imperandi genus, rogabat, qui iubere poterat, sanctus
imperator Valentinianus, vir meo iudicio eruditus.
nuptias quondam eiusmodi ludo descripserat, aptis

---

[1] = κέντρων. ἐγκεντρίζειν means "to plant slips" (of trees).
A late Greek word, κεντόνη, or κεντονάρων, meaning a patch-
work garment, is also found. A cento is therefore a poem
composed of odd fragments. Such works were common in

BOOK XVII

A NUPTIAL CENTO

Ausonius to Paulus, Greeting

READ through this also, if it is worth while—a trifling and worthless little book, which no pains has shaped nor care polished, without a spark of wit and that ripeness which deliberation gives.

They who first trifled with this form of compilation call it a "cento." [1] 'Tis a task for the memory only, which has to gather up scattered tags and fit these mangled scraps together into a whole, and so is more likely to provoke your laughter than your praise. If it were put up for auction at a fair,[2] Afranius would not give his straw, nor Plautus bid his husk.[3] For it is vexing to have Virgil's majestic verse degraded with such a comic theme. But what was I to do? It was written by command, and at the request (which is the most pressing kind of order!) of one who was able to command—the sainted Emperor Valentinian, a man, in my opinion, of deep learning. He had once described a wedding in a *jeu d'esprit* of this kind, wherein the verses were to

---

later antiquity : *e.g.* Falconia Proba dedicated to Honorius a *Cento Vergilianus* dealing with the events of the Old and New Testaments.

[2] On the Sigillaria see above, *Eclogues*, xxiii. 32 and note.

[3] *Rudens*, 580 : ciccum non interduim.

371

equidem versibus et compositione festiva. experiri
deinde volens, quantum nostra contentione praecelle-
ret, simile nos de eodem concinnare praecepit. quam
scrupulosum hoc mihi fuerit, intellege : neque ante-
ferri volebam neque posthaberi, cum aliorum quoque
iudicio detegenda esset adulatio inepta, si cederem,
insolentia, si ut aemulus eminerem. suscepi igitur
similis recusanti feliciterque et obnoxius gratiam
tenui nec victor offendi.

Hoc, tum die uno et addita lucubratione propera-
tum, modo inter liturarios meos cum reperissem,
tanta mihi candoris tui et amoris fiducia est, ut
severitati tuae nec ridenda subtraherem. accipe
igitur opusculum de inconexis continuum, de di-
versis unum, de seriis ludicrum, de alieno nostrum :
ne in sacris et fabulis aut Thyonianum mireris aut
Virbium, illum de Dionyso, hunc de Hippolyto[1]
reformatum.

Et si pateris, ut doceam docendus ipse, cento quid
sit, absolvam. variis de locis sensibusque diversis
quaedam carminis structura solidatur, in unum ver-
sum ut coeant aut caesi duo aut unus et sequens
<medius> cum medio. nam duos iunctim locare
ineptum est, et tres una serie merae nugae. diffin-
duntur autem per caesuras omnes, quas recipit[2]

---

[1] Hippolytus as rehabilitated by Aesculapius, after he had
been torn to pieces.

[2] *i.e.* the lines of the poet from whose works the cento is
compiled.

the point and their connections amusing. Then, wishing to show by means of a competition with me the great superiority of his production, he bade me compile a similar poem on the same subject. Just picture how delicate a task this was for me! I did not wish to leave him nowhere, nor yet to be left behind myself; since my foolish flattery was bound to be patent to the eyes of other critics as well, if I gave way, or my presumption, if I rivalled and surpassed him. I undertook the task, therefore, with an air of reluctance and with happy results, and, as obedient, kept in favour and, as successful, gave no offence.

This book, then hurriedly composed in a single day with some lamp-lit hours thrown in, I lately found among my rough drafts; and so great is my confidence in your sincerity and affection, that for all your gravity I could not withhold even a ludicrous production. So take a little work, continuous, though made of disjointed tags; one, though of various scraps; absurd, though of grave materials; mine, though the elements are another's; lest you should wonder at the accounts given by priests or poets of the Son of Thyone or of Virbius [1]—the first reshaped out of Dionysus, the second out of Hippolytus.

And if you will suffer me, who need instruction myself, to instruct you, I will expound what a cento is. It is a poem compactly built out of a variety of passages and different meanings, in such a way that either two half-lines are joined together to form one, or one line and the following half with another half. For to place two (whole) lines side by side is weak, and three in succession is mere trifling. But the lines [2] are divided at any of the caesurae which

versus heroicus, convenire ut possit aut penthe-
mimeris cum reliquo anapaestico, aut trochaice cum
posteriore segmento, aut septem semipedes cum ana-
paestico chorico, aut <ponatur> post dactylum atque
semipedem quidquid restat hexametro : simile ut
dicas ludicro, quod Graeci ostomachion vocavere.
ossicula ea sunt : ad summam quattuordecim figuras
geometricas habent.   sunt enim aequaliter triquetra
vel extentis lineis vel [eiusdem] frontis, [vel rectis] [1]
angulis vel obliquis : isoscele ipsi vel isopleura vocant,
orthogonia quoque et scalena.   harum verticularum
variis coagmentis simulantur species mille formarum :
helephantus belua aut aper bestia, anser volans et
mirmillo in armis, subsidens venator et latrans canis,
quin et turris et cantharus et alia huiusmodi innu-
merabilium figurarum, quae alius alio scientius varie-
gant.   sed peritorum concinnatio miraculum est, im-
peritorum iunctura ridiculum.   quo praedicto scies,
quod ego posteriorem imitatus sum.

Hoc ergo centonis opusculum ut ille ludus trac-
tatur, pari modo sensus diversi ut congruant,
adoptiva quae sunt, ut cognata videantur, aliena ne
interluceant : arcessita ne vim redarguant, densa
ne supra modum protuberent, hiulca ne pateant.

---

[1] So *Peiper* : aequilatera vel triquetra . . . vel frontis
angulis vel obliquis, *MSS.*

---

[1] *sc.* " A Battle of Bones."   For the nature of this puzzle
see Appendix, p. 395.

heroic verse admits, so that either a penthemimeris
($-\cup\cup-\cup\cup-$) can be linked with an anapaestic con-
tinuation ($\cup\cup-\cup\cup-\cup\cup--$), or a trochaic fragment
($-\cup\cup-\cup\cup-\cup$) with a complementary section
($\cup-\cup\cup-\cup\cup--$), or seven half-feet ($-\cup\cup-\cup\cup-\cup\cup-$)
with a choric anapaest ($--\cup\cup-$), or after a dactyl
and a half-foot ($-\cup\cup-$) is placed whatever is needed
to complete the hexameter: so that you may say
it is like the puzzle which the Greeks have called
ostomachia.[1] There you have little pieces of bone,
fourteen in number and representing geometrical
figures. For some are equilateral triangles, some
with sides of various lengths, some symmetrical,
some with right angles, some with oblique: the same
people call them isosceles or equal-sided triangles,
and also right-angled and scalene. By fitting these
pieces together in various ways, pictures of countless
objects are produced: a monstrous elephant, a brutal
boar, a goose in flight, and a gladiator in armour, a
huntsman crouching down, and a dog barking—even
a tower and a tankard and numberless other things
of this sort, whose variety depends upon the skill of
the player. But while the harmonious arrangement
of the skilful is marvellous, the jumble made by the
unskilled is grotesque. This prefaced, you will know
that I am like the second kind of player.

And so this little work, the *Cento,* is handled in
the same way as the game described, so as to har-
monize different meanings, to make pieces arbitrarily
connected seem naturally related, to let foreign ele-
ments show no chink of light between, to prevent
the far-fetched from proclaiming the force which
united them, the closely packed from bulging un-
duly, the loosely knit from gaping. If you find all

quae si omnia ita tibi videbuntur, ut praeceptum
est, dices me composuisse centonem. et quia sub
imperatore meo tum merui, procedere mihi inter
frequentes stipendium iubebis: sin aliter, aere
dirutum[1] facies, ut cumulo carminis in fiscum suum
redacto redeant versus, unde venerunt. vale.

I.—PRAEFATIO

ACCIPITE haec animis laetasque advertite mentes,[2]
ambo animis, ambo insignes praestantibus armis ; [3]
ambo florentes,[4] genus insuperabile bello.[5]
tuque prior,[6] nam te maioribus ire per altum
auspiciis manifesta fides,[7] quo iustior alter   5
nec pietate fuit, nec bello maior et armis ; [8]
tuque puerque tuus,[9] magnae spes altera Romae,[10]
flos veterum virtusque virum,[11] mea maxima cura,[12]
nomine avum referens, animo manibusque pa-
          rentem.[13]

non iniussa cano.[14] sua cuique exorsa laborem   10
fortunamque ferent:[15] mihi iussa capessere fas est.[16]

---

[1] cp. Festus, de Verb. Signif., ed. Lindsay, p. 61 : dirutum
vere militem dicebant antiqui cui stipendium ignominiae
causa non erat datum, quod aes diruebatur in fiscum, non in
militis sacculum.
[2] Aen. v. 304.   [3] Aen. xi. 291.   [4] Ecl. vii. 4.
[5] Aen. iv. 40.   [6] Aen. vi. 834.   [7] Aen. iii. 374 f.
[8] Aen. i. 544 f.   [9] Aen. iv. 94.   [10] Aen. xii. 168.

these conditions duly fulfilled according to rule, you will say that I have compiled a cento. And because I served at the time [1] under my commanding officer, you will direct "that pay be issued to me as for regular service";[2] but if otherwise, you will sentence me "to forfeit pay," so that this "lump sum" of verse may be "returned to its proper pay-chest," and the verses go back to the source from which they came. Farewell.

I.—The Preface

Give heed to these my words and hither turn gladsome minds, ye twain for courage, ye twain for prowess in arms renowned, ye twain who prosper— a breed invincible in war. And thou especially— for there is clear assurance that under high omens thou passest o'er the deep—than whom none ever was more strict in reverence of the gods, none greater in war and deeds of arms; thou and thy son, the second hope of mighty Rome, the flower and excellence of heroes of old time and my especial charge—he who in name is his grandfather's double, but in spirit and in might his father's. I sing as I am bidden. To each his own essay shall bring toil and event: for me 'tis lawful to perform a task enjoined.

[1] *i.e.* at the time of composition: the use of military phraseology suggests that the cento was composed while Ausonius was on active service, 368–9 A.D.

[2] Ausonius is here adapting the technical phraseology of military administration.

---

[11] *Aen.* viii. 500.   [12] *Aen.* i. 678.   [13] *Aen.* xii. 348.
[14] *Ecl.* vi. 9.   [15] *Aen.* x. 111 f.   [16] *Aen.* i. 77.

II.—Cena Nuptialis

Expectata dies aderat [1] dignisque hymenaeis [2]
matres atque viri,[3] iuvenes ante ora parentum [4]
conveniunt stratoque super discumbitur ostro.
dant famuli manibus lymphas [5] onerantque can-
    istris   15
dona laboratae Cereris [6] pinguisque ferinae [7]
viscera tosta ferunt.[8]   series longissima rerum : [9]
alituum pecudumque genus [10] capreaeque sequaces [11]
non absunt illic [12] neque oves haedique petulci [13]
et genus aequoreum,[14] dammae cervique fugaces:[15] 20
ante oculos interque manus sunt [16] mitia poma.[17]

    Postquam exempta fames et amor compressus
      edendi,[18]
crateras magnos statuunt [19] Bacchumque ministrant.[20]
sacra canunt,[21] plaudunt choreas et carmina dicunt.[22]
nec non Thraeicius longa cum veste sacerdos   25
obloquitur numeris septem discrimina vocum.[23]
at parte ex alia [24] biforem dat tibia cantum.[25]
omnibus una quies operum,[26] cunctique relictis
consurgunt mensis : [27] per limina laeta frequentes,[28]
discurrunt variantque vices [29] populusque patres-
    que,[30]   30
matronae, pueri,[31] vocemque per ampla volutant
atria : dependent lychni laquearibus aureis.[32]

[1] *Aen.* v. 104.	[2] *Aen.* xi. 355.	[3] *Aen.* vi. 306.
[4] *Georg.* iv. 477.	[5] *Aen.* i. 700 f.	[6] *Aen.* viii. 180.
[7] *Aen.* i. 215.	[8] *Aen.* viii. 180.	[9] *Aen.* i. 641.
[10] *Aen.* viii. 27.	[11] *Georg.* ii. 374.	[12] *Georg.* ii. 471.
[13] *Georg.* iv. 10.	[14] *Georg.* iii. 243.	[15] *Georg.* iii. 539.
[16] *Aen.* xi. 311.	[17] *Ecl.* i. 80.	[18] *Aen.* viii. 184.

A NUPTIAL CENTO

II.—The Marriage Feast

The looked-for day was come, and at the noble bridal, matrons and men, with youths under their parents' eyes, gather together and recline on coverlets of purple. Servants bring water for their hands, load in baskets the gifts of hard-won Ceres, and bear the roasted flesh of fat game. Most ample the list of their dainties: all kinds of fowl and flesh with wanton goat are present there, and sheep and playful kids, the watery tribe, and does, and timid stags: before their gaze and in their hands are mellow apples.

[22] When hunger had been put away and desire for food was stayed, great mixing bowls are set and wine is served. Hymns do they chant, they beat the ground in dances, and songs repeat. Withal, a long-robed Thracian priest accompanies on his seven strings their various tones. But on another side the flute breathes song from its twin mouths. All have the same repose from toil, and all arising leave the tables: passing in a throng over the jocund threshold, the company of fathers, mothers, boys, disperses into ever-changing groups, their voices echoing through the spacious halls beneath the lamps which from the gilded fretting hang.

---

[19] *Aen.* i. 724.   [20] *Aen.* viii. 181.   [21] *Aen.* ii. 239.
[22] *Aen.* vi. 644.   [23] *Aen.* vi. 645 f.   [24] *Aen.* x. 362.
[25] *Aen.* ix. 618.   [26] *Georg.* iv. 184.   [27] *Aen.* viii. 109 f.
[28] *Aen.* i. 707.   [29] *Aen.* ix. 164.   [30] *Aen.* ix. 192.
[31] *Aen.* xi. 476.   [32] *Aen.* i. 725 f.

III.—Descriptio Egredientis Sponsae

Tandem progreditur [1] Veneris iustissima cura,[2]
iam matura viro, iam plenis nubilis annis,[3]
virginis os habitumque gerens,[4] cui plurimus ignem   35
subiecit rubor et calefacta per ora cucurrit,[5]
intentos volvens oculos,[6] uritque videndo.[7]
illam omnis tectis agrisque effusa iuventus
turbaque miratur matrum.[8]   vestigia primi
alba pedis,[9] dederatque comam diffundere ventis.[10]   40
fert picturatas auri subtemine vestes,[11]
ornatus Argivae Helenae : [12] qualisque videri
caelicolis et quanta solet [13] Venus aurea contra,[14]
talis erat species,[15] talem se laeta ferebat [16]
ad soceros [17] solioque alte subnixa resedit.[18]   45

IV.—Descriptio Egredientis Sponsi

At parte ex alia [19] foribus sese intulit altis [20]
ora puer prima signans intonsa iuventa,[21]
pictus aɔu [22] chlamydem auratam, quam plurima
    circum
purpura maeandro duplici Meliboea cucurrit,[23]
et tunicam, molli mater quam neverat auro : [24]   50
os umerosque deo similis [25] lumenque iuventae.[26]

---

[1] *Aen.* iv. 136.   [2] *Aen.* x. 132.   [3] *Aen.* vii. 53.
[4] *Aen.* i. 315.   [5] *Aen.* xii. 65 f.   [6] *Aen.* vii. 251.
[7] *Georg.* iii. 215.   [8] *Aen.* vii. 812 f.   [9] *Aen.* v. 566 f.
[10] *Aen.* i. 319.   [11] *Aen.* iii. 483.   [12] *Aen.* i. 650.
[13] *Aen.* ii. 591 f.   [14] *Aen.* x. 16.   [15] *Aen.* vi. 208.
[16] *Aen.* i. 503.   [17] *Aen.* ii. 457.   [18] *Aen.* i. 506.

A NUPTIAL CENTO

III.—A Picture of the Bride as she comes forth

At length comes forth Venus' most lawful charge, already ripe for wedlock, already of full age for marriage, wearing a maiden's look and garb, o'er whose flushed cheeks a deep blush spreads, suffusing fire, while round she throws her eager eyes and inflames all with her gaze. At her the whole company of youths, gathered from house and field, and throng of matrons marvel. The whiteness of her advancing foot she displays,[1] her hair she had given to the winds to spread abroad. She wears a robe embroidered with thread of gold, apparel such as Argive Helen wore: as golden Venus is wont to appear before the gods in Heaven in beauty and in stature, so seemed she, and in such wise the joyful maid drew near the bridegroom's parents and sat supported on a lofty throne.

IV.—A Picture of the Bridegroom as he comes forth

But from the other side there entered by the lofty doors a youth whose unshorn cheeks bare token of early manhood, clad in a cloak bedecked with needlework of gold, about which ran an ample band of Meliboean purple in a double fret, and in a tunic wherein his mother had woven tissue of soft gold. In face and shoulders like a god was he, and in his

---

[1] The verb must be supplied from *ostentans* (in the original context).

---

[19] *Aen.* x. 362.   [20] *Aen.* xi. 36.   [21] *Aen.* ix. 181.
[22] *Aen.* ix. 582.   [23] *Aen.* v. 250 f.   [24] *Aen.* x. 818.
[25] *Aen.* i. 589.   [26] *Aen.* i. 590.

qualis, ubi oceani perfusus Lucifer unda[1]
extulit os sacrum caelo:[2] sic ora ferebat,[3]
sic oculos[4] cursuque amens ad limina tendit.[5]
illum turbat amor figitque in virgine vultus;[6]   55
oscula libavit[7] dextramque amplexus inhaesit.[8]

V.—Oblatio Munerum

Incedunt pueri pariterque ante ora parentum[9]
dona ferunt,[10] pallam signis auroque rigentem,[11]
munera portantes aurique eborisque talenta
et sellam[12] et pictum croceo velamen acantho,[13]   60
ingens argentum mensis[14] colloque monile
bacatum et duplicem gemmis auroque coronam.[15]
olli serva datur[16] geminique sub ubere nati:[17]
quattuor huic iuvenes[18] totidem innuptaeque
     puellae:[19]
omnibus in morem tonsa coma;[20] pectore summo   65
flexilis obtorti per collum circulus auri.[21]

VI.—Epithalamium Utrique

Tum studio effusae matres[22] ad limina ducunt;[23]
at chorus aequalis,[24] pueri innuptaeque puellae,[25]
versibus incomptis ludunt[26] et carmina dicunt:[27]
" O digno coniuncta viro,[28] gratissima coniunx,[29]   70

[1] *Aen.* viii. 589.	[2] *Aen.* viii. 591.	[3] *Aen.* iii. 490.
[4] *Aen.* iii. 490.	[5] *Aen.* ii. 321.	[6] *Aen.* xii. 70.
[7] *Aen.* i. 256.	[8] *Aen.* viii. 124.	[9] *Aen.* v. 553.
[10] *Aen.* v. 101.	[11] *Aen.* i. 648.	[12] *Aen.* xi. 333.
[13] *Aen.* i. 711.	[14] *Aen.* i. 640.	[15] *Aen.* i. 654 f.

A NUPTIAL CENTO

youthful eyes. As Lucifer when, bedrenched with
Ocean's waves, he lifts his sacred head in heaven,
so seemed this youth in feature and in glance, as in
wild haste he hastens to the threshold. Him does
Love o'erwhelm, and on the maid he fixes his gaze;
he tastes her kisses and, grasping her right hand,
holds it close.

V.—The Offering of Presents

THE boys advance and, all together before their
parents' eyes, bring their gifts, a robe stiff with em-
broidery of gold, carrying as offerings talents of gold
and ivory, a chair, a veil adorned with acanthus leaves
in saffron, a great piece of plate for the table, for the
neck a string of pearls, and a diadem of both gems
and gold. To her a slave-girl is given with twin
children at her breast: to him, four youths and as
many maids unwed, all with heads shorn as custom
is; while on their breasts hung pliant necklets of
twisted gold.

VI.—The Epithalamium Addressed to Both

THEN eagerly pressing forth, the matrons lead the
pair to the threshold; but the company of their
peers, boys and unwedded girls, make merry with
unpolished verse, and thus they sing: "O thou that
art mated with a worthy lord, bride most acceptable,

---

[16] *Aen.* v. 284.   [17] *Aen.* v. 285.   [18] *Aen.* x. 518.
[19] *Aen.* ii. 238.   [20] *Aen.* v. 556.   [21] *Aen.* v. 558 f.
[22] *Aen.* xii. 131.   [23] *Aen.* x. 117.   [24] *Georg.* iv. 460.
[25] *Aen.* vi. 307.   [26] *Georg.* ii. 386.   [27] *Aen.* vi. 644.
[28] *Ecl.* viii. 32.   [29] *Aen.* x. 607.

sis felix,[1] primos Lucinae experta labores [2]
et mater.   cape Maeonii carchesia Bacchi.[3]
sparge, marite, nuces;[4] cinge haec altaria vitta,[5]
flos veterum virtusque virum:[6] tibi ducitur uxor,[7]
omnes ut tecum meritis pro talibus annos   75
exigat et pulchra faciat te prole parentem.[8]
fortunati ambo,[9] si quid pia numina possunt,[10]
vivite felices." [11]   dixerunt "currite" fusis
concordes stabili fatorum numine Parcae.[12]

VII.—Ingressus in Cubiculum

Postquam est in thalami pendentia pumice tecta   80
perventum,[13] licito tandem sermone fruuntur.[14]
congressi iungunt dextras [15] stratisque reponunt.[16]
at Cytherea novas artes [17] et pronuba Iuno [18]
sollicitat suadetque ignota lacessere bella.[19]
ille ubi complexu [20] molli fovet atque repente   85
accepit solitam flammam [21] lectumque iugalem:[22]
"O virgo, nova mi facies,[23] gratissima coniunx,[24]
venisti tandem,[25] mea sola et sera voluptas.[26]
o dulcis coniunx, non haec sine numine divum [27]
proveniunt:[28] placitone etiam pugnabis amori?"[29] 90
     Talia dicentem iamdudum aversa tuetur [30]

[1] *Aen.* i. 330.	[2] *Georg.* iv. 340.	[3] *Georg.* iv. 380.
[4] *Ecl.* viii. 30.	[5] *Ecl.* viii. 64.	[6] *Aen.* viii. 500.
[7] *Ecl.* viii. 29.	[8] *Aen.* i. 74 f.	[9] *Aen.* ix. 446.
[10] *Aen.* iv. 382.	[11] *Aen.* iii. 493.	[12] *Ecl.* iv. 46 f.
[13] *Georg.* iv. 374 f.	[14] *Aen.* viii. 468.	[15] *Aen.* viii. 467.
[16] *Aen.* iv. 392.	[17] *Aen.* i. 657.	[18] *Aen.* iv. 166.

mayest thou be blessed when thou first hast felt
Lucina's pangs and art a mother. Take goblets of
Maeonian wine. O bridegroom, scatter nuts; wreathe
round these altars with fillets, thou flower and excel-
lence of heroes of old time : thou tak'st a wife to
live out all her years with thee—such is thy high
worth—and with fair offspring to make thee a father.
Blessed be ye both, if favouring gods aught avail,
live happily!" The Parcae, one in heart with the
unwavering power of Destiny, cried to their spindles,
"Speed on!"

VII.—The Entry into the Bedchamber

When they twain were come into the bridal chamber
with its soaring vault of stone, they enjoy such speech
as is at length permitted. Meeting, they clasp hands
and repose upon the couch. But Cytherea with Juno,
patroness of wedlock, stirs new-born arts in them, and
moves them to join contests hitherto unknown. And
when he fondles her in his soft embrace, and suddenly
has caught the flame inspiring wedded love, then he:
"O maiden, new to my sight, bride most acceptable,
thou art come at length, my only joy so long denied.
O my sweet bride, these feelings arise not save by
the will of Heaven, and wilt thou strive even against
lawful love?"

[91] While thus he speaks, she for a long while keeps
her eyes turned away, and hesitates through fear,

---

[19] *Aen.* xi. 254.   [20] *Aen.* i. 715.   [21] *Aen.* viii. 388.
[22] *Aen.* iv. 496.   [23] *Aen.* vi. 104.   [24] *Aen.* x. 607.
[25] *Aen.* vi. 687.   [26] *Aen.* viii. 581.   [27] *Aen.* ii. 777.
[28] *Aen.* xii. 428.   [29] *Aen.* iv. 38.   [30] *Aen.* iv. 362.

cunctaturque metu telumque instare tremiscit[1]
spemque metumque inter[2] funditque has ore lo-
    quelas :[3]
" Per te, per, qui te talem genuere, parentes,[4]
o formose puer,[5] noctem non amplius unam[6]   95
hanc tu, oro, solare inopem[7] et miserere precantis.[8]
succidimus : non lingua valet, non corpore notae
sufficiunt vires, nec vox aut verba sequuntur."[9]
ille autem : " Causas nequiquam nectis inanes,"[10]
praecipitatque moras omnis[11] solvitque pudo-
    rem.[12]   100

Parecbasis

Hactenus castis auribus audiendum mysterium
nuptiale ambitu loquendi et circuitione velavi.
verum quoniam et Fescenninos amat celebritas nup-
tialis verborumque petulantiam notus vetere insti-
tuto ludus admittit, cetera quoque cubiculi et lectuli
operta prodentur ab eodem auctore collecta, ut bis
erubescamus, qui et Vergilium faciamus impudentem.
vos, si placet, hic iam legendi modum ponite : cetera
curiosis relinquite.

VIII.—Imminutio

Postquam congressi[13] sola sub nocte per umbram[14]
et mentem Venus ipsa dedit,[15] nova proelia temptant.[16]
tollit se arrectum :[17] conantem plurima frustra[18]

[1] *Aen.* xii. 916.	[2] *Aen.* i. 218.	[3] *Aen.* v. 842.
[4] *Aen.* x. 597.	[5] *Ecl.* ii. 17.	[6] *Aen.* i. 683.
[7] *Aen.* ix. 290.	[8] *Aen.* x. 598.	[9] *Aen.* xii. 911.
[10] *Aen.* ix. 219.	[11] *Aen.* xii. 699.	[12] *Aen.* iv. 55.
[13] *Aen.* xi. 631.	[14] *Aen.* vi. 268.	[15] *Georg.* iii. 267.
[16] *Aen.* iii. 240.	[17] *Aen.* x. 892.	[18] *Aen.* ix. 398.

and dreads the threatened blow, half hoping and
half fearing, and so pours from her lips these words:
"By thyself, by the parents who begat thee, so goodly
a son, O beauteous youth, I beseech thee for this one
night alone to comfort my helplessness, and take pity
on my prayer. I am o'ercome: my tongue fails, and
its wonted strength deserts my frame; and neither
speech nor words are at command." But he: "In
vain thou weavest idle excuse," and hesitation casts
aside, and breaks the chains of shyness.

A DIGRESSION [1]

So far, to suit chaste ears, I have wrapped the
mystery of wedlock in a veil of roundabout and in-
direct expression. But since the concourse at a
wedding loves Fescennine songs, and also that well-
known form of merriment furnishes an old-established
precedent for freedom of speech, the remaining se-
crets also, of bedchamber and couch, will be divulged
in a selection from the same author, so that I have
to blush twice over, since I make Virgil also immodest.
Those of you who so choose, set here and now a term
to your reading: leave the rest for the curious.

VIII.—THE DEFLORATION

Once they came together, in the shadows of lonely night,
and Venus herself inspired them; they wage afresh the fight.
He raises himself erect; of one who resists in vain

---

[1] *Parecbasis* (παρέκβασις, *egressus*, or *egressio*), a technical
term used in oratory, is defined by Quintilian (iv. 3) as
"alienae rei, sed ad utilitatem causae pertinentis, extra
ordinem procurrens tractatio": its purpose, according to the
same authority, was to soften by anticipation the bad effect
which something following may produce.

occupat os faciemque,[1] pedem pede fervidus urget,[2]
perfidus alta petens :[3] ramum, qui veste latebat,[4] 105
sanguineis ebuli bacis minioque rubentem [5]
nudato capite [6] et pedibus per mutua nexis,[7]
monstrum horrendum, informe, ingens, cui lumen
    ademptum,[8]
eripit a femore et trepidanti fervidus instat.[9]
est in secessu,[10] tenuis quo semita ducit,[11] 110
ignea rima micans :[12] exhalat opaca mephitim.[13]
nulli fas casto sceleratum insistere limen.[14]
hic specus horrendum :[15] talis sese halitus atris
faucibus effundens [16] nares contingit odore.[17]
huc iuvenis nota fertur regione viarum [18] 115
et super incumbens [19] nodis et cortice crudo
intorquet summis adnixus viribus hastam.[20]
haesit virgineumque alte bibit acta cruorem.[21]
insonuere cavae gemitumque dedere cavernae.[22]
illa manu moriens telum trahit, ossa sed inter [23] 120
altius ad vivum persedit [24] vulnere mucro.[25]
ter sese attollens cubitoque innixa levavit,
ter revoluta toro est.[26]   manet imperterritus ille.[27]
nec mora nec requies :[28] clavumque adfixus et
    haerens
nusquam amittebat oculosque sub astra tenebat.[29] 125
itque reditque viam totiens [30] uteroque recusso [31]
transadigit costas [32] et pectine pulsat eburno.[33]
iamque fere spatio extremo fessique sub ipsam
finem adventabant :[34] tum creber anhelitus artus

---

[1] *Aen.* x. 699.   [2] *Aen.* xii. 748.   [3] *Aen.* vii. 362.
[4] *Aen.* vi. 406.   [5] *Ecl.* x. 27.   [6] *Aen.* xii. 312.
[7] *Aen.* vii. 66.   [8] *Aen.* iii. 658.   [9] *Aen.* x. 788.
[10] *Aen.* i. 159.   [11] *Aen.* xi. 524.   [12] *Aen.* viii. 392.
[13] *Aen.* vii. 84.   [14] *Aen.* vi. 563.   [15] *Aen.* vii. 568.
[16] *Aen.* vi. 240 f.   [17] *Aen.* vii. 480.   [18] *Aen.* xi. 530.

A NUPTIAL CENTO

he attacks the mouth and face, proceeds fiercely step after step,
treacherously steering for the deep: the rod within his garment,
with elderberries scarlet and with dye made ruddy,
its head left bare, as their legs together entwined,
a ghastly, shocking monster, huge, no sight in its single eye,
he draws forth from his flank and eagerly presses as she
    quivers.
In a spot secluded, where leads a narrow path,
there glows a fiery chink whose depths exude foul vapor.
No one chaste dare tread this wicked threshhold.
Here was an awful cave; such a breath pouring
forth from its black maw struck the nostrils with its stench.
Here the youth is drawn by a way that he knows,
and looming above with gnarled and native trunk
he casts his spear, applying all his force.
It finds the mark and, driven deep, imbibes the maiden's blood.
The hollows resound, the cavern gives a groan.
She tugs at the weapon with dying hand, but at the bone,
deep within the quick, the point sinks into the wound.
Three times she raised herself up, supported on her arm,
three times fell back on the bed. Undaunted he remains.
No rest there was, no respite: clinging and firmly
    attached
he never released the tiller, and kept his eyes on the stars.
Back and forth he plies his path and, the cavity reverberating,
thrusts between the bones, and strikes with ivory quill.
And now, their journey covered, wearily they neared
their very goal: then rapid breathing shakes his limbs

---

[19] *Aen.* v. 858.   [20] *Aen.* ix. 743 f.   [21] *Aen.* xi. 804.

[22] *Aen.* ii. 53.   [23] *Aen.* xi. 816.   [24] *Georg.* iii. 442.

[25] *Aen.* xi. 817.   [26] *Aen.* iv. 690.   [27] *Aen.* x. 770.

[28] *Georg.* iii. 110.   [29] *Aen.* v. 852 f.   [30] *Aen.* vi. 122.

[31] *Aen.* ii. 52.   [32] *Aen.* xii. 276.   [33] *Aen.* vi. 647.

[34] *Aen.* v. 327 f.

aridaque ora quatit, sudor fluit undique rivis,[1]   130
labitur exanguis,[2] destillat ab inguine virus.[3]

> Contentus esto, Paule mi,
> lasciva, Paule, pagina :
> ridere, nil ultra, expeto.

Sed cum legeris, adesto mihi adversum eos, qui,
ut Iuvenalis[4] ait, "Curios simulant et Bacchanalia
vivunt," ne fortasse mores meos spectent de carmine.

> "Lasciva est nobis pagina, vita proba,"

ut Martialis[5] dicit. meminerint autem, quippe eru-
diti, probissimo viro Plinio in poematiis[6] lasciviam,
in moribus constitisse censuram ; prurire opusculum
Sulpiciae, frontem caperare ; esse Appuleium in vita
philosophum, in epigrammatis amatorem ;[7] in prae-
ceptis Ciceronis extare severitatem, in epistulis ad
Caerelliam subesse petulantiam ; Platonis Symposion
composita in ephebos epyllia continere. nam quid
Anniani Fescenninos, quid antiquissimi poetae Laevii
Erotopaegnion libros loquar? quid Evenum, quem

---

[1] *Aen.* v. 199 f.   [2] *Aen.* xi. 818.   [3] *Georg.* iii. 281.
[4] *Sat.* ii. 3.   [5] *Epigr.* i. iv. 8.
[6] *e.g. Epist.* iv. xiv. 4 f.   [7] *cp. de Magia*, ix.

---

[1] Sulpicia, who flourished in the latter part of the first
century A.D., composed amatory poems addressed to her
husband Calenus.

[2] These letters are no longer extant. Dio Cassius, xlvi.
18, takes a sinister view of the relations between Cicero and
Caerellia ; but Caerellia was considerably older than the
orator (see Boissier, *Cicero and his Friends*, trans. A. D.
Jones, pp. 90 ff.).

and parched mouth, his sweat in rivers flows;
down he slumps bloodless; the fluid drips from his groin.

> Be satisfied, friend Paul,
> Paul, with this naughty page:
> Laughter—naught else—I ask.

But when you have done reading, stand by me to face those who, as Juvenal says—

" Put on the airs of Curius and live like Bacchanals,"

lest perchance they picture my life in colours of my poem.

"My page is naughty, but my life is clean,"

as Martial says. But let them remember, learned as they are, that Pliny, a most honourable man, shows looseness in his scraps of verse, rigour in his private life; that Sulpicia's[1] little work is wanton, her outlook prim; that in morals Apuleius was a philosopher, in his epigrams a lover; that in the precepts of Cicero strictness is prominent, in his letters to Caerellia[2] licence lurks; that Plato's *Symposium* contains rhapsodies upon favourites. For what shall I say of the Fescennine verses of Annianus,[3] what of the volumes of the *Jeu d'Amour* of Laevius,[4] that most ancient poet? What of Evenus,[5] whom Menander has called

---

[3] Annianus flourished under Trajan and Hadrian: *cp.* Aulus Gellius, vii. 7.

[4] Laevius, author of erotic poems burlesquing mythological subjects, flourished at the beginning of the first century B.C.: see Teuffel-Schwabe, *Hist. of Roman Lit.* (trans. Warre), § 150.

[5] Evenus of Paros, a writer of erotic verse, probably belongs to the fourth century B.C.: he is to be distinguished from a fifth-century namesake, also of Paros.

Menander sapientem vocavit? quid ipsum Menan-
drum? quid comicos omnes, quibus severa vita est
et laeta materia? quid etiam Maronem Parthenien
dictum causa pudoris, qui in octavo Aeneidos, cum
describeret coitum Veneris atque Vulcani, αἰσχρο-
σεμνίαν decenter immiscuit? quid? in tertio Georgi-
corum de summissis in gregem maritis nonne obsce-
nam significationem honesta verborum translatione
velavit? et si quid in nostro ioco aliquorum hominum
severitas vestita condemnat, de Vergilio arcessitum
sciat. igitur cui hic ludus noster non placet, ne
legerit, aut cum legerit, obliviscatur, aut non oblitus
ignoscat. etenim fabula de nuptiis est et, velit nolit,
aliter haec sacra non constant.

"the Wise"? What of Menander himself? What of all the comic poets, whose lives were strict for all the broad humour of their subjects. What also of Maro, called Parthenias (the Maidenly) because of his modesty,[1] who in the eighth book of the *Aeneid*,[2] when describing the intercourse of Venus and Vulcan, has gravely introduced a mixed element of lofty obscenity? And again, in the third book of the *Georgics*,[3] on cattle-breeding, has he not veiled an indecent meaning under an innocent metaphor? And if the primly-draped propriety of certain folk condemns aught in my playful piece, let them know that it is taken out of Virgil. So anyone who disapproves of this farce of mine should not read it, or once he has read it, let him forget it, or if he has not forgotten it, let him pardon it. For, as a matter of fact, it is the story of a wedding, and, like it or dislike it, the rites are exactly as I have described.

[1] *cp.* Donatus, *Vita Virgilii*, § 22 : vita et ore et animo tam probum fuisse constat ut Neapoli Parthenias vulgo appellaretur.   [2] *Aen.* viii. 404 ff.   [3] *Georg.* iii. 123 ff.

APPENDIX

THE puzzle here described in the Preface to the *Cento* (p. 374) is the *loculus Archemedius*, of which Caesius Bassus (*de lustris*, p. 271, ed. Keil) gives the following account: "loculus ille Archemedius qui quattuordecim eboreas lamellas, quarum varii anguli sunt, in quadratam formam inclusas habet, componentibus nobis aliter atque aliter modo galeam, modo sicam, alias columnam, alias navem figurat et innumerabiles efficit species." Marius Victorinus (*Ars Gramm.* iii. 1, pp. 100 f., ed. Keil) also describes the loculus as consisting of fourteen pieces, "nunc quadratis, nunc triangulis, nunc ex utraque specie." [1] The puzzle, then, consisted in a rectangle divided up into fourteen triangular or quadrilateral figures.

From another source we learn the principle on which this division was effected. There is extant in Arabic [2] a work entitled "The book of Archimedes on the division of the figure Stomâschion [3] into fourteen figures which stand in direct ratio to it" (*sc.* the whole). The method of division there set forth is as follows:

Take a parallelogram $ABGD$ (Fig. 1) and bisect BG at E. From E draw EZ at right angles to BG, and also

---

[1] The poem of Ennodius, *de Ostomachio Eburneo* (*Carm.* ii. 133, ed Hartel) is not enlightening.

[2] A fragmentary and incomplete Greek text (from a palimpsest MS.) is also extant: both are given by Heiberg in his *second* edition of Archimedes' works (Teubner, 1913), ii. pp. 416 ff.

[3] The Arabic is unpointed, and the vowels therefore uncertain: the Greek title is Στομάχιον; but the form Ὀστομάχιον is certainly right.

the diagonals, *AG*, *BZ*, *ZG*. Next, bisecting *BE* at *H* and drawing *HT* at right angles to *BE*, draw *HK* in the direction of *A*, cutting *BT* at *K*. When, further, we bisect *AL* at *M* and join *MB*, the half *AE* of the whole rectangle is divided into seven parts.

In the other half, *ZG*, bisect *GD* at *N*, *ZG* at *C*, and join *EC* and *CN*. From *C*, in line with the points *BC*,

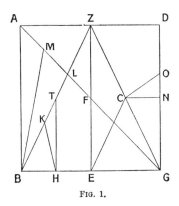

FIG. 1.

draw *CO* cutting *DN* at *O*. *ZG* also is now divided into seven, and the whole rectangle, *ABGD*, into fourteen figures.[1]

It is these fourteen figures which are to be fitted together to form the various objects mentioned by our authorities; and by way of an example an attempt is here made to reconstruct the "helephantus belua" of Ausonius (Fig. 2).

---

[1] The somewhat lengthy demonstration of the ratios (1:16, 1:24, etc.) of these figures to the whole rectangle is here omitted.

APPENDIX

The puzzle of Archimedes above described is in principle the same as the Chinese puzzle or Tangram which, however, has only seven pieces. On this latter and the

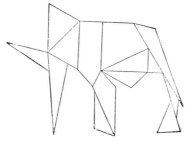

FIG. 2.

variety of forms which may be built up from the seven figures, see H. E. Dudeney, *Amusements in Mathematics* (Nelson, 1917), pp. 43 ff., with numerous illustrations.

397

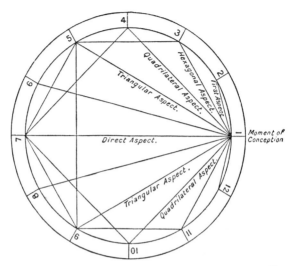

DIAGRAM TO ILLUSTRATE THE VARIOUS ASPECTS OF THE SUN
IN ITS PASSAGE THROUGH THE SIGNS OF THE ZODIAC.

(After the editions of Toll and Souchay.)

1 represents the Sign in which the Sun stands at the
moment of conception. Starting from here, the Sun's pass-
age through 1, 3, 5, 7, 9, 11 forms an equal-sided hexagon;
through 1, 4, 7, 10, a square; through 1, 5, 9, an equilateral
triangle. 1–4 and 1–10 therefore are lines of quadrilateral
aspect; 1–5 and 1–9, of triangular aspect. The diameter of
the zodiacal circle, 1–7, is the line of direct aspect. 1–6 and
1–8 cannot form the sides of any equilateral figure within the
circle; while 1–2 and 1–12 barely constitute aspects.